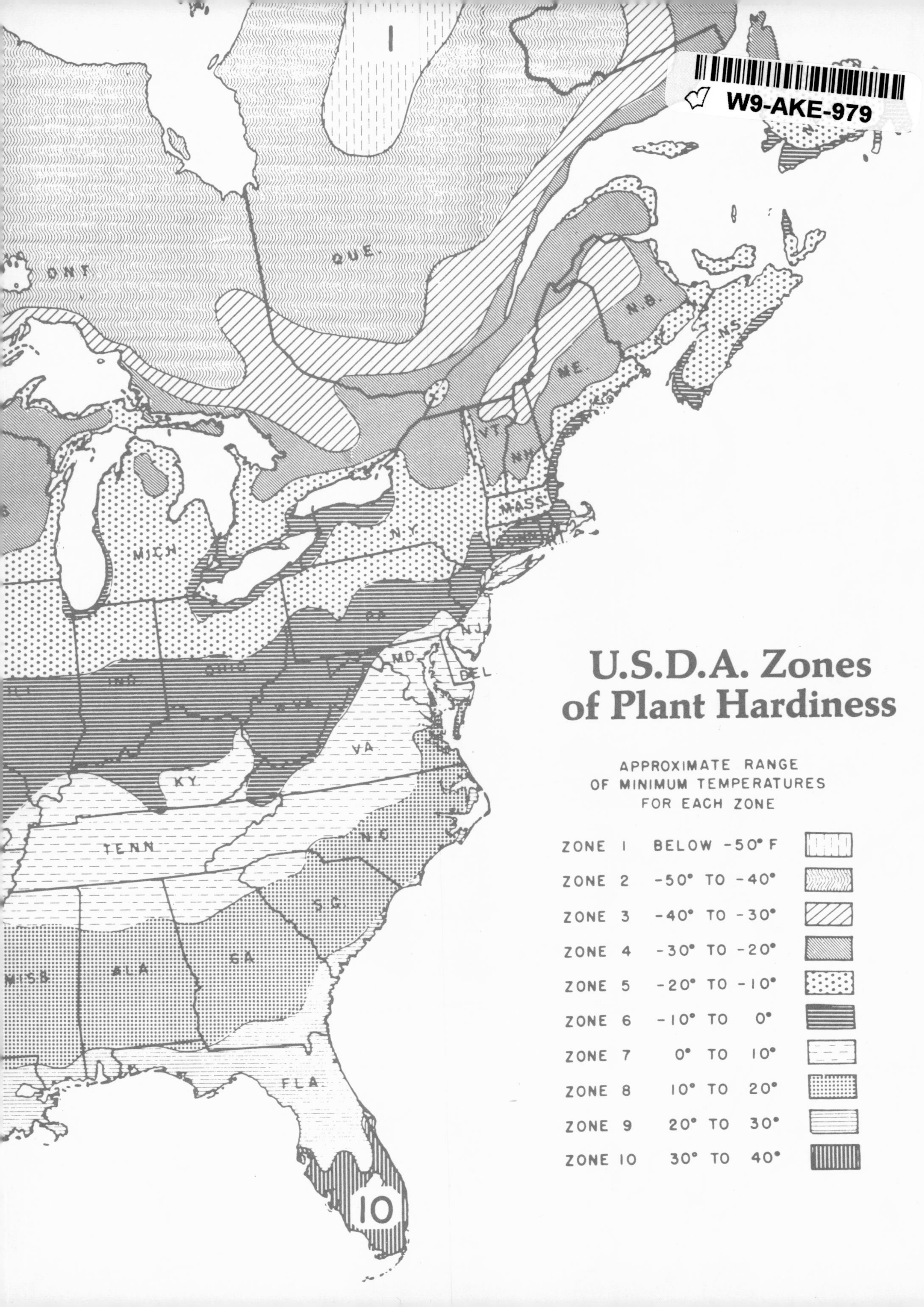

U.S.D.A. Zones of Plant Hardiness

APPROXIMATE RANGE
OF MINIMUM TEMPERATURES
FOR EACH ZONE

ZONE 1   BELOW −50° F

ZONE 2   −50° TO −40°

ZONE 3   −40° TO −30°

ZONE 4   −30° TO −20°

ZONE 5   −20° TO −10°

ZONE 6   −10° TO   0°

ZONE 7   0° TO   10°

ZONE 8   10° TO   20°

ZONE 9   20° TO   30°

ZONE 10   30° TO   40°

The
Good Housekeeping
Illustrated Encyclopedia
of Gardening

The Good Housekeeping Illustrated Encyclopedia of Gardening

in sixteen volumes

Volume One
Aaron's beard to annuus

Ralph Bailey
EDITOR-IN-CHIEF

Elvin McDonald
EXECUTIVE EDITOR

Compiled under the auspices
of the Editors of Good Housekeeping

BOOK DIVISION, HEARST MAGAZINES, NEW YORK

Library of Congress Catalog Card Number: 75–185478
ISBN Number 0–87851–200–4
Printed in the United States of America

Foreword

The *Good Housekeeping Illustrated Encyclopedia of Gardening* is a truly monumental new work. The culmination of nearly 15 years of research and testing by more than 40 distinguished American and Canadian writers, horticultural experts and practical gardeners, it is the first really new A to Z compendium of garden knowledge published in this country in more than 50 years.

Here, in a handsomely designed, beautifully written set of books, you will find answers to your every garden question. Comprehensive in every way, the *Good Housekeeping Illustrated Encyclopedia of Gardening* has been edited for the beginner as well as the more experienced gardener. You will find it useful whether your garden is an apartment terrace, a small plot or a formal English garden—whether you live in the Deep South, the Central Plains or the Pacific Northwest.

Here are just a few of the many useful, exciting features you will find in this Encyclopedia—features that make it unique among garden reference books.

● It is a three-in-one reference set that gives you 1) a complete how-to-do-it guide to all phases of gardening with articles and entries on literally thousands of plants and procedures; 2) fascinating articles by distinguished experts about every major gardening subject from roses to trees; shrubs and rock gardens to house plants; 3) *The Plant Finder*, a special section which lets you look up what you want to grow by the *results* you want.

● The *Good Housekeeping Illustrated Encyclopedia of Gardening* is magnificently illustrated. There are more than 700 drawings which help you to identify plants and show you techniques for planting, grafting, pruning and much more—2500 photographs, of which 800 are in full color—nearly half the space in the entire set is taken up by illustrations.

● It is *newly* written and edited by American and Canadian authors for American and Canadian readers. This first volume contains a 35-page section on the special climatic conditions of some 20 different sections of the U.S. and Canada, recommending the best plants for each region. In each case the plants selected are native to the region and will thrive with little care, or else they are plants the authors and other gardeners in that locality have found easily successful in the climate and growing conditions there and generally resistant to pests and diseases.

About the Editors

One of the most distinguished and most respected of American garden writer/editors, the late Ralph Sargent Bailey was for more than a quarter of a century garden editor of two distinguished magazines, *House Beautiful* and *House and Garden*. He not only loved gardening but brought to it and to his editorial work an irreplaceable knowledge, a warm sense of humor, and a brilliant talent for prose that made gardens bloom on paper and gardeners-at-heart of all his readers. These 16 volumes are the end-product of Ralph Bailey's life work. Designed as "an inclusive, readable and graphic guide to all aspects of gardening for pleasure" it is directed "to the interested gardener who is literate but not learned, who wishes to be informed but not patronized, enlightened but not dazzled."

Unfinished at the time of Mr. Bailey's death, the work has been completed, under the auspices of the *Good Housekeeping* staff, by the Garden Editor of *Good Housekeeping*'s sister publication, *House Beautiful*. Elvin McDonald has been an avid practicing gardener and garden writer since his early teens. Founder of the American Gloxinia and Gesneriad Society, he edited and published *The Gloxinian Magazine* for ten years. While still in school his gardening articles were published in virtually every garden magazine in this country. The author of half a dozen books on the subject, he also brings to the Encyclopedia practical dirt-gardening experience on a ranch in arid, western Oklahoma, suburban landscapes in Kansas City and Long Island and windswept terraces of New York's high-rise apartments.

The Editors
Good Housekeeping

CONTRIBUTORS

EDITOR-IN-CHIEF: **Ralph Bailey,** former garden editor of *House Beautiful* and *House & Garden* magazines, founding editor of House Beautiful's *Practical Gardener,* author of the *Gardener's Day Book.*

EXECUTIVE EDITOR: **Elvin McDonald,** Garden and Senior Editor of *House Beautiful,* former editor of *Flower and Garden,* author of many gardening books.

GENERAL EDITOR: **Jacqueline Heriteau Hunter,** noted amateur gardener, Horticultural Consultant for the *House & Garden Guides* and author of *The How To Grow and Cook It Book of Vegetables, Herbs, Fruits and Nuts.*

HORTICULTURAL CONSULTANT: **Dr. John Philip Baumgardt,** internationally recognized expert on a wide spectrum of gardening topics related to amateurs as well as professionals. He is Editor of the *American Horticultural Society Magazine,* President of the Men's Garden Clubs of America, and author of two books which are standard references: *How To Prune Almost Everything* and *Summer-Flowering Bulbs.*

ART EDITOR: **Kathleen E. Bourke,** specialist in container gardening, garden and landscape design, the art of espaliering and an expert rosarian. She is well-known as the illustrator of a major portion of today's gardening books, and serves as Senior Editor of *Bon Appetit* and *Bon Voyage* magazines.

TECHNICAL ADVISER FOR ART: **Rachel Snyder,** Editor-in-Chief, *Flower and Garden Magazine,* editor of *The Complete Book for Gardeners* and a notably successful home gardener.

EDITORIAL DIRECTOR: **Dale Benson**

LAYOUT AND DESIGN: **Susan Lusk**

ASSISTANT ART EDITOR: **John W. Stewart**

ASSOCIATE EDITORS

Joan Lee Faust, Garden Editor, *New York Times* and author of many *New York Times* volumes on gardening subjects; former instructor at the Brooklyn Botanic Garden; a graduate in the plant sciences.

Georgia J. Ingersoll, Senior Editor for *Field & Stream Magazine* and author of articles on gardening.

Margaret C. Perry, staff editor *Home Garden Magazine,* author and roving reporter on gardening topics, member of the Horticultural Society of New York.

Jeanne Richardson, Administrative Assistant, Princeton University.

Paul Sellers, lecturer and specialist in Southern gardening, frequent contributor to scholarly horticultural publications and agricultural trade magazines, and a Fellow of the Royal Horticultural Society.

CONTRIBUTING EDITORS

Betty Ajay, landscape designer and author of *Betty Ajay's Guide to Home Landscaping.*

Charles Marden Fitch, editor of *Orchidata* magazine, author of a book on tropical house plants.

Joan Meschter, specialist in children's garden projects, member of the Neighborhood Garden Association of Philadelphia and the Merrybrook Garden Club.

Francesca Morris writes for *Women's World* and has written a book on crafts; a successful indoor gardening enthusiast.

Lawrence V. Power is Garden Editor of *American Home* magazine and has been a frequent contributor for publications such as *House and Garden, Better Homes and Gardens* and *House Beautiful.* With Elvin McDonald he has co-authored *The Low Upkeep Book of Lawns and Landscape* and *Garden Ideas A to Z.*

Jerald P. Stowell, an expert on bonsai, has written *Bonsai, Indoors and Out* and is past president of The Bonsai Society of Greater New York and the American Bonsai Society.

Beth M. York spent her early years on a farm in the Oklahoma panhandle where her father used organic methods in his farming insofar as was possible, and she has retained an abiding interest in ecology.

ARTICLES AUTHORS

Catherine Smith Bailey, noted gardening and culinary amateur, is a newspaper woman by profession.

Dr. R. Milton Carleton is research director for Growth Systems, Inc. Previously he served in this capacity for a major seed company for 35 years.

Mary Deputy Cattell, dean of landscape architects, author of books, including *Garden Housekeeping.*

Marjorie Johnson Dietz, editor of *Plants and Gardens* for the Brooklyn Botanic Garden, author of several books including the *Encyclopedia of Wildflowers.*

James Fanning, landscape architect and editor.

Montague Free, lifelong plantsman and author.

George Graves, editor and author whose specialty is woody plants.

Elizabeth Lawrence, landscape architect, author of *The Little Bulbs,* and editor of the new Gertrude Jekyll anthology, *On Gardening.*

Dr. Roscoe Randell, Extension Entomologist at the University of Illinois, was formerly county agent and regional fruit specialist.

Stanley C. Schuler, gardener, editor, author of *Garden Lighting* and *How to Grow Almost Everything.*

Dr. Malcolm C. Shurtleff is Professor of Plant Pathology and Extension Plant Pathologist at the University of Illinois and author of a plant disease column for *Flower and Garden* magazine.

Kathryn Taylor, moving spirit of the N.E. Wildflower Preservation Society, lecturer, author of *The Sun-Heated Pit* and with Stephen Hamblin, *Handbook of Wildflower Cultivation.*

Dr. Cynthia Westcott, pre-eminent plant pathologist, lecturer, lifetime devotee of roses, author of *The Gardener's Bug Book* and *The Plant Doctor.*

REGIONAL EDITORS

How to use this book

This encyclopedia presents a selected list of all the plants most suited for home landscape and garden use, and gives for each key facts and opinions—an information capsule that will enable the reader to apply everyday gardening techniques successfully.

● **Where To Find It:** Plants are listed by genus under their botanical names and pronunciation appears beside each. A genus is a plant group including species that are alike in certain distinguishing characteristics. For instance, cabbage, brussels sprouts, broccoli, Chinese cabbage, kale, cauliflower, rutabaga and the various mustards all belong to the genus *Brassica*. The botanical name for cauliflower is *Brassica oleracea botrytis*. If you look up "cauliflower," it will lead you to the genus entry for *Brassica*, where specific information for the·cauliflower is given.

For the practical gardener there are many advantages in this presentation. For instance, it is not good garden practice to plant a species of *Brassica* where another *Brassica* was the last crop. By grouping *Brassica* species under the genus entry, the gardener can see which vegetables are *Brassicas* without guessing or time-consuming research.

Another reason for presenting entries under the Latin or botanical name is accuracy. From region to region, common names vary. What is "devil's paintbrush" in one area is "orange hawkweed" in another. In this encyclopedia, you can look up either of these common names, and the entry will send you to the genus entry, *Hieracium*, where information about this weed and related species is located.

Another advantage to this system of nomenclature is that facts about related species are readily made available. Would you have guessed that the sweet potato and the Irish potato aren't related? That eggplant, the nightshades and Jerusalem-cherry are all species belonging to the same genus as the common potato?

Species of each genus appear in every entry, along with any varieties and cultivars—natural variants or cultivated hybrids. The Index in Volume 16 carries a complete alphabetized listing of every subject entry, including all botanical and common names.

● **Plant Finder:** In Volume 16 several hundred important plants and plant groups have been arranged so that the gardener can view them in terms of use and purpose. Indexed in groups under, for instance, bog plants, cacti, ferns, greenhouse plants and by the height, color and time of bloom as well, are lists for any purpose and every gardening use.

● **How To Rate a Plant:** The encyclopedia offers a quality rating system for outstanding landscape plants and a guide to their selection for landscape and garden. Starred (★) are 37 plant groups, such as rhododendron, holly and juniper, one or more of which are virtually indispensable in American home landscapes today. Unusually outstanding species within generic entries throughout the A-to-Z section are indicated by a bullet (●).

● **Where To Grow a Plant:** General information appears with each genus, and each species where its culture differs. In addition, very detailed and specific cultural and propagation information for plant groups —annuals, biennials, trees and shrubs and wild flowers, to name a few—appears in definitive articles by noted specialists in each field. These are listed alphabetically throughout the A-to-Z entries; for instance, a comprehensive treatment for Pests and Diseases appears under "pests" in the "P" section.

● **Canada:** Horticulturally similar to the U.S., Canada is divided into five gardening regions. They are discussed by Canadian Regional Editor, Toronto garden writer and lecturer Lois Wilson, on page 42.

● **Conservation:** The preservation of native beauty is the task of the decade, and the Editors of the Encyclopedia have noted all plants that the state legislatures have ruled are not to be picked or dug up. These appear in the entry for each protected species.

● **Plant Societies:** A growing interest in gardening has led to the formation of hundreds of societies whose members are devoted to the development and improvement of specific plants—ferns for example— or growing techniques—The Indoor Light Gardening Society, for instance. Enthusiasts will find names and addresses of the various societies listed in the entry for each such plant or technique.

● **Candied Violets and Potpourri:** Imaginative gardeners of the past had hundreds of uses for flowers. A few outstanding ones have been recorded in this encyclopedia along with the plant entry. Projects to be undertaken with flowers also have been included as, for instance, an article on "potpourri."

UNDERSTANDING THE A-TO-Z ENTRIES

Star indicating genus indispensable to the home garden.

Genus, a plant group including many similar species.

Pronunciation key. Accent italicized syllable.

★ **BEGONIA** (bee-*gohn*-ee-uh). Begonia Family (*Begoniaceae*). An extremely large and diverse genus of herbaceous (usually) perennials from tropical America, though several Asiatic species of note are grown, also. Some species produce tuberlike corms, others remain fibrous rooted. Some develop a heavy rhizome, others send up tough, vertical canes that become al-

Common name of family to which this genus belongs.

Botanical name of the plant family.

Bullet indicates species of outstanding landscape merit.

Stands for *Berberis buxifolia*, a species belonging to the *Berberis* (Barberry) genus.

● **B. buxifolia** (bux-if-*foh*-lee-uh). MAGELLAN BARBERRY. Upright evergreen from Chile, growing to 8 ft. (usually much lower in cultivation), of compact habit. Oval leaves, to 1 in. long, wedge-shaped at the base. Orange-yellow flowers, one or two in a cluster. Dark purple fruit. One of the hardiest and best evergreen barberries. The variety *nana* (*nay*-nuh), to 18 in. high, is especially useful in small borders and low hedges. Zone 6.

Common name for *B. buxifolia*. Cross-reference entry appears listed alphabetically for Magellan Barberry, giving the correct botanical name, *B. buxifolia*.

Indicates this plant will survive cold weather generally prevailing in Zone 6. Zone map showing which areas of the continent this zone covers is on the inside front cover of each volume.

Hollies are remarkably hardy against disease and insect pests. The most serious pest is the holly leaf miner, which can be controlled by diazinon spray. Some damage from scales is evident in warm-weather

For complete information on dealing with pests and diseases, see "PESTS AND DISEASES" listed alphabetically in the "P" section.

Ingredients for Basic Potting Mixture appear inside back cover of all volumes.

house or greenhouse plant. It needs good drainage and an average garden soil. For pot plants use the Basic Potting Mixture. Outdoors, it is best grown in partial shade. After flowering, these plants lose their leaves and should remain dormant and fairly dry until new growth begins. Propagate by division in

For detailed information on all propagation methods, see comprehensive article on propagation listed alphabetically under "P."

Entry listed alphabetically under the plant's common name. All entries are listed under both the common and the correct botanical name so they can be located under either.

Velvet plant. See *Gynura aurantiaca*.

vegetus (*vej*-et-us), **-a, -um.** Vigorous.

Non botanical entries are listed alphabetically and without capital letters. Major articles on gardening subjects are listed alphabetically under the subject name.

Latin, or botanical, designation for "vigorous." The curious gardener can investigate the meaning of the botanical name for any plant by looking up each term alphabetically.

paving. The selection of paving materials for a walk, driveway or terrace depends on the decorative effect you wish to achieve, the ability of the material

Gardening Where You Live

Gardening is an inexact science, but one unshakable truth is that plants want to root, grow, bloom and propagate. The key to their success is location—the right plant in the right place will succeed. A plant provided with the right sunlight exposure in a setting where the native climate, moisture and soil conditions meet its needs will largely take care of itself.

Climate comes first. The A-to-Z entries in our volumes are zone-keyed to the United States Department of Agriculture Plant Hardiness Zone Map on the endpapers of each volume. *Flower and Garden* magazine has further divided the continental United States into gardening regions and along with these, our Regional Editors describe on the following pages the growing conditions to expect in each area. In addition, Canada is sectioned into five areas for gardening purposes and these have been keyed to the U.S.D.A. map by our Canadian regional editor, Lois Wilson.

The zones identified in the A-to-Z entries describe the coolest climate in which the plant usually will survive winter, but do not indicate the only region in which it will live. All temperate regions south, excepting high-heat belts, are usually suitable. The dictates of the zone map are an oversimplification, a generalization that ignores microclimates. An L-shaped wall with southern exposure, or a windbreak to the north, create pocket climates in which plants prove hardy well to the north of their normal range.

Plants have individual soil requirements as well as climate preferences. In fact, if the soil is ideal, the plant may stand up to adverse weather conditions. Most evergreens require well-drained, slightly acid soil, and most perennial flowers require more alkalinity—a higher pH. You can grow evergreens in a region where soils are alkaline if you take the trouble to create and maintain suitable soil conditions. But that plant won't really be "in the right place." It will demand higher maintenance and find the going tougher. You can grow tender cacti and other succulents in the North—in the heated indoors in winter—and bog plants in the desert—if you create a bog. But the low-maintenance way to success is to select plants that like to live where you garden.

The most accurate indication of which plants will thrive in your location, your microclimate and your soil conditions is a studied look at your neighbors' gardens. In the following regional articles, our Editors report their experienced views on climate, soil and which plants are likely to be the right plants in your neighborhood.

Elvin McDonald

ABOUT THE PLANT FINDER LISTS IN VOLUME 16

You can spend a lifetime gathering the information needed to plan a garden that blooms all season long, or a landscape whose plantings achieve specific purposes—offer shade, or scent, screening, or your favorite color. With the comprehensive lists in the *Plant Finder*, Volume 16, you can do it in minutes. This section includes hundreds of lists of plants grouped by specific use and purpose.

If you are looking for an annual, for instance, that is fragrant, grows in light shade and tolerates damp ground, a quick cross-check of the *Plant Finder* will tell you whether or not there is such an annual. If you want several species of fern for a rock garden in the sun, the *Plant Finder* will tell you which are suitable.

You can use the *Plant Finder* to select plants of all sorts for gardens by the seashore. Or trees with brilliant autumn coloring, or decorative bark; shrubs that provide fruit for the birds, or grow no taller than 2 feet or flower in winter.

In the *Plant Finder* you will find the exact answer to every landscape planning question. Along with your regional gardening guide, it is the key to fitting the right plant to the right place.

OPPOSITE: Here's the perfect example of how the Plant Finder section in Volume 16 can be used to answer specific landscape needs in a hurry. A spring-flowering tree with colorful foliage and berries in autumn? Dogwood. Evergreen, spring-flowering shrubs in light shade? Azaleas. Spring garden color and cut flowers? Tulips. Hardy perennials to interplant that flower in light shade in autumn? Aconite, anemone, hosta. The surrounding lawn? Bluegrass in sun, fine fescues in shade.

New England

By GEORGE TALOUMIS

Gardening in New England is both an adventure and a challenge. It is not unusual for temperatures to reach the 100-degree mark in summer and to plummet to 30 degrees below zero in winter. In spite of this rigorous climate, with the extremes of heat in summer and cold in winter, it has some of the loveliest—and oldest—gardens in the country.

The six-state region is bordered by the open Atlantic on the east, Long Island Sound along the south, New York State on the west and Canada on the north. The ocean has a tempering influence, cooling the coastal areas in summer and warming them in winter. Cape Cod's climate compares to that of Maryland, and plants that grow on the coasts of Connecticut and Rhode Island may be hardy on Maine's extended seacoast, though not inland.

Climate Comes First

The region is well watered. The average yearly rainfall of 40 in. for Boston is typical for the rest of the area. Though figures are nearly the same for each month, springs tend to be wet and cool, and autumns sunny and dry. Summers are variable. They bring high temperatures and high humidity. They may be rainy, but more often are dry.

Improving Your Soil

New England soils are on the acid side. This is a blessing for gardeners who can grow with minimum effort some of the handsomest of flowering trees and shrubs—dogwoods, azaleas, rhododendrons and mountain laurel. Even so, soils are not generally excessively acid. Many kinds of plants with alkaline requirements, as lilacs and clematis, can be grown with equal success. Soils on Cape Cod and in parts of New Hampshire are sandy.

Successful gardening in New England means proper soil preparation—the digging in of peat moss, leafmold, compost and other organics to condition them properly. It means feeding with organic or, if necessary, chemical fertilizers, and with bonemeal and superphosphate, which promote flowering and fruiting in plants. It means watering in dry spells and mulching to prevent moisture loss.

There is plenty of sunshine. Winters have dull days, yet many bright, sunny ones. It is these, in fact, which make gardening difficult, when strong sun and wind cause sunscald and windburning among needle and broadleaf evergreens, injuring barks of trees, as well.

Plants That Succeed

A wide variety of plants thrive in the region. These include the hardy woody plants—azaleas and crab apples—that are native to Japan and the colder areas of China where climatic conditions are similar. Sharp variations—warm days and cool nights—account for the brilliant coloring of native and Asiatic trees and shrubs in the fall—sugar, red and Tatarian maples, oaks, sassafras (*S. albidum*), sourwood, bottlebrush, shadbush, highbush blueberry (*Vaccinium corymbosum*), black tupelo (*Nyssa*), Japanese red maple and winged euonymus.

Among the best shade and flowering trees, in part because they are attractive and also because they are generally free of pests, are Norway maple, European linden, European and American beeches, red, scarlet and white oaks, the Moraine locust (*Gleditsia*). Crab apples, which are hardy in the far north, dogwoods, including the Japanese, hawthorns, halesia, and laburnum also are successful in New England gardens.

Early-flowering forsythias, Korean and other azaleas, mayflower (*Viburnum carlesii*) and other viburnums, spireas, rhododendrons, lilacs, mockoranges and rose-of-Sharon will give color among shrubs from early spring to fall. Roses are glorious.

Native pines, white, red and pitch, are among the most dependable large evergreens. Japanese black pine survives salt spray and hurricane winds along the coast. The best shrubby evergreen—in its myriad forms—is Japanese yew. Though common, it remains choice. Other good evergreens, needle and broadleaved, are Pfitzer and other low junipers, Mugho pine, Japanese and mountain pieris.

Even the smallest garden is not complete without iris, peonies, daylilies, phlox and chrysanthemums—the best of perennials. There is no limit, however, since towering delphiniums (they are superb in seaside gardens), Oriental poppies, columbines, gas plants, veronicas, hibiscus and fall asters do well here. All kinds of annuals flourish—petunias, marigolds, zinnias, sweet alyssum and snapdragons. In northern Vermont, New Hampshire and along the coast of Maine, gardeners succeed with those that like it cool—nemesia, nasturtium and stock.

Special plants—vines that grow vertically and ground covers which spread horizontally—complete the New England garden picture. Wisteria, the Chinese and the hardier Japanese, is every gardener's dream vine, except for roses, especially 'Paul's Scarlet' or 'Blaze,' its everblooming counterpart. Sometimes hybrid clematis do not succeed but gardeners never give up trying. Oriental and American bittersweets, actinidia, old-fashioned Dutchman's pipe (*Aristolochia durior*), Virginia creeper (*Parthenocissus quinquefolia*), Boston ivy, English ivy and the late-blooming sweet autumn clematis (*C. dioscoraefolia robusta*, formerly Clematis paniculata) and the Chinese lace-vine (*Polygonum auberti*) are grown.

Evergreen pachysandra is the outstanding ground cover. English ivy, more so the hardier Baltic ivy, luxuriates in shade of small city gardens. Running myrtle (*Vinca minor*), lily of the valley, variegated goutweed (*Aegopodium*), ground phlox, creeping thyme (*Thymus serpyllum*) and low junipers help to solve the problem of what ground covers to grow.

Where temperatures drop no lower than −20 degrees, the Carpathian strain of English walnut and the hardy strains of the shagbark hickory (a relative of the pecan) will bear. Chinese chestnut is hardy and bears where temperatures do not go below −15 degrees.

Cool-weather vegetables, as radishes, lettuce, peas, carrots and cabbages, can be started in the open ground in earliest spring. Corn, cucumbers, squashes, tomatoes and beans grow quickly in hot weather. Eggplants (set out as started seedlings) bear.

Bluegrasses, particularly 'Merion' and Kentucky, are the best grasses for lawns, followed by Chewings and red fescues and Colonial bentgrass. Weeds that plague the gardener are crabgrass, which can be controlled with pre- and post-emergence sprays, dandelions and plantains.

Well mulched, these Giant Pacific hybrid delphiniums will survive New England temperatures to 30 below; even less-hardy perennials are successful in microclimates along the Northeast Coast where the sea tempers the cold.

13

Middle Atlantic

By DR. JOHN W. MASTALERZ

Extending across three plant hardiness zones, the Middle Atlantic region takes in Pennsylvania, New Jersey, northern Delaware, New York (except north of the Mohawk Valley and Albany) and portions of Maryland and West Virginia.

There are three cold zones here. Zone 7, where average minimum temperatures range from 0 to 10 degrees, includes southeastern Pennsylvania, northern Delaware, the southern half of New Jersey, the Atlantic seacoast to New York City and all of Long Island. The Zone 6 portion of the Middle Atlantic Region, −10 to 0 degrees, extends across the southern half of Pennsylvania, northern New Jersey, the area surrounding New York City and the Hudson River Valley up to Albany. Sections south and east of Lake Erie and Lake Ontario also are in Zone 6. The Zone 5 area, −20 to −10 degrees, includes the northern half of Pennsylvania and upstate New York except for the areas adjacent to the Great Lakes.

Climate Comes First

The growing season is about 130 days in the mountains of Pennsylvania and adjacent New York counties and the Catskills. The spring frost-free date is May 20 and the first frost in the fall is about September 30. The season is 180 days on Long Island, in the suburban areas north of New York City and the Hudson Valley, most of New Jersey, Philadelphia and its immediate suburbs. Here the last frost in spring occurs before April 20 and the first frost in the fall after October 20.

For the balance of the region the last frost in spring

is on May 10, and the first frost in fall is October 10. With a few exceptions, the growing seasons are long enough to mature annuals and vegetables from seed sown directly in the garden. The exceptions are slow-growers such as tomatoes, begonias and eggplant which generally are started in the greenhouse or cold frame and set out when the weather warms. Gardeners extend the season in fall by protecting with plastic late crops of tomatoes and melons, and many use hotcaps to give vegetables an early spring start.

The average annual rainfall in the Middle Atlantic region ranges from 36 to 44 in. with as much as 52 in. in the Catskills of New York State. Almost one-half the total precipitation occurs in spring and summer months and is distributed relatively evenly throughout the growing season. The probability of receiving at least 1 in. of rain in a two-week period in summer is 70 per cent or greater. Short droughts do occur. Severe drought periods are abnormal and cannot be predicted on the basis of long-time precipitation records. The areas along the shores of the Great Lakes, Long Island and the coastal sections of New Jersey tend to be drier June through August. Plants growing in loamy soils with a high humus content can survive the shorter droughts with little supplementary watering.

Improving Your Soil

Soils in the Middle Atlantic region do not present serious problems except where subsoil drainage is poor. Relatively sandy soils are found along the Atlantic coast and on Long Island. They are easily cultivated but fail to hold moisture. Westward, soils become heavier. Silt loams derived from rock formations as a result of glacial activity are the predominant type.

Generally acid even where derived from limestone rocks, soils here benefit from the addition of lime and phosphorus (superphosphate). Most also are low in magnesium. Dolomitic lime (magnesium-containing forms) is preferred for sweetening the soil. Phosphorus is not readily available to plants in the red (iron oxide) soils of southern Pennsylvania and special efforts to supply the phosphorus requirements are necessary.

Because of relatively low levels of organic matter in the soil, it is desirable to add sphagnum peat moss and other forms of humus. Compost and cover crops, or even weeds, turned under at the end of the growing year, raise humus content and improve fertility as well.

Trace element deficiencies, especially iron and boron, do occur in the area, but indiscriminate applications of trace elements are not recommended because

Spring landscapes are breathtaking in this region whose climate is particularly suited to early-spring bulbs and some of the best of the flowering trees. Soils present few problems but benefit from additions of humus and the trace elements iron and boron. Dolomitic lime containing magnesium is recommended as a soil sweetener to offset magnesium shortages common to the area.

of the danger of producing toxic levels. Trace elements should be applied only when a deficiency has been confirmed by plant symptoms or leaf analysis.

Plants That Succeed

As specimen plants or members of a shrub border in this region, the viburnums have ornamental value every season—they provide spring flowers, summer foliage and in autumn and through winter vivid color in foliage and berry. Yews are the best evergreens for the climate, do well in both sun and shade, tolerate a wide variety of soil conditions and are vulnerable to few pests. Forsythias are just as easy as the yews and the flowering dogwoods do well, too. Another excellent selection is spirea, red- or white-flowered. *Spiraea vanhouttei* is the most popular. It does well in all soils and tolerates shade as well as sun, though it blooms most abundantly in full sun.

Other ornamental trees and shrubs particularly suited to the region are the rhododendrons (including azaleas), barberry, winged euonymus, cotoneaster and pyracantha. The sugar maple and the red oak are probably the most popular and trouble-free of the many handsome shade trees that flourish here.

In the Middle Atlantic region, petunias might win the vote as the most popular annual. Marigolds find use in many showy corners around the home, and will continue to flower even in dry weather; in fact they do best here when heavy applications of fertilizer and frequent watering are avoided. Zinnias make a brilliant show and the new low-growing cultivars are good edgers and fine rock-garden subjects. Fibrous-rooted begonias are highly successful, too. Daffodils of all varieties are the most durable of spring bulbs. Bearded iris (*Iris germanica*), daylilies and tulips are popular, and peonies, geraniums (which are not winter-hardy here), chrysanthemums and perennial phlox are also desirable and successful perennials.

Recommended lawn and ground cover materials are Merion' Kentucky bluegrass, 'Pennlawn' creeping red fescue, *Pachysandra terminalis*, *Vinca minor* (myrtle) and Baltic ivy.

Most of the home garden vegetables flourish—tomatoes (set out as started seedlings), snap beans, lettuce, sweet corn—as do strawberries, blueberries and hardy grapes.

Weeds to eradicate (if you can) as they appear are crabgrass (*Digitaria* species), dandelion, plantain (*Plantago major* or *P. lanceolata*), chickweed (*Stellaria media* or *Cerastium* species), knotweed (*Polygonum* species) and black medic (*Medicago lupulina*). A major article under the entry for *weeds* gives information on the elimination of these weeds from the garden.

The North

By ROBERT A. PHILLIPS

The North region includes all of Minnesota and Wisconsin, most of the northern peninsula of Michigan, eastern North and South Dakota and northern Iowa. This is a region of great contrasts in topography, climate, soils, weather, rainfall and season. Weather and climate for all four seasons can be characterized as decidedly variable, and to confuse gardeners further, the four seasons vary widely from year to year.

Climate Comes First

Spring is the short season and the most uncertain one because the weather usually changes suddenly and violently. Winter often lingers into spring as spring is designated on the calendar. Summers can be hot and cold, wet and dry. The same is true of fall, although autumn usually is fair. Winters are long and cold with several severe cold spells that take the temperature well below zero. There are winters with little snowfall and winters with much snow.

Because of the variance in the protection offered by snowfall and because of the subzero temperatures, winter protection must be provided for all garden perennials and for roses. A 6-in. covering of hay is usually adequate for perennials. Garden roses require special protection: A favorite method in this region is to hill roses at the base with 12 in. of soil and then to cover them with a foot or more of hay after the ground has frozen hard. Another method is to cover them with a 2-ft. mulch of tree leaves.

Improving Your Soil

Soils are as variable as weather and climate. They may be peaty, sandy, gravelly or clayey. Rarely are they rich and loamy or of adequate depth. The more successful gardens here are prepared beds composed of 10 in. of fertile loamy soil for annuals and bedding plants, 18 in. for most perennials and 24 to 30 in. for roses. There are both alkaline and acid soils here.

The annual rainfall ranges from 14 in. in the northwest to 30 in. in the south. Rainfall usually is not adequately distributed in most sections so some watering must be done. Gardens and lawns need one good rain or one thorough watering weekly. Newly-set woody plants, trees and shrubs also require a good weekly soaking. Watering during the region's not infrequent drought periods is necessary for several years to help newly planted ornamentals.

Plants That Succeed

The deciduous trees grown for shade and ornamental purposes in this area are mostly maples, ash, honeylocust, hackberry, mountain ash and basswood (American linden), all natives. Russian olive, not a native, is well adapted to the soils and climate of this region and it is extensively used on home grounds.

Only the narrow-leaf evergreens are widely used. Native pines, spruces and junipers are grown in all but the northwestern area. Many introduced horticultural varieties of junipers are also grown. Broadleaf evergreens, such as rhododendrons, are rarely planted, except by experienced gardeners.

The most commonly planted native shrubs are honeysuckle, dogwoods (unfortunately not the flowering dogwood of the East but red twig, yellow twig, and gray twig, with foliage and bark to provide fall and winter color), ninebark and viburnums.

Many introduced ornamentals are successfully grown here. Noteworthy among these are lilacs, spireas and euonymus. These are featured in local nursery catalogs. Gardeners and landscapers are urged to patronize local nurseries because they sell only those plants hardy in this region. Bare-rooted specimens can be planted in spring and fall and container-grown or balled-and-burlapped ones can be planted any time during the growing season.

All the popular annuals and perennials can be grown here. Plants may be home-grown or purchased from garden stores and nurseries. Zinnias, petunias, bachelor's-buttons (cornflower), marigolds, salvias, cleome, sweet alyssum, lobelia and snapdragons are among the favorite annuals. Peonies, delphiniums, phlox, iris, Oriental poppies, daisies, lilies, daylilies, blanket flower (*Gaillardia*), *Lythrum*, obedient flower

(*Physostegia*), Chinese bellflower (*Platycodon*), trollius, veronica and violas are popular perennials.

Chrysanthemums and roses have had a spectacular rise in popularity in the North. All varieties of roses can be grown very successfully and very high quality flowers can be obtained. Only the early-flowering varieties of chrysanthemums should be grown in the region because fall frost comes too early for the mid-season and late-flowering ones. The Horticultural Department of the University of Minnesota has developed many excellent varieties of mums especially adapted to the state and northern gardens. Two outstanding roses have been introduced because they combined superior flowers with more than average winter hardiness. They are sold throughout the nation. They are 'White Dawn' and 'Viking Queen.' Both are very floriferous. 'White Dawn' is a lovely floribunda type that has double white flowers resembling gardenias. It blooms on the current season's growth as well as last year's canes, and is in bloom most of the time from mid-June to late fall. 'Viking Queen' is a climber with large, double pink flowers.

Nearly all kinds of bulbs, corms and tubers can be grown with success. Most popular of these are gladiolus, dahlias, crocus, cannas, tulips, hardy narcissus, hyacinths, scillas and grape-hyacinths. Tuberous begonias are increasing in popularity every year. Here the tubers must be started in pots indoors, then moved outside as soon as all danger of frost is past. They must be in sites protected from wind and have shade or semishade from 10 A.M. to 3 P.M. Exposure to full sun too many hours burns the leaves.

Small fruits such as strawberries and raspberries are grown by home gardeners. Apples are largely grown commercially on selected sites. Some apples, however, are grown on home grounds and crab apples are widely planted for ornamental effects.

Nut trees are rarely planted in the region. Butternuts and black walnuts will succeed.

By far the most popular vegetable for the home gardener is the tomato. Other vegetables grown are asparagus, cabbage, beans, beets, carrots, corn, lettuce, kohlrabi and peas. Rhubarb flourishes here, too.

Most lawns are Kentucky bluegrass with fescues planted in shady areas. There are a few bentgrass lawns but this grass is most used on golf greens.

Most common lawn weeds are dandelion, plantain, ground ivy, quackgrass and crabgrass. The latter is the most difficult to control. However, there are new selective herbicides that are very useful in keeping this pest under reasonably good control. There are two types of crabgrass herbicides, pre-emergence and post-emergence. The first is by far the most effective. Other broad-leaved lawn weeds are easily eliminated by 2,4-D, but great care must be exercised in its use.

Key to success in this region's highly variable climate and soil is to plant only species recommended by local garden centers. Early chrysanthemums like this red hybrid flourish here, and the ball dahlia, 'Lark,' is a popular ornamental.

17

Northern Plains

By GLENN VIEHMEYER

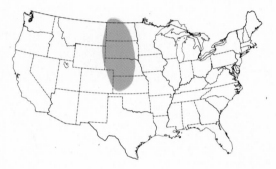

Early explorers named this area the Great American Desert. It is a sea of grass stretching from the Canadian prairies to the Texas panhandle and rolling westward to break against the foot of the Rocky Mountains. The accompanying map outlines the area but does not show extensions of the mountains that run into the prairies nor the arms of grassland that reach into the mountains.

This is a transition zone between the humid East and the arid West. Variability in temperature, precipitation and soils is a rule, not an exception. Irrigation is a must for growing many ornamentals.

Climate Comes First

The weather pattern is one of violence. Perpetual winds freeze in winter and burn in summer. Movement of dry air desiccates plant tissues and tatters tender leaves and flowers. Windbreak protection for the garden is essential. Thin-barked eastern shrubs and trees may die of physiological drought during winter unless protected by windbreaks or sprayed with an antidesiccant to reduce transpiration.

Winter temperatures may fall as much as 40 degrees in an hour or less. The "January thaw" may break dormancy of nonnatives and be followed by temperature drops that winterkill plants hardy to much lower temperature.

Drought is an ever-present threat that increases from north to south and from east to west. Supplementary water is needed for effective gardening. Mulches and wide spacing are used to help conserve moisture.

Summer rainfall follows a pattern of violence. Wind may rip leaves and twigs from trees and flatten gardens and crops. Rainfall is erratic and ranges from showers so light as to be ineffective to heavy rain and hail that may wipe out a season's work.

Winter precipitation is equally violent. Snow drifts often expose plant crowns to the bitter winter cold or move onto shrubs and tear them apart as the snow melts. This is the land of the "killer" blizzards that may destroy the unwary traveler or unprotected livestock.

Improving Your Soil

Soils are as variable as climate, ranging from dune sand to the heavy gumbo (clay) soils. In the eastern part of the area soils may be acid and require lime. In the west they are often alkaline and iron chlorosis is a major problem. Irrigation water is frequently high in dissolved minerals and adds to the alkali problem. Iron in available form must be frequently applied to control the chlorosis that may destroy the beauty of ornamental plantings.

In this region the length of the growing season ranges from 100 frost-free days in the north to 200 days in the south. Temperatures may drop below −50 degrees north but less than half that in the south. Length of frost-free periods and low temperatures are important in selecting plants for the area.

Plants That Succeed

Despite environmental variation, certain groups of plants are widely adapted in the region. Annual flowers and vegetables are examples. In woody plants, junipers, ash, bur oak, American elm and many shrubs range widely over the plains. The use of locally selected material is advisable.

In the northern states, fir, pine and spruce are important ornamentals. Here broadleaf evergreens, excepting the very hardy *Pachistima canbyi* and *Euonymus nana*, are failures. Southward many euonymus, yews and the hardier firethorns can be used.

Flowering crab apples do well throughout the northern plains and are widely planted. An excellent but seldom used small tree is the Japanese lilac, *Syringa amurensis* variety *japonica*, which bears huge trusses of creamy-white flowers in June after other lilacs have stopped blooming.

In the north the blaze of mountain-ash berries rivals the brilliant fruit of the firethorns of warmer

The bush cinquefoil, *Potentilla fruticosa*, cultivar named
'Klondike,' native to the Northern Hemisphere,
is a low-maintenance ornamental easy to grow in
this region where perpetual winds make windbreaks
and well-timed watering musts for all of the
imported species if they are to survive
winter's variable temperatures and lack of snow cover.

areas. Among the cotoneasters are species to fit any part of the Northern Plains. Red-berried elderberries brighten the shrub border in summer and fall. Lilacs and viburnums are excellent in shrub borders as are the many honeysuckles.

Overlooked by most gardeners are the evergreen yuccas. These range from foot-high pygmies to head-high giants. Though cursed by the cattleman as a range weed, yucca is at home in the garden where the giant bloom clusters thrust to the sky, so spectacular that the mission fathers dubbed them "Our Lord's Candles."

Among perennials the chrysanthemum is perhaps most important, followed closely by phlox, iris and hemerocallis. Delphinium is spectacular in the north but less well adapted southward. In the drier western plains penstemon, a relative of the snapdragon, is receiving attention from plant breeders and promises much as an ornamental.

Kentucky bluegrass from the wild and in its various selected forms is the most important lawn grass here. Zoysia and Bermudagrasses are of limited use in the south. In places where irrigation water for lawns is lacking the very drought-tolerant gramagrass and buffalograss make tough, hardy turf.

Many plants native to the region merit a place in the garden. Unfortunately many of the best are offered by only a few dealers or not at all. In the latter case it may be necessary to collect seed from wild stands. Remember that National Forests and Parks do not permit collectors to collect plants without special permits, which are sparingly issued.

One widely offered native is the shrubby cinquefoil, *Potentilla fruticosa*, an everblooming, yellow-flowered, rose relative. A second subshrub is the sundrop, *Oenothera serrata,* which blooms continually in the garden. Another low shrub is the lead plant, *Amorpha canescens.* This and the smaller *A. nana* have purple and gold racemes in July held above ferny, gray-green foliage.

A worthwhile perennial, native in the drier southwest, is a wild four o'clock, *Mirabilis multiflora,* which carries its 2-in. lilac-pink blooms above a mound of glaucous foliage that may reach a diameter of 4 or more ft. in old plants. Another is the bush morning-glory with 4-in. pink trumpets and narrow foliage.

Many other natives add interesting possibilities to the Northern Plains garden, which is a fascinating as well as a challenging adventure in horticulture.

Plants protected by law are so designated in this encyclopedia; protected means that they may be neither picked nor dug up even for transplanting to nearby gardens.

Among imported plants that flourish here are crab apple, apple, pear, apricot and ornamental as well as fruiting members of the *Prunus* genus. Cherries, haws and cotoneasters do well also.

Ornamentals that succeed including the new chrysanthemums, handsome specimen irises and hemerocallis are annuals such as marigolds, zinnias and asters. Some of the new hardy roses should be tried. All will do well with winter protection.

High Plains

By F. L. STEVE O'ROURKE

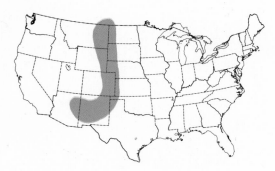

The High Plains, stretching nearly 2,500 miles from the far reaches of Saskatchewan and Alberta to the Rio Grande at an average altitude of four to six thousand feet, lies mostly west of the 100th meridian and extends to the foothills of the Rockies. This is "short grass" country where herds of buffalo once grazed on undulating plains marked by buttes and mesas.

Rivers and dry water courses occur at intervals. These carry off the sparse and spasmodic rainfall and nourish the only native trees and shrubs, cottonwoods, box-elders, willows and hackberries. Ancient maps called this the "Great American Desert." It was not until the white settlers came, after the mid-half of the nineteenth century, that water was diverted from mountain streams, irrigation canals constructed and crops planted.

Climate Comes First

The High Plains has a "continental climate," characterized by hot, dry summers and cold, windy winters. There are no seas and few lakes and rivers to moderate the extremes of temperature. The rainfall ranges from 5 or 6 in. to 15 or 20, mostly in spring or in the thunderstorms of early summer. Winters are dry with little snowfall and strong winds under bright skies draw moisture from exposed plants. Alternate freezing and thawing of the surface soil exhausts soil moisture and plant roots often freeze or desiccate.

The greatest hazards to woody plants here are the unpredictable storms and blizzards of late spring and early fall. Trees in full foliage may be so covered with snow that branches break. Cold snaps which follow a storm often freeze back succulent growth.

One of the best means of protection for tender plants is a tight windbreak north and west. It may be of either or both evergreens and deciduous trees and shrubs. Evergreens such as Colorado and Black Hills spruce, Ponderosa or Austrian pine, Rocky Mountain or other junipers are good-looking.

Improving Your Soil

A protective layer of mulch over soil surfaces will compensate for light snowfall. A mulch conserves moisture and protects the soil from wind erosion, reduces the effects of fluctuating temperatures and adds organic matter as it decomposes. Wood chips, hay and straw are excellent for mulching.

Supplemental watering is as necessary in the High Plains region as winter mulch. Only a few plant species can exist under the natural rainfall conditions. Most ornamentals should be watered at intervals.

Soil types of the High Plains vary widely. There are the light-textured "sand hills," the well-structured loamy alluvial soils of river valleys, and the stony glacial till of other sections. The great majority of the soils are compact and highly alkaline. Very light rainfall limits vegetative growth and therefore the humus content of most soils is low. The structure of the soil —the amount of pore space to hold air and water—is generally poor but can be improved by the addition of organic matter such as manure or peat moss.

Most of the soils are satisfactory from the fertility standpoint, and contain quantities of calcium and potassium salts. Phosphorus is usually present but may be unavailable owing to the high alkalinity. This is also true of iron. It is often necessary to apply phosphorus and particularly iron to assure good plant growth. "Iron chlorosis," the yellowing of the foliage from lack of iron, is common. The nutrient element always in short supply is nitrogen. The deficiency is easily overcome by two or three light applications of inorganic nitrogen or one of the "slow release" nitrogen carriers per year. The usual rate for grass and ornamental shrubs is three to four pounds of active elemental nitrogen per 1,000 square feet per year.

Plants That Succeed

There are few native plants of ornamental value, but a number of exotic species from the cold, dry areas of Siberia adapt well here.

The following list indicates in a descending sequence of value plants which are commonly grown or have high potential for the special climate of the High Plains area.

Code: T = Tree; S = Shrub; W = often used in Wind-breaks in rural areas.

RUSSIAN OLIVE	T,W	*Eleagnus angustifolia*
HACKBERRY	T,W	*Celtis occidentalis*
HONEY LOCUST	T,W	*Gleditsia triacanthos*
KENTUCKY COFFEE-TREE	T	*Gymnocladus dioicus*
ROCKY MOUNTAIN JUNIPER	T,W	*Juniperus scopulorum*
EASTERN RED-CEDAR	T,W	*Juniperus virginiana*
COMMON JUNIPER	S	*Juniperus communis*
PONDEROSA PINE	T,W	*Pinus ponderosa*
PINYON PINE	T	*Pinus cembroides edulis*
GAMBEL OAK	S	*Quercus gambelii*
STAGHORN SUMAC	S	*Rhus typhina*
SIBERIAN PEA-SHRUB	S,W	*Caragana arborescens*
HEDGE COTONEASTER	S,W	*Cotoneaster acutifolia*
SQUAWBUSH	S,W	*Rhus trilobata*
BUSH CINQUEFOIL	S	*Potentilla fruticosa*
COMMON LILAC	S	*Syringa vulgaris*

Perennials recommended are: columbine (*Aquilegia caerulea* hybrids); iris (*Iris germanica*); peony (*Paeonia albiflora*); Oriental poppy (*Papaver orientale*); Shasta daisy (*Chrysanthemum leucanthemum*); chrysanthemum (*Chrysanthemum morifolium* hybrids); hollyhock (*Althaea rosea*); blanket flower (*Gaillardia aristata*); larkspur (*Delphinium cultorum*); bleeding-heart (*Dicentra spectabilis*); daylily (*Hemorocallis* hybrids); perennial sweet pea (*Lathyrus latifolius*); and coneflower (*Rudbeckia laciniata*).

All the commonly used annuals may be grown in prepared beds and window boxes. Petunias are the favorite, followed by geraniums, marigolds, ageratum, balsam and zinnias.

Strawberries are commonly grown. The hill type varieties developed for the region are most satisfactory and are available from local nurseries. Red raspberries, particularly the fall-fruiting varieties, are grown in gardens; also gooseberries and currants.

Warm days and relatively cool nights during the short growing season favor vegetable production. Lettuce, radishes, beets, carrots, cabbage and its relatives, peas and snap beans are widely planted. In warmer valleys, melons, cucumbers, tomatoes, squash and other warm-season species flourish.

Nut trees are seldom seen in the High Plains. In the southern region there are a few pecans and occasional Carpathian walnuts. Northward only the black walnut survives.

Common Kentucky bluegrass is preferred for most of the region. Its vegetative varieties 'Park,' 'Merion,' 'Windsor,' 'Fylking' and the like are successful.

The importance of specific weed species varies from place to place. The following noxious weeds are considered serious pests throughout most of the High Plains: Canada thistle (*Cirsium arvense*); Russian thistle (*Salsola pestifer*); field bindweed (*Convovulus arvensis*); leafy spurge (*Euphorbia esula*); silverleaf poverty weed (*Franseria discolor*); woollyleaf poverty weed (*Franseria tomentosa*); Russian knapweed (*Centaurea repens*); Mexican fireweed (*Kochia scoparia*) and tumble amaranth (*Amaranthus albus*).

Peonies like these succeed in the High Plains' extremely fertile soil if well mulched against subzero winters. Phosphorous and iron are needed in soils here for optimum success.

Western Mountains

By MARION BLACK WILLIAMS

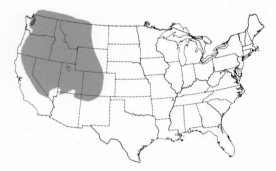

The Western Mountains area includes the chain of Rocky Mountains running north and south from Canada to the southwest ranges of New Mexico and Arizona, and is bordered by the High Plains on the east, desert to the west and portions of the Pacific Mountain States. It is the combination of latitude and altitude that determines plant habitation and survival. The climatic conditions of moisture, sun, wind and temperature, as well as soil, are widely variable.

Climate Comes First

The average yearly precipitation including moisture from snow is eight to 20 in. in population centers at lower elevations. High mountain areas receive more rain, plus deep winter snow packs which also supply water for the cities. Metered water for hose irrigation is expensive. It is essential to learn to water thoroughly, using enough at one time to penetrate to root zones and to the subsoil, and then to use surface mulches to conserve moisture.

Frequent overhead sprinklings, except to create a moist surface for newly set bedding plants, wastes water and retards deeper penetrating root development. Deliver water by lawn sprinklers (systems), open-end hoses, open-end soakers, root feeders.

The length of the growing season varies with the location. The number of daylight hours is influenced by the proximity to the mountains. The intense sunlight increases the value of frost-free days so that most crops can be grown. The season is too short for much gardening at the high elevation resorts. Winter sun makes indoor gardening successful.

Improving Your Soil

Generally, native soils are overly alkaline and lack humus because there is not enough rain to wash away the excess of mineral salts nor enough natural plant growth to use them, die, and decay, thus providing organic matter for the soil. This poor physical condition may be corrected by the continual addition of organic matter such as animal manures, peat, leafmold, compost, wood chips and mulches. Sand is added to lighten and increase the porosity of clay soils. Nitrogen and phosphorus are usually lacking and must be supplied. Available iron locks up in the soil, causing chlorosis; the remedy is iron sulfate or chelated iron. Alkalinity is lowered by agricultural sulfur, into a suitable pH range for acid plants.

In this region drying winds and sun evaporate moisture, causing low humidity year around. Plants manage to thrive in spite of erratic weather which includes mild or cold winters with sharp night temperature drops, hot and cool, dry and wet summers, chinook winds, low chill factor winds on sunny winter days, wet April snows, summer hailstorms and late spring and early autumn frosts.

There is a wide choice among trees, shrubs, vines, ground covers, herbaceous perennials, bulbs, annuals and vegetables known to be reliably hardy to use for framework plantings. Ornamentals are recommended as much for their resistance to sunscald as to cold and drought. It is often necessary to protect young tree trunks against sunburn for several years. Varieties hybridized for short-season development should be selected rather than those needing a long, even-temperature season to reach maturity.

Broad-leaved evergreens, deciduous trees, shrubs and perennials that prefer acid soils and humidity are not successful outdoors here because of the lack of humidity and the difficulty in maintaining the soil pH. These plants, along with warm-climate tropicals, are easily container-grown indoors in winter.

Exposure conditions differ within a yard. It is sometimes necessary to relocate a shrub or tree to either a more open or more protected spot. The flowering time of the same variety of a perennial can be advanced or retarded as much as two weeks by location alone. Walls, solid fences and windbreaks of trees and shrubs should be planned both for decorative effects and weather control.

In the Western Mountain region cold frames and hotbeds are all-season garden adjuncts used in the early spring for seed starting. They are also useful in the summer for growing perennial seedlings and for tomatoes. Screens should replace glass lids to shield against hail damage in warm weather.

In this area the times of the year to move woody ornamentals, particularly natives and herbaceous perennials, depend upon their dormancy, flowering time, re-establishment condition and care. Usually, nursery stock is handled best during late February through April, depending upon whether it is balled and burlaped, bare-rooted or container grown.

Natives growing at higher elevations become dormant in October and can be dug with a ball of soil and moved to lower elevations where the ground will not freeze for another month. In the spring, by the time higher soil can be dug, dormancy has broken and the move to a warmer temperature is not as successful. Try to duplicate native soil and exposure conditions when relocating wild plantings. Attractive

natives to cultivate are: thimbleberry, aspen, cinquefoil, Oregon grape, seedlings of Apache-plume, wax and yellow flowering currant, mountain mahogany, chamisa, three-leaf sumac, chokeberry, wild plum, yucca and evergreens.

Varieties of bluegrass and fine fescues are used for lawns. Seed beds should be enriched with organic matter and thoroughly prepared prior to planting. One inch of water a week should be sufficient to maintain turf built on a good base and fed regularly.

Designs combining small lawn areas with open spaces covered with indigenous materials (not fields of crushed stone) are becoming increasingly popular and practical in this semiarid climate.

Plants That Succeed

Among the most successful plants for this region are: American linden (*Tilia americana* 'Redmond') Zones 3–8, 60–75 ft. high, deciduous; blue spruce (*Picea pungens* and varieties) Zones 3–8, 100 ft. high, evergreen; Norway maple (*Acer platanoides* and variety 'Crimson King') Zones 4–8, 40–60 ft. high, deciduous; locusts 'Sunburst' and 'Moraine' (*Gleditsia*), Zones 4–9, 40–50 ft. high, deciduous; junipers (*Juniperus* species and varieties) Zones 3–8, 1–30 ft. high, evergreen; pinyon pine (*Pinus edulis*) Zone depends upon altitude, to 25 ft. high, evergreen; crab apples (*Malus* species and varieties) Zones 4–8, to 25 ft. high, deciduous; Kentucky coffee-tree (*Gymnocladus dioicus*) Zones 5–8, 40–60 ft. high, deciduous; *Euonymus* (species and varieties) Zones 3–8, vine to 10 ft. high, deciduous to semi-evergreen; firethorn (*Pyracantha* species and varieties) Zones 5–8, 5–6 ft. high, deciduous; and weeping birch (*Betula pendula*) Zones 3–8, 30–40 ft. high, deciduous.

Fruits that succeed include: apple, cherry, plum, peach, apricot, Zones 4–8, 6–25 ft. high.

Most cool-weather vegetables will do well if care is given to soil preparation and watering—so will most favorite annual and perennial flowers and bulbs.

The most common weeds in the region are dandelion; ragweed, giant and common; Russian thistle (tumbleweed); plantain, broadleaf and buckhorn varieties; wild morning-glory (bindweed); chickweed; grasses such as quack, nut, crab, foxtail, common or annual thistle; prickly lettuce; purslane; mallow; and clover.

Sunscald is a hazard in this region, but intense sunlight also increases the value of frost-free days so plants such as the firethorn (*Pyracantha*), shown in fruit, make a good show. Use of soakers, root feeders and mulches offsets seasonal droughts and the high cost of water for irrigation.

Pacific Northwest

By CHARLES H. POTTER

The gardener of the Pacific Northwest may be a resident of northern California, Oregon or Washington. He falls generally into one of two divisions—either on the seaward side of the area which is divided by the Cascade Mountains in the northern part and melts into the Sierra Nevadas further south, or eastward of the mountains where gardening is a different story.

The Japanese ocean current greatly modifies the weather picture for the whole of the Pacific Northwest. It carries with it a mildness of temperature unequalled anywhere else in this latitude. Its influence is felt primarily along the coast but some penetrates inland, and causes climatic surprises.

Climate Comes First

Such a region contains all the varieties of climate and rainfall under which most gardening takes place. The gardens of the Puget Sound area of Washington and the Willamette Valley of Oregon grow in a climate that is generally moist with mild winters and summer temperatures mostly in the 70's and 80's. Coastal gardens reckon with temperatures more often in the 60's during the summer than above that, and winters soaked with Pacific winds laden with water. Coastal areas of northern California are less wet and temperatures more mild.

The "other half" of the gardens, those eastward of

the mountains of the area, face severe frost, freezing winter weather and hot summer days.

In the coldest portions of the region it may get down to a minus 35 or 40 degrees. In summer temperatures have been known to soar as high as 110 to 115 degrees, though rarely.

Knowing something about the annual precipitation can be a big help to the home gardener, especially if he uses that knowledge in his soil preparation, selects plants suitable to his available irrigation or natural rainfall and knows when best to apply water where natural moisture is critical.

Indicating the wide variation of annual precipitation in the Northwest are these figures: Tatoosh Island (northwestern point of Washington State, adjoining the rain forest of the Olympic National Park), 77.69 in.; Seattle, Washington, 38.94 in.; Yakima, Washington, 7.86 in.; Portland, Oregon, 37.18 in.; Pendleton, Oregon, 12.38 in.; Lakeview, Oregon, 14.11 in. and Eureka, California, 38.43 in.

Improving Your Soil

Generally speaking, the soils of the wetter areas are the result of accumulated foliage from huge forests which once blanketed the entire western half of the Pacific Northwest and in many places still do. Built over a millennium of pine, fir and hemlock needles and compatible undergrowth shrubs, the percentage of organic matter is high and the soils mostly very retentive of moisture.

But even in these formerly forested areas are pockets—such as Canby, Oregon—where the deposits of soil run to sand. The latter type is quick to drain, easy to cultivate even after rainfall, but moisture soon disappears and fertilizers are leached away more rapidly than in soils containing a better percentage of organic matter.

Compost, peat moss, well-rotted manure, barkdust and sawdust are materials readily available to most Northwest gardeners for improving the moisture retention and aeration qualities of the soil.

Fertilizer must be supplied in accordance with the soil's needs. If fresh sawdust is used, nitrifying organisms turn their attention to breaking down the raw sawdust, and the nitrogen which would ordinarily go to the plants is robbed. To offset this, it is necessary to apply ammonium sulfate. And every gardener, no matter what he may "think" to be the nutrient situation of his soil or its acidity or alkalinity factor should not guess about it in this variable region. There is no substitute for soil testing.

To bring a heavy, clayey soil into line and improve its texture, sand or vermiculite and organic matter must be added. All plants require a well-aerated soil for root systems so that the pockets in the soil may be alternately filled with air and moisture. A heavy, compacted soil contains few pockets and root development is hampered by this poor texture. Sand alone is not enough to improve such soil. Sand helps drainage—and good drainage is a must—but does not improve texture.

Surveys show that a big majority of the coastal soils in the Northwest is highly acid with a pH of below 5.5 and most of the rest slightly above that point. Coastal soils are low in phosphorus and deficient in potassium, and these must be supplied if plants are to flourish.

Between the coast and the mountains most of the soils are moderately acid; phosphorus is needed and potassium is low. About half the soils east of the mountains in the more arid regions are below the mid-

point of 7.0 between acid and alkaline. In the eastern parts of the area some require a moderate amount of phosphorus; others require a lot. Others in that part of the Northwest run high in phosphorus content. The important point here is for the gardener to be absolutely sure of his soil's needs before attempting to make corrections. Use a home soil testing kit to determine your soil's specific needs, or consult the local Agricultural Extension Service. You will find the address listed under *Experiment Station*.

Plants That Succeed

The home gardener can make gardening much easier by growing the plants that do best in the type of soil he has. There are many wonderful plants native to the Northwest, including the Pacific dogwood, Oregon grape, California fuchsia, Oregon trillium, dwarf rhododendron, coast rhododendron, western azalea, lupines, squawgrass, camas, Douglas-fir, various maples, red and blue elderberries, oaks, pines, mock-orange and willows. All of these and many more succeed in "captivity" if given the care they require.

Walnuts and filberts are the principal nuts for the Northwest and in the western part of the area raspberries, black caps, blueberries, blackberries, loganberries, youngberries and strawberries do exceptionally well. Except for the tropical or subtropical flowers, there is hardly an annual or perennial which will not be at home in the Northwest. The same is true of vegetables, all the leafy types, root sorts and those which grow on vines produce exceptionally good crops. Corn is most successful in the hotter parts of the Northwest.

Much of the nation's lawn grass seed is produced in Oregon. The bentgrasses, fescues and bluegrasses are best in most lawn situations and are used in various combinations or singly. Those grasses used in the South are not suited for the Northwest.

No Northwest gardener would give the same list of favorites among the ornamentals. Most heavily grown, however, are roses, rhododendrons, azaleas, dogwoods, camellias, holly, *Daphne odora, Pieris japonica*, the heaths, delphinium, petunia and marigold, especially the new hybrids.

The area is not without its weeds. Some of the worst are quackgrass, Canada thistle, horsetail rush, crabgrass, dandelion, plantain, creeping buttercup, oxalis, nutgrass, chickweed, bracken and bindweed.

Rhododendrons as handsome as the hybrid 'Boursoult' shown ABOVE originated in this region warmed by Japanese currents. Understanding annual patterns of rainfall is the key to success in the Northwest's varying climates.

East Central

By VICTOR M. RIES

This area comprises Ohio, Indiana, Illinois, Kentucky, southern Michigan, southern Wisconsin and western West Virginia. It is extremely variable in climate. Much of it is in the Corn Belt with searing summers in which nights as well as days are hot. The bulk of the area is in Zones 5a/b and 6a/b. But Kentucky includes Zone 7, and the northern part of southern Michigan and south central Wisconsin include Zone 4b. The areas around large bodies of water, as the Great Lakes, are milder than those a few miles away. The letter a designates cooler, and b warmer, areas in each Zone.

Climate Comes First

Since most of the central part of this area is without snow much of the winter, damage can be expected, especially with herbaceous plants. Heavy winter mulching will help, and it is important to make sure plants are well watered before winter sets in.

The number of days between killing frosts in the growing season varies: Illinois 160–210, Indiana 150–190, Kentucky 180–200, Michigan 130–170, Ohio 140–200, West Virginia 150–170 and southern Wisconsin 150–170.

Rainfall in the region is considerably varied: Illinois 32–46 in., Indiana 34–44 in., Kentucky 40–50 in., Michigan 26–36 in., Ohio 32–44 in., West Virginia 30–32 in. and Wisconsin 38–48 in.

Improving Your Soil

Soils vary from heavy clays to sandy, and there are good loams and muck soils as well. The soils are acid through neutral to alkaline according to the rock underneath. The acid soils may be made less so by the addition of agricultural lime. Soils may be made more acid by the addition of iron sulfate, or aluminum sulfate and powdered sulfur. Add at the rate of 1 oz. per square yard every three weeks until leaves turn dark green.

Most ornamental plants are highly tolerant of soil reaction despite much advertising to the contrary. All of the soils and all plantings will be benefitted by a regular application of a complete commercial or organic fertilizer.

Deficiencies of elements such as iron, zinc and magnesium can be determined only by soil tests. Your County Agricultural Agent can usually tell you what is needed. All soils here will be improved by the addition of organic matter in the form of peat moss, compost or similar humus material. Sand may also be used to lighten clayey texture.

Plants That Succeed

Annual flowers that flourish include petunias, zinnias and marigolds. Sweet alyssum, portulaca, verbena, annual phlox, cornflower, snapdragon, annual foxglove and Shirley poppies are also highly successful. Among perennials that do well here are lilies, daylilies, iris, peonies, phlox, bleeding-heart, columbines, hardy pinks, hardy alyssum, hardy candytuft and bellflower (*Campanula*).

Bulbs for the East Central area are tulips, hyacinths, narcissus, snowdrops, crocus, squills and alliums.

For shade trees use long-living ones such as red oaks, sugar maples, red maples, thornless honey locust (named varieties only), small-leaf linden, pin oak (only if soil is acid) and ginkgo. Try sweetgum in Zone 5b and south.

Introduced species of shrubs are often more satisfactory than natives for home planting, especially around smaller houses. Among low shrubs recommended are cranberry cotoneaster (*Cotoneaster apiculata*), slender deutzia (*Deutzia gracilis*), glossy abelia (*Abelia grandiflora*), kerria (*K. japonica*), Froebel spirea (*Spiraea bumalda*).

Medium-tall shrubs to try include: spreading cotoneaster (*C. divaricata*), Regel privet (*Ligustrum obtusifolium regelianum*), Korean spice viburnum (*V. carlesii*) and 'Bristol Ruby' weigela. And among the tall shrubs select Amur maple (*Acer ginnala*), Cornelian cherry (*Cornus mas*), showy forsythia (*F. intermedia spectabilis*), Sargent crab apple (*Malus sargentii*),

The mixed bouquet is a sample of the multitude of flowers that thrive in this region.
Cold temperatures and sparse snowfall make winter mulching the key to survival for many perennial species.

Chinese lilac (*Syringa chinensis*), wayfaring tree (*Viburnum lantana*) and Japanese snowball (*Viburnum tomentosum sterile*).

Before planting any fruit, berry or grape plants check with your local County Agricultural Agent for a list of varieties recommended for your area. These do not always agree with the catalogs; there is considerable difference in quality of fruit and productiveness.

Since most fruits require a regular application of pesticides, get a spray schedule for home fruits from the County Agent. Apples may not be worth the effort it takes to keep them free of pests here. Peaches are best when spring planted. Use several varieties for a succession of fruit. Sour cherries succeed well but sweet require two or more varieties for pollination. Fire blight may be a problem with pears so select 'Seckel' and 'Kieffer,' which are immune to it. Plant 'Callery' pear and 'Bradford Callery' as ornamentals. Use only those plum varieties recommended by County Agents. Spraying may be a problem.

Strawberries, raspberries, black raspberries, blackberries, currants and gooseberries are usually good. Blueberries require an acid soil which is not always available. Grapes are successful in the East Central; new varieties are being introduced and it will be worthwhile to check with the County Agent.

Named varieties of black walnuts and hickories are good for this area but English walnuts seldom are fruitful. Hard-shell pecans are good only in Zone 6 and south.

Most vegetables can be grown in this area except early peas in southern areas only. Try kale, broccoli, Brussels sprouts, salsify, parsnips, summer and winter squash and, up through Zone 5, try sweet potatoes. White potatoes require so much spraying that they may not be worth the effort. Make second sowings of lettuce, endive, beets, carrots and beans for fall enjoyment.

Kentucky bluegrass and its varieties 'Merion,' 'Pennstar' and 'Windsor' are the best in East Central areas. Zoysia and Bermuda will be brown from early October to mid-May. Do all grass seeding before early May or early in October for best results. Spring and fall are the best seasons to plant sod lawns.

Weeds will vary depending on your type of garden, the amount of sunlight and nearby sources of seed. Crabgrass, controlled by a pre-emergence spray, and a southern grass working northward, nimblewill (which can be controlled only by hand pulling), are the worst weeds. Dandelion, ground ivy, broadleaf plantain, buckhorn and white clover can be controlled by commercial sprays. In flower beds and gardens, purslane, Canada thistle, oxalis, quackgrass and lamb's-quarters can be controlled by cultivation or pulling by hand while they are young.

Heartland

By ROSE ROSS

Heartland's northern boundary point is Des Moines, Iowa. From there the line circles down through Peoria and Springfield, Illinois, to eastern Missouri at Saint Genevieve, cutting off the southeastern section of the state, but including Springfield and the Missouri Ozarks. It crosses the northwestern tip of Arkansas and the northeastern section of Oklahoma, circling between Bartlesville and Tulsa. From there it enters Kansas northwest of Ponca City and Blackwell, Oklahoma, to include Wichita and Salina. It continues to circle through mid-Kansas and into Nebraska north of Smith Center, Kansas. The circle passes through Lincoln and Omaha, Nebraska, and is completed at Des Moines.

Climate Comes First

In the Heartland area, the gardener is challenged by a climate that can change drastically and rapidly from warm to cold—and from cold to hot. In winter there occasionally is a lasting blanket of snow to be counted on as insulation for and protection to plantings that aren't quite hardy. But generally, the ground lies bare and exposed and the gardener will have to supply man-planned protection. But there is a bonus—we are neither North, South, East nor West, but the center of all, and plants from both cold and warm climates can do well here—in any case, are worth a try in the microclimate of your own back yard. But plan to mulch valuable plants that may not be rugged, as azaleas, and if they have been planted in open spaces shelter them with windbreaks, such as stands of sturdier growing materials, or behind staked burlap.

The northern area of Heartland lies in Zone 4 with the limits of the annual average minimum temperature of −30 to −20 degrees; the middle area falls in Zone 5 with a minimum of −20 to −10 degrees and the southern area in Zone 6 with a minimum of −10 to 0 degrees.

Frost dates vary widely within each state as well as from state to state in Heartland. Roughly, in the warmer areas the last killing frost in the spring is likely to fall between April 15–10 while it may come as late as April 30–25 in the colder areas. The first killing frost in the fall usually occurs between October 15–10 in the colder areas of Heartland and as late as October 25–20 in the warmer zones. Estimate of the growing days for the region is 160–180.

The pattern of rainfall varies widely throughout Heartland with a rough average of 29–30 in. Most areas suffer from hot, dry conditions during the months of July and August.

Improving Your Soil

The soils of Heartland cover a wide range. In the western half, basically northern prairie soils predominate, and in the eastern half the gray-brown podzolic soils are most common. All areas produce crops with adequate soil management. By using barnyard manures, decayed compost, cover crops and commercial fertilizers the soil is maintained in optimum condition. It is necessary to lime soils that are too acid.

Plants That Succeed

Although Heartland has some summer daytime temperatures of 100 degrees, below-zero winter temperatures occasionally and late-spring frosts, there is a fine choice of plant material that gives excellent crops under the growing conditions that exist.

Good shade trees for Heartland are the white ash, fast-growing, fall coloring; Norway maple, brilliant fall foliage, compact crown; sweetgum, interesting bark, good form; white oak, handsome bark, fall coloring; pin oak, good form, fall coloring; sugar maple, excellent form, fall coloring.

Small ornamental trees of value are 'Hopa' crab, red flowers; 'Bob White' crab, yellow fruit, dense foliage; 'Radiant' crab, pink flowers, bright fruit; white redbud, white flower, early; eastern redbud, pink bloom, early; and fringetree, white flowers.

There is a wide selection of shrubs and flowers adapted to Heartland's growing conditions, but many gardeners believe a regular fungicide and insecticide spray schedule is advisable to prevent the buildup of insect populations and of diseases particular to this area.

Shrubs with excellent performance records in this area are dwarf burning bush, handsome bark and leaf coloring; slender deutzia, graceful form, good bloom; red osier dogwood, white flowers, red twigs; Siberian dogwood, good form, white flowers; 'Sarcoxie' euonymus, upright growth, glossy leaves; 'Lynwood' forsythia, good form, yellow bloom; 'Arnold Tartarian' honeysuckle, red bloom; inkberry, abundant fruit; 'Esther Staley' lilac, fine color; 'Minnesota Snowflake' mock-orange, attractive bloom; doublefile viburnum, fruit and flowers; 'Mariesii' viburnum, excellent fruit; 'Peace' hybrid tea rose, fine bloom, vigorous growth; and Hick's yew, upright.

Reliably hardy perennials are 'Pearl' achillea; yellow aconitum; 'Basket of Gold' alyssum; 'Silver Mound' artemisia; 'Snowflake' candytuft; 'Chau-

baud's Giant' carnation; 'McKana's Giant' columbine; 'Pinwheel' gloriosa daisy; 'Snow Cloud' Shasta daisy; 'Chinese Lantern' dahlia; 'Hyperion' daylily; 'Excelsior' foxglove; 'Fire Sprite' heuchera; 'Pompadour' hollyhock; 'Tampa Dwarf' iris; 'Tahiti Sunrise' iris; 'Crown Imperial' and 'Minnpink Cushion Mum' chrysanthemums; 'Indian Jewels' penstemon and Oriental poppy.

Hardy bulbs that have many uses in landscape plans are chionodoxa, crocus, camassia, eranthis, grape-hyacinth, *Amaryllis hallii*, galanthus, lily, narcissus and tulip.

Annuals of merit are 'Blue Mist' ageratum; 'Rosie O'Day' alyssum; 'Early Splendor' amaranthus; 'Salmon Rose' balsam; 'Golden Triumph' celosia; 'Rusty Splendor' coleus; and 'Persian Carpet' dianthus; dwarf mixed impatiens; 'Carefree' geraniums; 'Southern Belle' hibiscus; 'Summer Carnival' hollyhock; 'Golden Climax' marigold; 'Silver Medal' and 'Pink Cascade' petunias; and 'St. John's Fire' sage (salvia).

Some favorite fruit varieties are: grape, 'Concord,' 'Niagara'; apple, 'Lodi,' 'Golden Delicious'; strawberry, 'Blakemore,' 'Surecrop'; peach, 'Red Haven,' 'Alberta'; and pear, 'Kieffer' and 'Seckel.'

Black walnut, American hazelnut; hardy pecan and shagbark hickory are major nut varieties.

Some choice vegetable varieties are: 'Martha Washington' asparagus; snap bean, 'Top Crop,' 'Contender'; beets, 'Early Wonder'; cabbage, 'Earliana,' 'Marion Market'; carrot, 'Tender Sweet'; corn, 'Marcross'; lettuce, 'Black-seeded Simpson'; muskmelon, Burpee Hybrid; mustard, 'Green Wave'; onion, 'Yellow Globe,' 'Early Harvest'; parsnip, 'Hollow Crown'; peas, 'Little Marvel'; pepper, 'California Wonder' and tomato, 'Moreton Hybrid.'

Kentucky bluegrass is the most satisfactory lawn for Heartland. Once established it withstands heavy traffic and extremes in rainfall and temperature.

A seed mixture of 60 per cent topgrade Kentucky bluegrass seed with 40 per cent Chewing's fescue will produce an attractive, serviceable lawn. Regular mowing and feeding is advisable.

Some weed pests of both garden and lawn are field bindweed, common chickweed, hairy crabgrass, smooth crabgrass, dandelion, goosegrass, pigweed, broad-leaved plantain, purslane, smart weed and ragweed. Clean cultivation is the major control and will spare the gardener the need for pulling or spraying programs later.

Most warm- and cool-weather ornamentals succeed in this region whose main challenge is drastically variable winter temperatures. Heartland's popular globe flower, *Kerria japonica pleniflora*, is shown here in full bloom.

Southeast

By DR. FRED J. NISBET

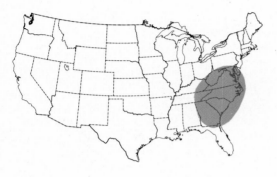

For gardeners, the Southeast means the two Virginias, both Carolinas and Georgia, with eastern slices of Tennessee and northeast Alabama. Elevations range from sea level to more than 5,000 feet and the climate from subtropical to subalpine, which permits growing a wide range of plants. Here southern and northern plants grow together.

Climate Comes First

There are three different climates in the region. The subtropical is in the Coastal Plain, with minimums of 20 degrees or higher; the northern limit of the humid, subtropical climate, with minimums 0 to −10 degrees, includes the Upper Piedmont and lowest foothills. Elevations of 1,500 to 2,500 feet, except in the Virginias, generally have minimums of −10 degrees; higher elevations can go to −35 degrees. Frost-free days range from about 275 to 140 or less.

Rain is adequate, ranging from 30 to 70 in. plus, and is well distributed; all areas with less than 44 in. lie in the two Virginias.

Improving Your Soil

Most soils here tend to be acid, fine for camellias, azaleas and other acid-loving plants. The Coastal Plain has sandy soils, elsewhere clays are general; a few locations have good loams. High temperatures and humidity burn humus rapidly, so it needs to be dug into the soil and replenished often in decomposed organic forms such as peat moss, leafmold or decayed wastes. These soils respond well to fertilization.

Plants That Succeed

Camellias are the glamour plants of the region. Once planted only on the Coastal Plain, they have now spread over the Piedmont and a few selected varieties have climbed up into the mountains. Cultivars of *C. japonica* are most common, but those of *C. sasanqua* are gaining favor. Azaleas are grown in vast numbers and are the colorful basis of spring gardens. The so-called Southern Indicas dominate the Coastal Plain. Some Kurume hybrids, such as 'Hinodegiri,' are grown there too, but they really take over in the Upper Piedmont and up to the middle elevations of the mountains. Usually only a few cultivars are planted, resulting in about three to five weeks of bloom. With the addition of early and late varieties of the Glenn Dales and Satsukies, the blooming season can be made to extend to three months or more. Exbury, Mollis hybrids and native kinds add gold, peach and coral tones to the color scheme.

Dogwoods (*Cornus florida*) are found everywhere, in both white and pink. Another month of bloom can be had by planting the Japanese dogwood (*C. kousa*). Boxwoods are still widely planted, even though troubles, such as nematodes, are increasing. Roses grow beautifully in this region and are widely planted. Many local rose societies sponsor fine rose shows.

The Southern magnolia (*M. grandiflora*) is a favorite. The saucer and star magnolias should be more widely planted, for they thrive. Daffodils are found everywhere, from naturalized clumps in farmyards to fine collections of the newest kinds. There are many daffodil shows. Crape-myrtles, both bush and tree types, bloom from June to September and are popular. Hollies are favorites. Many of these are the native American holly, and some of the cultivars of the Japanese and the Burford hollies are also gaining ground. New hybrids, such as Foster, have been introduced here and are growing in popularity. Daylilies are well adapted to the region and are seen everywhere. For autumn color, chrysanthemums are tops. Oaks are favorites among shade trees. Live oaks are common where hardy. Willow, water and white oaks fill in elsewhere.

Peaches, the favorite fruit here, are grown in all areas, while apples and a few pears start in the Upper Piedmont and gain quality at the higher elevations. Grapes are widely grown in the Upper Piedmont and in the mountains, with 'Scuppernong' and 'Muscadine' in milder areas. Strawberries are the most popular small fruit; select varieties for your conditions from your local garden-supply center. They will do better than imported varieties which may look wonderful in catalogs but may not be suitable here.

Pecans are favored where they are hardy, and black walnuts and Chinese chestnuts take over as the preferred nut crops in colder areas. In the milder sections of the Southeast, vegetables can be grown most of the year. "Greens" such as mustard, collards and kale are popular during cool seasons. Okra, black-eyed peas and sweet potatoes are, too. Many gardeners grow "roastin' ears," field corn that is tough and coarse, but modern sweet corn is far superior and recommended instead. Watermelons are a major crop and succeed without making great demands on the gardener.

The "warm-season grasses," from the Upper Piedmont down, are St. Augustine, Bermuda, centipede (for the poorest soils) and Matrella strains of zoysia. The "cool-season grasses," Kentucky bluegrass and the fine-leaved fescues, are for the Upper Piedmont and the mountains. Meyer zoysia is hardy here, too. Bermuda and zoysia lawns are frequently overseeded with annual ryegrass in the late fall, and provide a green lawn all winter. Close mowing is necessary in the spring to allow the perennial grasses to recover. Some gardeners dye the permanent grass as soon as frost turns it brown; repeat treatments may be necessary to keep the color a promising green.

The high soil temperature of the region favors crabgrass as a weed, but this is easily controlled with either a pre-emergence chemical before the seeds sprout or a post-emergence chemical in early summer. Bermudagrass is another story; clean cultivation or hand weeding, followed by a heavy mulch, is the answer. Hand weeding or hoeing wild artemisia just spreads it, so use Casoron, preferably in the fall. Johnson, nut and quackgrass can be controlled with EPTC; repeat treatments are usually necessary. Poison ivy, poison oak and honeysuckle will yield to amino-triazol; this must be kept from desired plants and used in the quantities and with all the precautions recommended on the label.

A lovely evergreen, the camellia, blooms in the warmer
areas of this section from fall to spring and the
magnolia, showiest of flowering trees, blossoms as
early as February. The *Magnolia soulangeana*, ABOVE, and the
Camellia 'Adolph Audusson,' BELOW, are glamour plants
of the Southeast, but the generally acid soil
is well suited to the needs of azaleas as well
and they dominate spring gardens. Indica azaleas are
most successful in the coastal plains
and the Kurume hybrids flourish in the Upper Piedmont.
Careful selection of azalea hybrids by growing season
extends the flowering period many weeks. A well-
distributed rainfall, mild climate and elevations ranging from
sea level to 5000 feet above, create microclimates both
subtropical and subalpine. In most areas high temperatures
and humidity burn humus which needs frequent
replenishing to keep soils in top condition.

Florida

By MARY NOBLE

Florida is the most versatile state of all in its plants and gardens. Five hundred miles across from the top of Florida to Key West, 367 miles across the panhandle and there is water on three sides. The coastline is so jagged that there are 8,000 miles of waterfront. Within the land mass are many rivers and 10,000 named lakes plus thousands of small bodies of water.

The topography is mainly flat and at sea level. But in the west, the end of the Appalachian Mountain chain makes hills with the highest point in the state rising 345 feet. Some plants grow here that find the peninsula too tropical. (Hardiness is a measure of how much cold a plant can stand. In Florida, heat tolerance is a factor and many cold-hardy plants do not survive here.)

Climate Comes First

All this water warms the air when cold waves sweep in from the North and West, but Florida's climate is not entirely tropical.

Across the northern third of the state, where azaleas, wisteria and dogwood make of every garden a pastel fantasy in spring, the annual minimum temperature averages between 20 and 30 degrees. Several nights of subfreezing occur between mid-October and mid-March but the cold is not consistent. There are balmy spells between.

In the central citrus area the average minimum is 25 to 30 degrees, but the periods of freezing temperatures may be only a few hours long. Plants of the northern tier and tropicals of south Florida meet in central Florida gardens.

South Florida is subtropical. The temperature may dip below 32 degrees during a few nights and cause havoc, but most years the royal poincianas (*Delonix regia*) and flame vines (*Pyrostegia ignea*) flower unharmed. Plants protected by windbreaks, buildings or water survive cold better than those in exposed locations, especially in low-lying ground.

Improving Your Soil

Florida soil needs large amounts of humus material worked into it prior to planting to improve the texture and the ability to retain moisture and the elements that make soil fertile. Most of it is porous sand from which water and nutrients leach out rapidly. Some is compact red clay. Marl is low in organic matter and is alkaline in nature. In parts of south Florida the layer of soil over limestone may be too thin for planting, which requires that a hole be blasted in the limestone and filled with imported soil. An easier solution is to plant in containers.

Oak leaves and pinestraw, available in abundance, are excellent for mulching, help to retain moisture and improve the soil as they decay.

Plants That Succeed

Useful and popular low-maintenance plants include these: (*If restricted in growth area, the initials indicate North, Central and South.*)

Trees: Palms in variety, some limited to S. Cabbage-palm (*Sabal palmetto*) is the state tree and good anywhere. Thirty species of oak grow here including the patriarch live oak (*Quercus virginiana*). White dogwood (*Cornus florida*, N) is native, needs well-drained soil. Pink dogwood is not adaptable. American holly (*Ilex opaca*, N) comes in several horticultural varieties. 'Burford' variety of Chinese holly (*Ilex cornuta*, N) is good. Bauhinia (*B. variegata*, C and S), called orchid tree, is colorful. Also: Australian pine (*Casuarina*, C and S); crape-myrtle (*Lagerstroemia indica*) for summer bloom; *Jacaranda mimosifolia* (C and S) is a beautiful blue tree; *Magnolia grandiflora* (N) is the classic tree of the Deep South; royal poinciana (*Delonix regia*, S only) is the most spectacular flowering tree; pine trees for shifting shade.

Shrubs: Azalea (N and C), attractive evergreen for landscaping with glorious flowers in the spring. Roses are not low-maintenance, but more than six million bushes are imported into the state annually. In addition, gardeners buy locally grown plants grafted onto *Rosa fortuniana* rootstock. Hibiscus (mostly C and S) are available in handsome named varieties or the old

dependable single red. *Hydrangea macrophylla* (N and C) is deciduous, has enormous pink or blue flower clusters. *Camellia japonica* (N and C) is a beautiful evergreen. By planting carefully selected cultivars, blooms can be had for six months. Croton (*Codiaeum variegatum*) has exotic foliage in a variety of colors and patterns.

Also important: *Nerium oleander,* bottlebrush, seagrape (*Coccoloba uvifera*), poinsettia, boxwood, podocarpus, pittosporum and ligustrum.

Philodendrons, self-heading and climbing, are valuable landscape plants in south and central Florida but are less suited to the cooler areas.

Annuals and Perennials: In the north, annuals are divided into two groups, cold-tolerant and heat-resistant. Pansies, petunias and snapdragons are for winter; zinnias, marigolds and amaranthus for summer. Daylilies (*Hemerocallis*) grow in masses in gardens everywhere.

The tomato, our most popular food plant, is grown in home gardens along with annual flowers and many of the kitchen herbs.

Fruits and Nuts: Mango (*Mangifera indica*), papaya, and avocado in the south; citrus in central and pecan in the north.

Grass: Centipede (*Eremochloa ophiuroides*) is a low-maintenance grass for sandy soil. St. Augustine (*Stenotaphrum secundatum*) grows in sun, shade or on the oceanfront, but it is attacked by chinch bugs. Bermudagrass (*Cynodon dactylon*) needs sun and constant maintenance. Bahia (*Paspalum notatum*) grows on sandy soil and endures foot traffic, but needs frequent mowing. Italian ryegrass (*Lolium multiflorum*) is planted as a temporary winter cover over the permanent turfs which turn brown in cold weather.

Weeds: Most noxious to Florida gardeners are betony (*Stachys floridiana*), with square stems and small leaves and white tubers (no herbicide controls it); ragweed, a summer annual with purple stems; dollar weed (*Hydrocotyle umbellata*) or pennywort, has round leaves and creeping stems and grows in moist areas of the lawn; nutgrass, several species of *Cyperus,* infests the lawn, as does the universal crabgrass; and tea weed (*Sida acuta*), with dark green leaves, stems to 3 feet, small white flowers and deep roots. Most can be controlled by cultivation or kept out with the help of mulches. Those best handled with chemicals are discussed in the article on weeds.

Everything from the royal poinciana, LEFT, palms and papayas
—to dogwoods—succeeds in Florida's diversified climate.
Soils here benefit from additions of humus; mulch is
the low-maintenance trick that preserves moisture
through hot, dry spells.

Mid-South

By CAMILLA BRADLEY TRUAX

The Mid-South is composed of approximately a quarter of a million miles of flat, sometimes rolling land. Owing to its temperate climate and ample rainfall this is a region where gardening is a year-round delight. It is a section in which the choice of plant material, both native and introduced, is almost limitless.

The area includes Arkansas and west Tennessee, Alabama, Mississippi, Louisiana and a shallow, lateral portion of east Texas. It extends south to the Gulf of Mexico and is dominated by the Mississippi River and its many tributaries. It is interlaced with lesser waterways and dotted with lakes. The only mountains are the Ozarks in the upper portion of Arkansas, and the foothills of the Appalachian Range which taper off in northern Alabama. Nowhere must we contend with rugged peaks or altitudes higher than 1000 feet. Most of the region is lower than 100 feet. New Orleans, Houston and other coastal communities are practically at sea level.

Climate Comes First

Average annual rainfall is about 50 in., but unfortunately it is not distributed evenly throughout the year. October is usually a dry month and, by contrast, January is notably a wet one. The wise gardener provides good drainage for his plants at all times and keeps them well mulched for their protection through alternate dry periods.

Snow is not uncommon in and above the Texarkana-Greenwood-Birmingham belt. Although it may occur frequently, intermittent warm spells bring quick thaws. It is this fluctuation in temperature that prevents soil from remaining frozen long enough to interfere with planting.

Actually, November through February are our best months for planting or transplanting deciduous trees and shrubs, and we wait for winter to set out tulip bulbs and Dutch hyacinths in order to get maximum performance. The average last frost date in this belt is late March. Moving south toward the coast, it graduates to mid-February. As in all parts of the country, there can be some unpleasant surprises and we must be prepared to protect tender plants against "unusual" weather until April.

Extreme heat is a greater consideration than extreme cold for we experience it every summer. In selecting "hardy" plants we must consider their ability to withstand long periods of hot weather. The average summer daytime temperature is in the 90's, with readings of 100 degrees not uncommon, while relative humidity varies with proximity to water.

Improving Your Soil

Soil is as variable as climate. Its components may change not only from state to state but within the same county. The Extension Division of the U.S.D.A. offers an excellent soil analysis service. Its County Agents are equipped to take soil samples for free analysis and will recommend the necessary corrective measures.

Rule-of-thumb suggestions to those who do not wish to avail themselves of professional assistance are: (1) lighten heavy clay with coarse, salt-free sand; (2) improve sandy soil by adding organic matter; (3) acidify soil with agricultural sulfur or aluminum sulfate; or (4) alkalize it with bonemeal, lime or ashes.

When selecting woodland, desert or marshland plants for domestication, try to duplicate the growing conditions of their native habitat. Give shade and acid soil to wild ferns, mandrake and trilliums; full sun and neutral or slightly alkaline soil to phlox, liatris and yucca.

Most ornamentals need acid or neutral soil, but some, such as bearded iris, nasturtiums, lilac, deutzia and the legumes, of which sweet peas and the brooms are important species, need liming if soil is naturally acid. Japanese and Louisiana iris are acid-loving and, as opposed to bearded iris, require abundant moisture during the growing season.

Plants That Succeed

Azaleas are probably the most popular flowering shrub in the entire Mid-South. Their specific soil requirements are easily met by mixing peat moss or compost with sand and loamy soil. Deciduous species are the hardiest although the evergreen Glenn Dale hybrids grow well as far north as the District of

Columbia. Smaller species, such as the Kurumes and Belgian hybrids make beautiful potted plants to feature in whatever spot needs color when they are in bloom.

A fine companion plant for an azalea, and one having identical soil and moisture requirements, is the camellia. *C. japonica* is the traditional outdoor species of the lower South and is a popular greenhouse subject beyond its range of hardiness. *C. sasanqua* blooms early and can stand more cold than *C. japonica*. It makes a beautiful hedge used either alone or in combination with *Photinia glabra* whose new spring growth is such a brilliant red that it gives the effect of flowers.

The most majestic tree of the lower South is the live oak with *Magnolia grandiflora* as a close second. Both are evergreen. The latter is hardier and is famous for its fragrant, creamy-white blossoms. Other oaks, such as willow, water and southern red oak, are also good shade trees, but reserve all of these large trees for spacious grounds and select smaller trees for street planting and for landscaping the average home site. Substitute redbud, crab apple, crape-myrtle, Oriental magnolia or mimosa and enjoy the added bonus of colorful blossoms. These will screen out summer sun but admit it in the winter when its warmth is most desired. Native pines serve a dual purpose: They admit light and air and also provide high shade and a protective covering for semihardy undergrowth and they are decorative as well.

Pecans are an important commercial crop in upper Louisiana, Mississippi and east Texas. Walnuts supplant them farther north. Either makes a fine shade tree that pays dividends in nuts where home grounds are large enough to support one or two specimens. These are low maintenance food plants.

Among successful fruit trees in the warmest sections of the Mid-South region are figs, citrus, pomegranates and loquat (Japanese plum). Peaches, plums and pears succeed readily in cooler areas when rigid spray programs are carried out and benefit from regular fertilization.

The importance of a healthy, well-kept lawn in the Southern landscape cannot be overstressed. Either carpetgrass or Bermuda will make a beautiful lawn in full sun. Zoysia will remain green in high shade, requires less frequent mowing than most grasses and chokes out weeds when well established. East Texas is noted for its success with St. Augustinegrass, which is the most shade-tolerant of all. Centipedegrass makes a thick mat in sandy soils.

Just as the rose has its thorns, so do all growers have weeds to fight. Johnsongrass and cockleburs are the bane of the farmer in this region. The home gardener's worst fights are against nutgrass, goosegrass and crabgrass. Pre-emergent herbicides and diligent weeding are the best controls to date. For the vegetable garden the heavy mulching that helps to retain moisture during the October droughts also helps to keep weeds from making any headway.

Azaleas, in reality species of *Rhododendron*, make brilliant spring displays here when planted in a mix of peat moss or compost and sand or loam. Gardening is year-round but plants require protection through April weather changes. Popular are *Azalea japonica*, LEFT, and *Malus floribunda japonica*, RIGHT, the flowering crab apple, one of the region's favorites.

Southwest

By M. E. "GENE" GRAVES, JR.

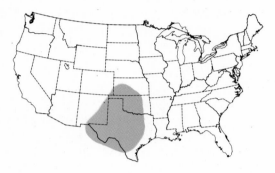

Most of Oklahoma and Texas, with the exception of the humid eastern part and the Gulf coastal area, are included in the Southwest region. There are tremendous variations in climatic and soil conditions here but the areas of the region have one thing in common: periodic severe drought conditions.

The average annual rainfall varies from eight to 60 inches. Generally the amount of moisture decreases as we go west.

Climate Comes First

Annual distribution of moisture and the rate that it falls are more important than the total amount. The entire Southwest is noted for receiving large amounts of rainfall in short periods of time with most of the water lost in runoff. Supplementary watering is necessary, especially during establishment of new plantings and during the drought periods.

Seasonal weather extremes make themselves felt on all plants throughout the region. High temperatures and wind velocity, bright sun and low humidity are common throughout the summer months.

Average annual minimum temperatures range from minus 10 degrees in northwest Oklahoma to 28 degrees in Laredo, Texas, on the Mexican border. The growing season varies from 170 to 340 days.

Improving Your Soil

Soil requirements for the plants grown in the Southwest vary widely. Most landscape plants need at least medium soil fertility for best growth. Fertility is judged by the amount of nitrogen, phosphate and potash in the soil as well as organic matter and trace minerals.

In general, from the central area eastward the soil reaction is neutral to acid. The western half is generally alkaline. Variations can be found in most areas.

High lime soils—alkaline—tend to tie up both phosphate and iron, causing a chloritic condition in a great number of ornamental plants. Iron must be added or the soil made more acid, releasing available iron to species needing pH on the acid side.

Large areas of the region are infested with cotton root rot fungus that infects the roots of some 2,000 species of plants, eventually killing them. It is important to avoid species that are susceptible.

Plants That Succeed

Trees (30 feet and over) that will grow throughout the state of Oklahoma and all except the extreme western and southwestern parts of Texas are: American elm (*Ulmus americana*) which is perhaps the most beautiful tree in the region, and Siberian elm (*Ulmus pumila*) which is often sold under the name of Chinese elm and has been planted perhaps more widely than any of the other introduced species, even though highly susceptible to cotton root rot.

The sycamore or American plane tree (*Platanus occidentalis*) is the largest hardwood tree in North America and a good selection for the region. Eastern poplars or cottonwoods (*Populus deltoides*) are abundant. Select male trees for planting. The honey locust (*Gleditsia triacanthos*) is excellent for the drier sections of the region.

Trees that grow well in the eastern half of the region include: silver maple (*Acer saccharinum*); silk tree or mimosa (*Albizia julibrissin*); common mulberry (*Broussonetia papyrifera*); and eastern redcedar (*Juniperus virginiana*). The southern magnolia (*Magnolia grandiflora*) is one of the best known trees in east Texas. American sweetgum (*Liquidambar styraciflua*) prefers the eastern part, but is growing nicely in the Fort Worth–Dallas area. Natural habitat for the bald-cypress (*Taxodium distichum*) is near water; however, it will grow in Lubbock, Texas.

Deciduous large shrubs or small trees (10 to 25 feet) that do well here are: fruitless mulberry (*Morus alba*), eastern redbud (*Cercis canadensis*) and crapemyrtle (*Lagerstroemia indica*).

Narrow-leaf evergreens that make good choices include: Oriental arborvitae (*Thuja orientalis*) and Rocky Mountain juniper (*Juniperus scopulorum*). Broadleaf evergreens are: loquat (*Eriobotrya japonica*), yaupon (*Ilex vomitoria*), glossy privet (*Ligu-*

German irises native to central and southern Europe flourish here and some of the loveliest of the new hybrids are featured in early-summer gardens. The cultivars 'Party Dress,' ABOVE, and 'Lady Ilsa,' BELOW, are among the best. The growing season varies from 170 days in cooler stretches to 340 days on the Mexican border and rules the selection of ornamentals. Periodic droughts in western areas are the gardener's greatest challenge, and efforts must be made to avoid water lost in run-offs after heavy rains. Alkaline soils common to the western half of the area tie up phosphate and iron and should be improved by additions of iron or acidifying elements. Soils from central areas eastward are neutral to acid, suited to the needs of many fine deciduous species.

strum *lucidum*) and Chinese privet (*Ligustrum sinense*).

Medium evergreen shrubs (6 to 9 feet) most favored in the home garden include: Chinese holly (*Ilex cornuta*), Burford Chinese holly (*Ilex cornuta* 'Burfordii'), Pfitzer Chinese juniper (*Juniperus chinensis* 'Pfitzeriana'), Japanese privet (*Ligustrum japonicum*) and nandina (*Nandina domestica*). Bridal-wreath spirea (*Spiraea prunifolia*) is an excellent deciduous plant.

Small evergreen shrubs (3 to 5 feet) are: glossy abelia (*A. grandiflora*), Japanese aucuba or golddust plant (*A. japonica variegata*), Japanese littleleaf box (*Buxus microphylla japonica*) and dwarf yaupon (*Ilex vomitoria*).

Dwarf evergreen shrubs (1 to 3 feet) for the region are: dwarf gardenia (*G. radicans*), dwarf Chinese holly (*Ilex cornuta rotunda*) and Adam's needle yucca (*Y. filamentosa*). A deciduous plant for the drier areas is Texas sage (*Salvia coccinea*).

Ground covers that improve the landscape in shaded or otherwise difficult areas include: Japanese star jasmine (*Trachelospermum asiaticum*) and English ivy (*Hedera helix* and varieties). A common evergreen vine is the yellow Carolina jessamine (*Gelsemium sempervirens*). Virginia creeper (*Parthenocissus quinquefolia*) is deciduous; all wisteria, semi-evergreen.

The primary fruit and nut trees grown in this climate are pecan (*Carya illinoesis*), pear, plum and peach. Grapes and strawberries also do well.

The list of flowering annuals and perennials is almost endless. Some of the more popular ones are rose, pansy, petunia, portulaca, vinca, zinnia, daisy, chrysanthemum, iris and tulip.

Most garden vegetables are grown throughout the region. The higher elevation of the high and rolling Plains, with cool nights, permits growing Irish white potatoes, celery, rhubarb and eggplant.

Bermudagrass (*Cynodon dactylon*) makes up about 90 per cent of the turf grass in Oklahoma, with some zoysia and buffalo (*Buchloe dactyloides*). Approximately 50 per cent of the lawns in Texas are Bermudagrass. St. Augustine (*Stenotaphrum secundatum*) is found primarily south and east of Fort Worth.

Weeds causing problems are: common chickweed (*Stellaria media*), henbit (*Lamium amplexicaule*), mouse-ear chickweed (*Cerastium vulgatum*), purslane (*Portulaca oleracea*), many-flowered aster (*A. ericoides*), sandbur (*Cenchrus pauciflorus*), annual bluegrass (*Poa annua*), dandelion, spurge-milk purslane (*Euphorbia supina*), goathead or puncture vine (*Tribulus terrestris*) and knotweed. Nutgrass or nutsedge (*Cyperus esculentus*) is one of the hard weeds to control because of its root runners.

Warm Southwest

By MARGARET TIPTON WHEATLY

Weather is today's temperature, rain, wind and humidity. Over a period of time these factors make up what we call "climate." All are important to plant growth, but temperature and rainfall are primary in determining which plants we can grow in our gardens, regardless of their location on the map.

The terrain and climate of the Warm Southwest are among the most diversified in the western United States. Included are seacoast, mountain and below-sea-level areas. In a single hour's drive in this area the traveler can pass from subtropical, ocean-damp climates to bone-dry desert, so that no one set of gardening rules holds for the entire region.

Climate Comes First

In San Diego and San Francisco, the frost-free season is almost all year, and most tender plants will flourish with little special attention. At Salinas, frosts arrive about November 22 and depart about March 17. Inland, in Phoenix, Arizona, the average frost season is from December 6 to February 15. Along the coastal areas, lush subtropical plants succeed. In the foothills and higher in the mountains hardy eastern lilac thrives, and there are apple and pear orchards which could not produce in the more tropical areas of the Warm Southwest. Imperial Valley, well below sea level, grows commercial crops of vegetables throughout the winter. In these areas supplemental watering may not be necessary.

Arid areas of the Warm Southwest, on the other

hand, have truly bone-dry climates. Rainfall (or more properly, "precipitation," since some snow falls in the mountains) occurs only during half the year from November through March—the "rainy" season. Here supplemental water is generally a year-long requirement for vegetables, flowers, subtropical fruits and ornamentals.

Improving Your Soil

Soils of these low rainfall regions are basically alkaline, or at best neutral. In order to grow plants in high pH alkaline soils, acid reacting chemicals need to be used. Most deciduous plants, excepting roses, will grow well in a neutral soil (pH 7.0), but broadleaf evergreens and conifers require an acid soil (pH 6.0–6.5). Native plants of wooded areas also need humus and a slightly acid soil. By using acid peat moss or composted forest humus, soil may be maintained at a suitably low pH to meet growth requirements for acid-loving plants.

Plant species and varieties that have low water needs come from Australia, China and the Cape of Good Hope. There are some native to the western United States which will also thrive in the slightly alkaline soil here. Orchard fruits need medium moisture, except citrus and avocado, which require high moisture, as do most vegetables and annual flowers, and should not be attempted in bone-dry areas unless the gardener is willing to water heavily.

Plants That Succeed

Outstanding ornamentals that will do well in almost all other areas of the region—coastal, mountains and inland—include the California live oak (*Quercus agrifolia*) and hollyleaf and Catalina cherry (*Prunus ilicifolia* and *lyonii*), all natives. The carob (*Ceratonia siliqua*) and the maidenhair tree (*Ginkgo biloba*) also succeed in the desert. Ornamentals that grow well on the coast and inland include *Jacaranda acutifolia* and the smaller evergreen pear (*Pyrus kawakami*).

Three outstanding shrubs are the native Oregon grape (*Mahonia aquifolium*), Burford holly (*Ilex cornuta* 'Burfordii') and *Plumbago capensis*, which will succeed in the desert as well. Bougainvillea, one of the most decorative warm-climate vines, is a favorite for coast and inland, and the trumpet-vine (*Bignonia*) does well everywhere. *Clematis armandii*, a beautiful species, succeeds along the coast, in the mountains and inland as well.

If you are interested in a food garden, you will find it possible to grow most of the familiar nuts and fruits, but ask local nurserymen for species and varieties adapted to your particular segment of the Warm

The Argentinian cactus, *Parodia aureispina*, shown here blooms along with many Australian plants of note in Warm Southwest desert gardens. Citrus, avocado, annuals and vegetables succeed in the region's high-moisture areas. With terrain and climate ranging from subtropical seacoast to bone-dry desert, this is a region where no one set of gardening rules applies.

Southwest. Apricots, peaches and plums are popular. Dwarf citrus are replacing the standard sorts because they often prove hardier and, being smaller, are easier to protect in unseasonably cold weather. Avocado grows here and is about as hardy as the standard size citrus, but too tall to protect if frost threatens. In the colder regions, plant either in a pocket microclimate or in areas safe for standard citrus.

Almonds and walnuts are current crops in most areas, and the delicious macadamia nut is beginning to appear commonly in home gardens.

Cool-weather vegetable crops (many vegetables are cold-weather crops) can be counted on, providing the gardener investigates the cool season (usually winter) in his area, and times his crops accordingly. Giant African marigolds, a common summer display, give way in winter to French marigolds and to a host of cool-weather bulbs and perennials.

Lawn materials for cool areas include the fescues, bentgrass and bluegrass. Grasses more suitable for hot areas are hybrid Bermuda and rye. Ground cover for foot traffic includes *Ajuga reptans* for shaded spots, and *Dichondra repens* for partial shade or sun. Ground covers for landscaping include the low-growing *Ceanothus* species, all species of Manzanita, which grows to about 12 inches, creeping *Baccharis pilularis* and the native strawberry plant, *Fragaria chiloensis*.

The most annoying weeds here are wild morning-glory (bindweed), oxalis, puncture vine and the many perennial thistles, all hard to eradicate. Annual weeds that can be kept down if they are eliminated before they go to seed include mallow ("cheese weed"), scarlet pimpernel, spurge and mouse-ear chickweed, a particular nuisance here in the Warm Southwest.

Creeping grasses that should be dug up before they get too strong a hold on plantings are nutsedge (nutgrass), Bermudagrass, kukuyu and St. Augustine. Sandburgrass can also be troublesome. Crabgrass is as much of a nuisance here as elsewhere and can best be handled with a pre-emergent control program instituted in earliest spring. Close mowing and other post-emergent crabgrass controls discussed in the article under *lawns* are measures worth undertaking to keep it out of lawn and flower beds.

Southern Shores

By RUTH STUART ALLEN

The nearly 3,000-mile boundary of the Southern Shores region extends from Chesapeake Bay to the southern tip of Texas, and includes Plant Hardiness Zones 9a/b and 10a/b. The area also extends inland to the extent of brackish water penetration. Zone 9a/b winter temperatures range between 20 and 30 degrees, Zone 10a/b between 30 and 40 degrees. The letter a designates the cooler, and b the warmer, reaches of each Zone.

The Zone 9a range is spotted from the Bay to the northeast coast of South Carolina, and from there it extends unbroken to Jacksonville, Florida. Here it is joined by 9b and travels south to Cape Kennedy, the terminus of Zones 10a/b.

Zone 10b skirts the eastern shore from the Cape around the tip of the Florida peninsula where it is joined by the inland, almost parallel 10a, and continues to St. Petersburg. This forms the area of south Florida, which is part of Southern Shores. Here 9b picks up for 100 miles, joining 9a, and reaches along the coast to Corpus Christi, Texas. Once more, it is joined by 9a, and forms what is known as the "Valley." The small southern tip of Texas is included in Zone 10a.

Climate Comes First

Zone 10 on the east coast, and subsequently 9a/b and around the Gulf states and the Texas coast, are subject to hurricanes from mid-June to November 14. "N'easters" attack from Daytona Beach north, December through February; the west coast of Florida often suffers from southwest winter winds, and cold "plains" winds reach the Texas coast. Only Zone 10 enjoys relatively frost-wind-free weather during winter months. However, the entire coastline is warmed by the Gulf Stream and this makes year-round gardening possible in Zone 10 and only slightly restricted in 9.

A second spring begins in Zone 10 in October for home and commercial gardeners. Only limited planting is possible in this area from mid-May to mid-September. Days and nights are too hot and humidity is high.

The Texas coast and the tip of the Florida Keys are the driest regions in the area. Southern Shores on the whole has enough rainfall to produce lush growth. By cities, yearly rainfall is: Brownsville, Texas, 28 in.; Galveston, 48 in.; New Orleans, 64 in.; Mobile, 68 in.; Pensacola, 63 in.; Tampa, 52 in.; Fort Myers, 53 in.; Key West, 40 in.; Miami, 60 in.; West Palm Beach, 62 in.; Jacksonville, 53 in.; Savannah, Georgia, 46 in.; and Charleston, S.C., 46 in. New Orleans is considered the wettest big city in the United States.

Improving Your Soil

Coastal soils are composed of high alkaline, shell-infiltrated sands which shift with the wind if not stabilized by sod or ground cover. Periodic applications of topsoil are necessary and a frequent fertilization program is required. Local County Agricultural Extension service centers will give formulas and suggest schedules for your area.

The Shores' three prime gardening problems are wind, salt spray and sand. All plantings need to be prepared for by supplemental additions of good soil and organic materials, and need to be protected by heavy mulches. Planting is limited along the beachline, but a wide variety of ornamentals and trees are usable 100 ft. or so inland when sheltered by proper wind breaks which will also act as traps for blown salt spray.

Plants That Succeed

One tree that thrives in all coastal zones is the live oak (*Quercus virginiana*). It is as Southern as hot biscuits. *Magnolia grandiflora*, a flowering beauty, is at home in Zones 9a/b as are several of the hollies including *Ilex cassine*, *I. opaca*, *I. vomitoria* and *I. cornuta*. So are many of the pines.

Some useful shrub-trees in Zones 9 and 10 are cherry-laurel, wax myrtle, crape-myrtle, shore juni-

per, callistemon, poinsettia, gardenia, *Ligustrum lucidum* (a privet of the Olive Family) and viburnum such as the sweet *V. odoratissimum.*

Shrubs suited to Zone 9 include: Japanese ardisia, Japanese box, *Camellia japonica* (common camellia) and *C. sasanqua,* a hardier, smaller species. Pyracantha, hydrangea and most varieties of azalea also do well here.

Shrubs to try in Zone 10 include codiaeum (croton), rose-of-China (Chinese hibiscus), ixora, thunbergia (clock-vine), orange jessamine and *Jatropha hastata.*

Palms and palmlike plants that thrive in both 9 and 10 are sabal (palmetto), phoenix (both *P. canariensis* and *reclinata*), washingtonia, Chinese fan palm and yatay or butia palms (*Butia capitata,* also known as *Cocos australis*). Palmlike plants include *Cycas revoluta,* prickly pear (a cactus), *Agave* species including the century plant, and *Yucca aloifolia,* commonly called Spanish bayonet.

Two picturesque palms which flourish only in Zone 10 are roystonea and the coconut.

Trees for Zone 10 include the many ficus (figs), *Bischofia javanica,* silk oak (*Grevillea robusta*), black olive (*Bucida*) and *Pongamia pinnata,* the poonga oil tree. Flowering trees for this region are the many bauhinias, poinciana, the pink tecoma-tree (*Tabebuia pallida*), *Peltophorum inerme* (related to the royal poinciana) and queen's crape-myrtle, *Lagerstroemia.*

Weeds common to most sections of Southern Shores are creeping charlie (*Lippia nodiflora*), the spurges, the pennyworts, purslane including Florida purslane or "pusley" (*Richardia scabra*), heartleaf drymary (*Drymaria cordata*), *Centella erecta,* chickweed and certain oxalis. Annual sedge, often mistaken for hybrid Bermudagrass, if not controlled, will overrun a depressed turf.

Virtually all cut flowers and annuals grown in the temperate zones will produce most of the year in Zones 9 and 10, but protective measures against frost are necessary in Zone 9. Also, only the sturdiest annuals, such as marigolds and zinnias, should be planted in Zone 10 from mid-May to mid-September.

The rules governing annuals in Zones 9 and 10 also govern most vegetables. Fruits, including loquats, kumquats, calamondin and other citrus produce best in Zone 9. Zone 10 is a treasure trove of backyard tropical fruits—avocado, mango, white sapote, carambola, sugar apple, surinam cherries (*Eugenia uniflora*), Barbados cherries and governor's plum.

The semitropical *Nerium oleander,* ABOVE, grows well
here and a real tropical, the coconut palm, succeeds
in coastal areas of Zone 10, a region that
supports plants grown no where else on the continent.
Hydrangea, BELOW, boxwood and azaleas flourish
in cooler areas of the Southern Shores' benign climate.

Canada

By LOIS WILSON

Canada, politically divided from the United States by a 3,000-mile border, is, in many ways, horticulturally similar. Its southernmost point in Ontario matches the northwest tip of Texas in plant hardiness; much of its Atlantic region's growing weather is similar to the Central and East Coast states; its prairie lands compare to the northern plains; its gentle-weathered Pacific coast to the United States Northwest; its far north to inland Alaska. Flower seeds move freely back and forth by mail and most plants can be exported and imported by government permit. Gardening practices are almost identical; the main differences are in plants that can be recommended as hardy for different Zones.

Plant lists, keyed through this book to established plant hardiness Zones in the United States (see endpapers), can be used also for Canada by adapting middle range figures to match Canada's Map of Plant Hardiness Zones. Canadian and United States Zones 1, 2, 3, 4, 9 are similar. From Zone 4b to 8 of the United States lists, read one-half Zone higher for Canada.

The Atlantic Provinces (Newfoundland, Prince Edward Island, Nova Scotia, New Brunswick)

Sunny spring, summer and fall days are clear and sparkling, with, near the coast, the tonic smell of salt in the air. Nights are cool and ideal for growing Temperate Zone plants—sweet peas and nasturtiums, roses and mignonette, pansies, dahlias as big as soup plates and mountain ash so red with berries autumn could be Christmas.

Sweeping storms can carry ocean spray miles inland from the sea, so salt-tolerant plants such as the evergreen Koster's blue spruce (*Picea pungens* 'Koster,' Zone 2) or the Japanese black pine (*Pinus thunbergi,* Zone 5) should be chosen for planting. On the Gulf Stream-warmed coasts of Nova Scotia and Newfoundland, hardy rhododendrons do superbly and everywhere wild flowers are breathtaking—ladies' slippers and grass pinks in sphagnum bogs, bright red pigeon berries (Newfoundlanders call them cracker berries, botanists, *Cornus canadensis*) on the mossy green forest floor, sweeps of fragrant purple violets everywhere, blue asters and goldenrod banding the roadsides.

Most soil is acid. Peat moss is locally available for added humus. Seaweed, used as a conditioner, is available for the picking.

Governments in all four provinces have excellent advisory services for home gardeners and a subsidized nursery on Prince Edward Island sells plants at lower than regular trade cost to residents of the Island.

Ontario and Quebec

Canada's highest concentration of people and gardens stretches along the St. Lawrence River to Lake Ontario and within a triangle from the capital city of Ottawa to Windsor and Niagara Falls. Here one finds the new gardens adapted to high-rise apartment balconies hundreds of feet up in the air—some converted to small winter greenhouses—and architect-designed gardens in the inner cities and suburbs display the best in contemporary materials and ornament and a choice of plants second to none.

Deep insulating snow cover makes it possible to grow such tender treasures as the blue poppy of Tibet (*Meconopsis baileyi*) in the coldest parts of Quebec and lack of it is often the greatest challenge in bringing plants successfully through the winter in more temperate Ontario. Soil is varied, some heavy clay, some sandy, but material and advice to improve it is easily available.

New cultivars of fine plants are tested at three excellent places, all open to the public—the Montreal Botanic Garden, the Royal Botanical Gardens in Hamilton and the Central Experimental Farm in Ottawa. Many Canadian-bred ones have won world renown: lilies, lilacs, Siberian and bearded iris, euonymus, linden, junipers and roses are but a few of the plants hybridized here.

In this region the latest in gardening methods are practiced: innovations such as container-grown plants that can be moved into gardens successfully at any time of the growing year; instant lawns laid in less than a day with named varieties of sod; full-size trees transplanted at any time with the use of antidesiccants; self-watering window boxes—all are available here. Government departments have excellent publications and soil-testing services and subsidized horticultural associations attract many thousands to membership.

Favorite flowers are tulips and flowering shrubs in spring; iris, peonies, roses in June; delphiniums, lilies, daylilies in July; annuals all summer; phlox, dahlias, michaelmas daisies, asters in August; and mums in

September. Fall color in the foliage of maple, birch, spindletree, Virginia creeper, sumac, pear and shadbush is brilliant.

The Prairie Provinces
(Manitoba, Saskatchewan, Alberta)

Gardening on the prairies, because of winter cold, great sweeps of drying wind and a fairly short growing season (180 days at Winnipeg, Regina and Calgary), is more chancy than in either the east or west of Canada. Yet flowers bloom with a brilliance here, under the wide prairie sky, they show nowhere else. Gardeners have to be wary in what they choose to grow and knowledgeable especially about best methods to protect their plants from dehydration and sunburn in winter, from drought in summer. Shelterbelts—windbreaks—are useful to cut the thrust of the wind, and shields between plant and sun effectively prevent late winter burning. Summer can be hot and rainfall light, so knowledgeable gardeners use mulches to preserve moisture and keep soil well supplied with water-holding humus and organic material. The famous chinook winds of southeast Alberta, when temperature in winter can fly up 60 degrees in an hour (melting snow cover) and fall to below zero almost as quickly, puts a terrific burden

Most heavily populated regions of Canada are horticulturally similar to hardiness zones in the northern U.S. and most of the desirable ornamentals flourish here. Dahlias, for example the Mignon types, LEFT, thrive in gardens on the East Coast, in Ontario and Quebec where nights are cool and conditions ideal for Temperate-Zone plants. Deep insulating snow cover makes many tender perennials safer through this country's cold winter than they are in snowless regions south.
Under open prairie skies bulbs such as the lovely daffodil, RIGHT, bloom with a brilliance they show nowhere else. Windbreaks, deep fall-watering, training shrubs and small trees to be multistemmed, are techniques used to help plants survive violent temperature fluctuations when chinook winds sweep the country in midwinter. Yukon and Northwest Territories gardens produce giant specimens seen nowhere else on the continent.

on a plant's life system. Deep watering in late fall and training small trees and shrubs to be multistemmed are two methods that help to guarantee plant survival.

Soil is variable. In some areas it is already high in potash, in others heavy with salt. Fertilizers and humus should be chosen with local experts.

Nurserymen and amateurs have developed a fantastically wide range of plants for prairie gardens—many exchanged with similar climate areas in China, Japan, Russia, Finland and the United States. Flower-

43

were born here. It is flowering dogwood country. The newly introduced 'Eddie's White Wonder' with bracts 5½ in. across and a whole month of bloom is spectacular. It's heather and holly country and home for many of the best flowers and shrubs—daffodils in January, fern and mosses, broom and rhododendrons. Natives such as mahonia and salal (*Gaultheria shallon*) move into cultivated gardens as though they had always been there. Growing seasons are long on the coast; fall, winter and spring have ample rainfall, summer is often dry. Soil is, for the most part, sharply drained glacial till, so frequent watering and extra fertilizing are essential in summer.

Booklets and advice are available from the Department of Agriculture. Butchart's Gardens in Victoria is a famous place to go for ideas and unusual seeds and Little Mountain Park in Vancouver has one of the best displays of old roses, lilies and annuals anywhere.

The Yukon and Northwest Territories

To most people the Far North, with its reputation for icebergs and biting blizzards, sounds like an impossible place to make a fine garden. In fact, it's exciting. The growing season is short—only 90 degree days at Aklavik—and the permafrost is truly perma, but 24-hour daylight from May into July can produce 8-foot delphiniums and 50-pound cabbages because the plants are never, during that critical time, in darkness.

Soil in many areas is heavy and the breakdown of organic material necessary to plant growth is slow because of the unthawing cold below ground. Added peat moss, immediately available chemical fertilizers, the use of hot caps and clear plastic mulches can raise temperatures as much as 15 degrees—no mean feat. Most Far North gardeners pre-start seedlings indoors and sprinkle during dry spells with drum-caught rain which is warmer than water from wells or lakes.

Research is going on to develop more good plants for gardens in this region, notably with saskatoons (*Amelanchier alnifolia*, Zone 1). This shrub can produce fine edible fruit as well as early spring flowers and a vivid fall color. Advice for this region is given by the Beaverlodge Research Station, Alberta.

ing crab apple, cherry, hawthorn, junipers, honeysuckle, lilac, mock-orange, hardy shrub rose cultivars such as 'Austrian Copper,' 'Betty Bland,' 'Father Hugo,' saskatoon, spirea, weeping willow, aster, chrysanthemum, coral bells, lily, lythrum, shrubby cinquefoil, double petunias and plums are only some of those now available for prairie gardens. The government of each province offers an excellent advisory service and booklets to the home gardener.

British Columbia

The well-tempered weather of this Pacific Coast province grows almost all Temperate Zone plants superbly. There is keen interest in fine gardening and easily accessible supplies of excellent nursery stock. Victoria, where many English have retired, is world famous for rock gardens and Vancouver is known for imaginative garden architecture that weds land to sea with cantilevered decks and terraces. This is rose country. The top-rated 'Miss Canada' and 'Burnaby'

The
Good Housekeeping
Illustrated Encyclopedia
of Gardening

Volume One
Aaron's beard to annuus

ABOVE: *Abelia floribunda*, Mexican abelia, is an excellent specimen shrub in regions where winter temperatures don't go below 10°. It grows to a height of 6 to 10 ft., and makes an outstanding hedge planting. Showy rose-colored flowers bloom in summer.

Aaron's beard. Common name given to several garden plants. See *Hypericum calycinum*, which is a St. John's wort with beardlike stamens; also *Saxifraga sarmentosa*, the strawberry-geranium; also *Cymbalaria muralis*, Kenilworth-ivy. Aaron's beard cactus is *Opuntia leucotricha*.

Aaron's rod. See *Thermopsis caroliniana*.

Abaca. See *Musa textilis*.

Abele tree. See *Populus alba*.

ABELIA (ab-*beel*-ee-uh). Honeysuckle Family (*Caprifoliaceae*). Graceful, bushy shrubs from Asia and Mexico; small to medium in size, and widely useful in landscaping where winter temperatures are not too severe. Opposite, simple, pointed, small leaves. Tubular flowers are small but profuse and pretty, produced in leafy terminal clusters over a long period in summer and early fall. Sun encourages flowering, but abelias tolerate considerable shade. Plant in a well-drained sandy loam, rich in humus. Indoors, use Basic Potting Mixture. Propagate by cuttings, either of soft tip growth rooted outdoors in June or of ripened wood rooted indoors in late summer for planting out the following spring. Outstanding among unusual hedge plantings. See Hedge Plants index in Plant Finder section of Volume 16, where other materials suited for use in hedges are listed.

A. floribunda (floh-rib-*bund*-uh). MEXICAN ABELIA. A pleasing evergreen shrub, growing 6 to 10 ft. high, with showy, purple-rose flowers in summer. Excellent specimen shrub. Zone 8.

● **A. x grandiflora** (gran-di-*floh*-ruh). GLOSSY ABELIA. Hybrid of *A. chinensis* and *A. uniflora*. Grows from 3 to 6 ft. high. The lustrous, semi-evergreen leaves, on arching stems, assume a lovely bronze color in the fall. The bell-shaped, white or pinkish flowers bloom continuously from June to Nov. The top may be killed back in severe winters, but new growth from the base is vigorous and produces flowers the same summer. Especially useful for landscape and unusual hedge plantings for border accent; even for single specimen display. The variety 'Edward Goucher' is a desirable semi-evergreen hybrid of *A. x grandiflora* and *A. schumannii*. It grows to 6 ft. and bears lilac-pink flowers all summer. Zone 6.

A. triflora (trye-*floh*-ruh). This species is deciduous, and taller than most, sometimes reaching 12 ft. in height. The leaves are lance shaped, an intense and attractive green and about 3 in. long. The flowers are a rosy-white, about 2 in. long and grow on terminal clusters rather thickly. The over-all effect is of a spray of bright little stars. *Triflora* is native to the Himalayas, and hardier than other species. Zone 6.

ABELIOPHYLLUM (a-beel-ee-oh-*file*-um). Olive Family (*Oleaceae*). There is only one species, a deciduous shrub from Korea. Propagate in midsummer by cuttings of half-ripened shoots.

A. distichum (*diss*-ti-kum). KOREAN ABELIA-LEAF. Grows 3 to 4 ft. high. Oval, opposite leaves to 2 in. long, on slender, arching stems. When young, it is an awkward shrub, becoming bushy with maturity. Dense clusters of small, white, fragrant flowers, often in mid-April, before the leaves appear—making it well worth planting in the shrubbery border, and an excellent companion for the spring-flowering bulbs. Zone 6.

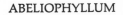

UPPER LEFT: *Abelia grandiflora*. UPPER RIGHT: *Abelia triflora*.
LOWER LEFT: *Abelia grandiflora* in bloom, used as a clipped
hedge. LOWER RIGHT: *Abeliophyllum distichum*, the Korean
abelia-leaf, grows to a height of 3 or 4 feet, and bears
dense clusters of small, white, fragrant flowers. It is
a charming companion for spring-flowering bulbs in bloom.

ABERIA. See DOVYALIS.

ABIES (*ay*-bih-eez). FIR. Pine Family (*Pinaceae*). Evergreen trees of pyramidal form, most growing fairly rapidly to 50 ft. or more. They are distinguished from spruces by flatter leaves (needles), which usually have two white bands beneath. The cones are erect and shatter soon after maturity. Firs grow best in moist and sheltered positions, becoming sparse under hot, dry conditions. They are primarily forest trees, suitable only for large-scale landscapes. With a few exceptions, these are listed chiefly for identification. Propagate by seeds or grafting.

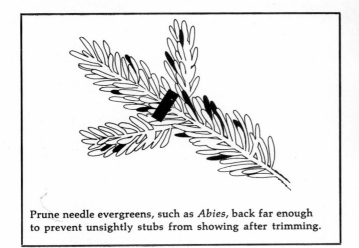

Prune needle evergreens, such as *Abies*, back far enough to prevent unsightly stubs from showing after trimming.

A. balsamea (bal-*say*-mee-uh). BALSAM FIR. Native to the northeastern U.S., this species may reach a height of 60 ft., but is generally lower. Rounded leaves to ¾ in. long and violet-purple cones to 2 in. long. Difficult to establish in cultivation, but among the most popular Christmas trees. There are several varieties, including dwarf forms. Zone 3.

A. cephalonica (sef-a-*lon*-ik-uh). GREEK FIR. Grows to 90 ft., with grayish-brown bark and shiny green leaves about 1 in. long. Greenish-purple cones, 3 to 5 in. long. Zone 6.

A. concolor (*kon*-ko-lor). COLORADO FIR. WHITE FIR. Native to the southwestern U.S., this is a handsome tree, growing to 120 ft. Gray bark, bluish-green leaves about 2 in. long, and greenish-purple cones, 3 to 5 in. long. Hardier than most firs. Several "blue" cultivars available. Zone 4.

LEFT: *Abies concolor*, the Colorado fir, or white fir, seen as a young lawn specimen here, grows to 120 feet at maturity.
LOWER RIGHT: *Abies grandis*, the giant fir, will soar to 300 feet and flourishes in the Far West where it is native.
UPPER RIGHT: Cones of the balsam fir will shatter soon after maturity, releasing slow-to-germinate seeds.
Shape and size of the cones are typical of the fir species.

A. fraserii (*fray*-zer-ee). FRASER BALSAM FIR. SOUTHERN BALSAM FIR. Native to the mountains of W. Va. and Tenn., it resembles the balsam fir that grows in the North. Excellent in cool, moist mountain areas. A clone 'Prostrata' grows close to the soil surface in a semiprostrate shape. Zone 6.

A. grandis (*gran*-diss). GIANT FIR. Leaves are up to 2¼ in. long, rounded and notched at the apex. Cones of the giant fir are cylindrical, bright green and about 4 in. long. Grows from Vancouver Island as far south as Calif. and as far west as Mont. Zone 5.

A. homolepis (ho-*mol*-ep-iss). NIKKO FIR. A valuable Japanese tree, growing to about 80 ft., with lustrous, dark green leaves about 1 in. long. Purplish to brown cones about 4 in. long. Zone 5.

A. koreana (koh-ree-*ay*-nuh). KOREAN FIR. Grows to about 50 ft., with lustrous green leaves less than 1 in. long. The violet-purple cones are up to 3 in. long. Zone 5.

A. lasiocarpa (lay-see-oh-*karp*-uh). A mountain fir that is native from Alaska to northern Calif. The cones are purple, about 3 in. long, and the leaves are to 1½ in. long. Bark of the variety *arizonica* (ar-iz-*zon*-ik-uh) is a creamy white, and has a corky texture. This species does less well in the East. Zone 6.

A. magnifica (mag-*niff*-ik-uh). RED FIR. Grows well on the West Coast where it is native from Ore. to Calif. Variety *argentea* (ar-*jen*-tee-uh) has bluish-white leaves. The variety *glauca* (*glaw*-kuh) has leaves whose glaucous coating gives them a bluish cast, and it is called azure fir. *Magnifica* will grow in the East in moderate regions. Zone 6.

● **A. pinsapo** (pin-*say*-poh). SPANISH FIR. This beautiful fir grows to 80 ft., with rigid, dark green leaves to ¾ in. A tree of great distinction when adequately displayed. The purplish-brown cones are 4 to 5 in. long. Zone 7.

● **A. veitchii** (*veech*-ee-eye). VEITCH FIR. A very handsome and hardy fir from Japan, growing to 80 ft. The leaves are crowded in a forward direction. They are about 1 in. long and a lustrous dark green, conspicuous with two silvery bands underneath. Bluish-purple cones, each about 2½ in. long. Zone 3.

abortive. Term referring to plants that do not develop properly; particularly to those failing to produce seeds.

UPPER: Close-up of the upright Korean fir pine cone.
CENTER: A compact variety of *Abies lasiocarpa*, the alpine fir, a tree native to the mountains from Alaska to northern Calif. The species does not succeed in the eastern reaches of the country, but makes a beautiful specimen in its native areas.
LOWER: *Abutilon* x *hybridum maximum* is a flowering-maple species suited to culture as a house plant. Showy bell-like flowers are red, purple, white or yellow.

ABRONIA (ab-*roh*-nee-uh). SAND VERBENA. Four-o'clock Family (*Nyctaginaceae*). A large genus of low or trailing plants native to western N. America. The most commonly grown species, described below, thrives in poor, sandy soil and is a great little ground cover, also useful for edgings, borders, or rock gardens. Fragrant, verbenalike flowers in colorful shades of red and pink. For early bloom start seeds indoors in March or sow outdoors when the ground is warm. As the seeds are slow to germinate, remove husks before planting. Resists drought. Sand verbena, *Abronia latifolia,* is on the preservation list of Calif. and is protected, that is, is not to be picked or dug up. For other rock-garden plants that resist dry conditions study Plant Finder section of Volume 16.

A. latifolia (lat-if-*foh*-lee-uh). YELLOW SAND VERBENA. Was formerly known as *Arenaria.* Prostrate species that grows along the seacoast from Calif. to British Columbia.

A. umbellata (um-bel-*lay*-tuh). PROSTRATE SAND VERBENA. A tender vinelike perennial usually grown as an annual for its attractive rose-pink flowers, which are small (½ in. long) but bloom in showy, umbel-like clusters. Finely cut, opposite leaves. Blooms from July to Sept. An unusual plant for hanging baskets. *A. u. grandiflora* (gran-di-*floh*-ruh) is a variety with larger flowers. Zone 9 (performs as a perennial where temperatures do not drop below 20°).

ABRUS (*ay*-bruss). Pea Family (*Leguminosae*). A tropical genus with a single species in cultivation.

A. precatorius (prek-uh-*tor*-ee-us). ROSARY-PEA. NECKLACE PLANT. CRAB'S EYES. WEATHER-PLANT. TELEGRAPH-PEA. From the East Indies. An intriguing climber because the pinnate leaves respond to temperature and light changes, variously folding or drooping. The flowers are pale purple, followed by pods that open to reveal shiny scarlet seeds, each with a single black spot. These seeds are used as beads. Grow in a large pot, in Basic Potting Mixture with double loam. Keep evenly moist, minimum night temperature of 60°. Plant in the open garden in tropical Fla. Propagate by seeds or firm cuttings in deep sand with bottom heat. Zone 10.

Absinthium. See *Artemisia absinthium.*

ABUTILON (ab-*yew*-til-on). FLOWERING MAPLE. Mallow Family (*Malvaceae*). A large group of herbs and shrubs, mostly small, from tropical countries. With long petioles, the alternate leaves are sometimes lobed and maplelike. The showy, bell-shaped flowers are borne singly in the leaf axils and are mostly drooping. Popular for summer bedding, in home greenhouses and as house plants. Upright forms may be trained as standards, especially in a greenhouse or sunny plant room. Indoors, they need Basic Potting Mixture and sun. Watch especially for whitefly, scale, but also for mealybug. Control by spraying with malathion. Propagate by seeds or cuttings. Zone 10.

A. x hybridum (*hib*-rid-um). A mixture developed in cultivation. The attractive leaves are lobed or simple, sometimes speckled. The showy flowers may be red, pink, purple, white or yellow. The variety *savitzi* (sav-*vitz*-eye) is notable for silvery leaf variegation.

A. megapotamicum (meg-ap-poh-*tam*-ik-um). A bountiful basket plant from Brazil, with drooping stems sometimes several ft. long. Plain, narrow leaves to 3 in. long and showy flowers, yellow with red calyx

Abronia, sand verbena, is a trailing plant native to the West. It bears fragrant red or pink blooms and makes an excellent ground cover for poor sandy soils.

and protruding stamens. The leaves of variety *variegatum* (vay-ree-eg-*gay*-tum) are flecked and splashed with gold.

A. striatum (strye-*ay*-tum). The leaves of this flowering maple are five- to seven-lobed, and the middle lobe narrows at the base. The flowers are almost 2 in. long, orange veined with crimson. The variety *thompsonii* (tom-*soh*-nee-eye) has green and yellow leaves and orange flowers. Native to Guatemala, it is sometimes used in flower borders for its colorful leaves. Zone 10.

A. vitifolium (vye-ti-*foh*-lee-um). A sturdy shrub from Chile, growing to 15 ft. or more. The leaves, to 5 in. across, have three to seven long pointed lobes and are white-woolly underneath. Light blue flowers.

LOWER: *Abutilon megapotamicum variegatum* is another species of flowering maple and has leaves flecked with gold. Originally from Brazil, it is a basket plant with drooping stems. UPPER: Close-up shows its flowers which bear a resemblance to Chinese lanterns.

Abyssinian banana. See *Musa ensete*.

ACACIA (ak-*kay*-see-uh). Pea Family (*Leguminosae*). A large group of fast-growing evergreen trees and shrubs, natives of many tropical and subtropical regions, Australia in particular. The leaves are usually bipinnate with numerous small leaflets, but in some cases are reduced to flattened, leaflike stems called phyllodes. Showy yellow flowers in attractive clusters or spikes, blooming in spring. Some are grown in tubs in cool greenhouses. A number are handsome and popular plants to grow outdoors in Calif. and Fla., where they are free-flowering and reach considerable size. Propagate by seeds or cuttings. Zone 9.

A. baileyana (bay-lee-*ay*-nuh). Showy shrub or small tree with beautiful, feathery, gray foliage and clusters of small yellow flowers. Bluish-green pods, to 4 in. long. Very popular in Calif.

A. decurrens (dee-*ker*-renz). GREEN WATTLE. Tree to 60 ft., with dark green leaves and light yellow flowers, blooming later than other species. The pods are 4 in. long. The variety *dealbata* (dee-al-*bay*-tuh) has silvery-gray foliage and heads of soft yellow flowers (the "mimosa" of florists). Widely grown in Calif. as a florist's flower.

A. farnesiana (far-neez-ee-*ay*-nuh). POPINAC. SWEET ACACIA. An attractive, thorny, much-branched shrub, growing to 10 ft., with leaflets that are ⅛ in. long and heads of dark yellow, very fragrant flowers. Blooms all winter in the greenhouse.

A. longifolia (lon-jif-*foh*-lee-uh). SYDNEY GOLDEN WATTLE. Shrub or small tree with phyllodes to 6 in. long and lemon-yellow flowers produced over a long season in spikes 2 in. or more long. No prickles. Pods to 5 in. long.

A. pendula (*pen*-dew-luh). WEEPING MYALL. Small tree with drooping branches, gray phyllodes to 3 in. long and clusters of round flower heads. Chiefly valued for its weeping habit.

A. pruinosa (prew-in-*noh*-suh). Small tree, the leaves bronze when young, cream and yellow fragrant flower heads in racemes, pods to 3 in. long.

Acacia, rose. See *Robinia hispida*.

ACAENA (ass-*see*-nuh). Rose Family (*Rosaceae*). Predominantly evergreen, trailing perennials that make attractive ground covers in mild regions or in the North with mulch (evergreen boughs) over winter. The species below are native to New Zealand. Com-

RIGHT: *Acacia decurrens* variety *dealbata* has silvery-gray foliage and heads of soft yellow flowers. Grown in Calif. as "mimosa." INSET: tree of *A. d. baileyana* in bloom.

Acanthocereus, a member of the Cactus Family, is a trailing or climbing form from the tropical South.
Single funnel-shaped flowers that bloom after sunset make it an interesting subject for gardens designed to be lighted at night.
The species *pentagonus* produces greenish-white flowers 6 to 8 inches long, followed by red berries and is grown outdoors in the frost-free regions of Zone 9.
Acanthocereus may be grown in greenhouses in Basic Potting Mixture with double the amount of sand. It propagates readily from cuttings rooted in moist sand. This variety may reach a height of 20 feet at maturity, has strongly angled stems, no leaves and stiff spines.

pound leaves with many-toothed leaflets, inconspicuous flowers and bristly fruit. Excellent in rock gardens, where they form fine-textured mats close to the ground. Sandy loam and sun give best results. Propagation by seeds, division or cuttings. Zone 7.

A. buchananii (bew-kan-*nan*-ee-eye). Dwarf plant with beautiful, silvery-gray leaves to ¾ in. long. Tiny, whitish-green flowers.

A. microphylla (mye-kroh-*fill*-uh). NEW ZEALAND BUR. Not over 3 in. high with gray-green leaves to 2 in. long. Crimson flowers with purplish-red spines.

ACALYPHA (ak-al-*lye*-fuh). Spurge Family (*Euphorbiaceae*). Annuals and shrubs for warm, humid greenhouses. They have attractive green leaves and showy spikes of small flowers. Outdoors in frost-free regions they may be used for bedding out or even as hedges. Not always successful as house plants unless a moist atmosphere can be maintained. Basic Potting Mixture, double peat. Propagate by cuttings.

A. hispida (*hiss*-pid-uh). CHENILLE PLANT. From the East Indies, where it may grow as high as 15 ft. In cultivation, however, this shrub generally is 1 to 3 ft. high and bears long, striking, drooping tassels.

Acanthaceae. See Acanthus Family.

ACANTHOCALYCIUM (a-*can*-tho-cal-*ih*-see-um). Cactus Family (*Cactaceae*). These S. American cacti closely resemble those in the related genus *Echinopsis* (which see) and require the same culture and conditions. Argentinian species occasionally encountered in collections include *A. spiniflorum,* flowers pink; *A. thionanthum,* flowers yellow; and *A. violaceum,* flowers pale lavender.

ACANTHOCEREUS (ak-anth-oh-*seer*-ee-us). Cactus Family (*Cactaceae*). Climbing or trailing cacti from tropical America, these plants have strongly angled stems, no leaves and stiff spines. The single, night-blooming, funnel-shaped flowers are not as showy as those of other night-blooming cacti. Grown outdoors in frost-free regions or indoors in a greenhouse, they need good drainage, plenty of sun and light and Basic Potting Mixture with double the amount of sand. Propagate by cuttings.

A. pentagonus (pen-ta-*goh*-nus). May reach a length of 20 ft. Greenish-white flowers 6 to 8 in. long, followed by red berries. Zone 9.

ACANTHOLIMON (ak-anth-oh-*lye*-mon). PRICKLY THRIFT. Thrift Family (*Plumbaginaceae*). Desirable, prostrate evergreen rock garden perennials with many species not in cultivation. These grow in sandy soil in full sun. Suitable for the dry wall. Propagate by seeds or by late summer heel cuttings rooted in sand and overwintered in the cold frame, or by layering. Zone 5.

A. acerosum (ass-er-*roh*-sum). Rose-colored flowers to 6 in., in midsummer; from Asia Minor.

A. androsaceum: *A. echinus.*

A. echinus (eh-*kine*-us). Pink flowers to 6 in., in midsummer; from China and perhaps Japan.

A. glumaceum (glew-*may*-see-um). Rose-colored flowers in early summer, rising 6 to 9 in.; from Armenia. This is the commonly encountered species.

A. venustum (ven-*nuss*-tum). Dark pink flowers on 9-in. stems, in midsummer; from Asia Minor.

ACANTHOPANAX (ak-anth-oh-*pay*-nax). Aralia Family (*Araliaceae*). Shrubs and trees from eastern Asia, valued chiefly for their handsome foliage. They grow well in shade and withstand city conditions. Propagate by seeds sown in autumn or by cuttings.

A. pentaphyllus: *A. sieboldianus.*

A. sieboldianus (see-bold-ee-*ay*-nus). FIVELEAF-ARALIA. This deciduous shrub from Japan is the best-known garden species. (Often listed in catalogs as A. pentaphyllus). It grows about 10 ft. high and has prickly, arching branches. The bright green leaves have five- to seven-toothed leaflets. Flowers are greenish white and inconspicuous. A good shrub for shady corners and useful as a hedge, since it stands hard clipping. This plant bears flowers and fruits only rarely. Zone 4.

ACANTHOPHYLLUM. The plant sometimes listed as Acanthophyllum spinosum is *Dianthus noeanus*, which see. The genus *Acanthophyllum* is not represented by species in cultivation.

ACANTHUS (ak-*kanth*-us). BEAR'S-BREECH. Acanthus Family (*Acanthaceae*). Only one species is in common cultivation, a perennial of southern Europe. The elegant, elongated leaves are irregularly scalloped along the edges and the lobes of most species end in spines. These leaves are familiar in sculptured form on the capital of the Corinthian column. The stately plant is striking in the border and makes a dramatic accent among shrubbery in landscape plantings. Full sun, rich, well-drained soil and not too much water give best results. North of Zone 7 protect by mulching in winter. Propagate by seeds or root division in spring.

A. mollis (*moll*-iss). A large plant, to 3 ft. and more. The leaves are up to 2 ft. long and 6 to 9 in. across. White or purple flowers with spiny bracts at the base of the blossoms, which grow in bold spikes 2 to 4 ft. high and bloom in July and Aug. The variety *lat-*

UPPER: *Acalypha hispida,* the chenille plant, is most often seen in the North as a flowering greenhouse specimen 12 to 36 inches tall, but in its native habitat, the East Indies, it grows to a height of 15 feet. The related *A. wilkesiana macafeana* is grown for its large red leaves, splashed crimson and bronze.
LOWER: *Acanthus,* bear's-breech, is a perennial from southern Europe but will flourish in regions south of Zone 7. Its scalloped spiny leaf is the model for sculptured motifs on the capitals of the Corinthian columns. The species here, *A. spinosa,* bears showy purple flowers and blooms in July and August bringing color to the summer border.

ifolius (lat-if-*foh*-lee-us) grows to 4 ft. or more and is much less spiny (and more hardy) than the type. The purple flowers grow in a loose spike. Zone 6.

A. spinosa (spye-*noh*-suh). One of the important species of Acanthus, *spinosa* is native to southern Europe and to Asia Minor. The leaves are cleft, the lobes toothed or cut, and spiny. The flowers are purplish and grow in dense spikes and bloom in July and Aug. Height rarely exceeds 3 ft. Sometimes grown in greenhouses, the species succeeds outdoors in Zone 9.

Acanthus Family (*Acanthaceae*). Mostly tropical plants with simple, opposite leaves and irregular flowers (usually one- or two-lipped). Grown in greenhouses or outdoors for the showy flowers and striking foliage. The following genera are included in this encyclopedia: *Acanthus, Beloperone, Crossandra, Fittonia, Jacobinia, Mackaya, Ruellia* and *Thunbergia*.

acaulescent (ak-*kaw*-less-ent). Tending not to exhibit or develop a stem.

acaulis (ak-*kaw*-liss), **-e.** Apparently stemless (sometimes having an underground stem); acaulescent.

accent. A plant, rock or structure that, because of its size, shape or color attracts attention and thus emphasizes that particular part of the garden or grounds where it is situated. To be successful, an accent should complement its surroundings. It should be obtrusive enough only to catch your eye for the moment before you take in the whole surrounding scene and perhaps for an instant afterward. Handle accents carefully. If you select the wrong shapes or colors, if you put them in the wrong places or if you employ too many of them, they will make the garden a disturbing, rather than a pleasantly restful place.

acclimate. To accustom to an unfamiliar climate. Unfortunately, in the case of plants, this is much easier to talk about than to accomplish. Plants that are native to one region may not respond favorably to another region having a completely different climate. For example, citrus fruits will not grow in the North, while white birches will not survive in the South, and the American elm grows poorly west of the Rockies. Even when seeds and cuttings from one region are planted in a region with only a slightly different climate, they may not be successful. With annuals, there is little trouble, but perennials require extra care —particularly against the rigors of winter. Actually, the successful acclimatization of plants is a job for the hybridizers, who, by crossing different species or varieties, can often develop new cultivars that will thrive where the parents were not adaptable.

★ **ACER** (*ay*-ser). MAPLE. (BOX-ELDER.) Maple Family (*Aceraceae*). Trees (usually deciduous) ranging in height from 20 to 120 ft. and native to North Temperate Zones. They make good shade trees—some almost too good (offering stiff competition to lawn grass)—but as a group they are among the most valuable landscape trees. The lobed or compound, opposite leaves turn a brilliant color in the fall. Clusters of small flowers in spring and, in some species, colorful seed keys.

The handsome qualities of the maples are apparent when they are seen either in the woods, in spacious landscapes or in collections of fine trees, where their competitive position is outstanding. In small home landscapes their use is limited either to screening (*A. campestre*), or to strategic placement for specimen use (especially the good forms of *A. palmatum* and the more refined of its cut-leaved varieties). The striped maple or moosewood (*A. pensylvanicum*) is a bold but airy species, suited to shady woods. Of the medium-sized trees, three introduced species are distinctive as lawn or shade trees if the lawn is large and the shade really desired. Where a truly magnificent specimen may be given an adequate location, the sugar maple (*A. saccharum*) is in the very first rank of ornamental trees, of whatever kind. Its handsome proportions know no season, and its autumnal appearance is beyond compare.

Easily grown, maples thrive in ordinary soil and are mostly very hardy. Established specimens grow better if fertilized from time to time and are often improved by removing weak and poorly placed branches. Occasionally attacked by aphids, caterpillars, cottony scale and borers. Norway and sugar maples are sometimes infected with a wilt disease. Leaf spot and blotches are likely to appear in a wet season. A good spraying program (best carried out by professional tree men) will combat most of these pests and diseases. Leaves of Japanese and sugar maples may appear scorched, due to drying conditions as they are developing. The remedy for the latter is watering and mulching, rather than spraying. Propagate by seed stratified four months at 40°; special shapes, color forms and foliar variants usually are budded or grafted.

Sugar maple, *Acer saccharum*, was declared the official tree of N.Y. in 1955; of W. Va. and of Wisc. in 1949.

A. argutum (ar-*gew*-tum). A graceful small tree from

RIGHT: *Acer saccharum,* the sugar or hard maple, is common throughout Canada and the eastern United States where the first frosts color leaves from gold to red. Sap of this tree is collected in late winter and boiled down to make maple sugar.

Japan, growing to 20 ft. The leaves have five to seven lobes. Small clusters of greenish-yellow flowers. A good shade tree for a small property. Zone 5.

A. buergerianum (burr-*jerr*-ee-*ay*-num). TRIDENT MAPLE. A low, globe-shaped tree from Japan; leaves three-lobed, small. To 20 ft. Usually good fall color. Zone 6.

● **A. campestre** (kam-*pest*-ree). HEDGE MAPLE. Shrub or round-headed tree to 40 ft., with corky branchlets. The leaves, to 4 in. across, have three to five lobes. Greenish flowers in loose, erect corymbs (clusters). Makes an excellent bold screen or clipped hedge because of its dense growth. *Compactum* (kom-*pak*-tum) is lower growing, exceptionally dense; *postelense* (poh-*stel*-ense) leafs out yellow, but foliage soon turns green. Its chief fault, to be noted, is a shallow, invasive root system. Zone 4.

A. capillipes (ka-*pill*-ih-peez). From Japan, this rare maple, to 30 ft., is valuable for small gardens. The three-lobed leaves unfurl red, then turn green. Mature bark is striped white. Good autumn color. Zone 5.

A. cappadocicum (cap-puh-*do*-sik-cum). COLISEUM MAPLE. From the Caucasus Mts. and Asia Minor, this grows to 60 ft., with a spreading crown. Leaves are five- to seven-lobed and the broken petiole exudes milky sap as does the Norway maple. Several varietal names are based on the variously colored new foliage, but all quickly turn green. Zone 6.

A. carpinifolium (car-*pine*-ih-*fohl*-ee-um). HORNBEAM MAPLE. A vase-shaped Japanese species. Usually with several trunks to 30 ft., and a dense crown of bright green, unlobed leaves resembling those of hornbeam. Poor autumn color. Zone 5.

A. circinatum (ser-sin-*nay*-tum). VINE MAPLE. A thicket-forming small tree or ascending bush (to 25 ft.) from the Pacific Northwest, this is a good landscaping species, with attractive trunks, showy red fruits in summer; colored foliage in the fall. Zone 5.

A. dasycarpum: *A. saccharinum*.

A. davidii (day-*vid*-ee-eye). DAVID MAPLE. A bulky upright tree to 45 ft., this Chinese species unfurls bright red leaves in spring that soon expand to 8 in. across and turn green. Bark is striped white. Fall color is bright yellow overlaid with purple. Zone 6.

A. diabolicum (dye-ah-*bol*-ih-cum). DEVIL MAPLE. A small tree, to 30 ft., with exceptionally handsome leaves but little else to recommend it. The flowers, young foliage and fruits of variety *purpurascens* (purr-pew-*rass*-senz) show a purplish cast. Zone 5.

● **A. ginnala** (gin-*nah*-la). AMUR MAPLE. A picturesque small tree to 20 ft.; craggy, with silver bark and a spreading, open crown. Often multiple-trunked or low-branched. Leaves small, toothed, shiny, with three lobes and coloring brilliantly in autumn. This maple is disease-free and tolerant of adverse con-

ditions. The variety 'Durand Dwarf' is bushlike and quite dense. Zone 2.

A. glabrum (*glay*-brum). ROCKY MOUNTAIN MAPLE. Rather like *A. ginnala* in its loose, decorative growth habit, this maple grows to 25 ft. The leaves are three-lobed or, rarely, three-parted, 3 to 5 in. across. Bright yellow autumn color. Zone 5.

● **A. griseum** (*gree*-zee-um). PAPERBARK MAPLE. A nondescript tree to 25 ft., but valuable in certain settings for the mature bark, which is papery, cinnamon-colored and peels freely. The three-leaflet leaves are small, glossy green. No fall color. Zone 5.

A. japonicum (jap-*pon*-ik-um). FULLMOON MAPLE. A small, bushy tree to 35 ft. that responds well to pruning and shaping. This is not the red-leaved Japanese maple (*A. palmatum*), but a fine ornamental in its own right. The leaves, with seven to eleven lobes, are 3 to 6 in. across, green in summer, scarlet in the fall. Of the several varieties, *aconitifolium* (ak-oh-nye-tif-*foh*-lee-um), with deeply indented lobes, and *aureum* (*aw*-ree-um), with yellow-green foliage, are most valuable. Zone 5.

A. lobelii (low-*bell*-ee-eye). LOBEL MAPLE. This is a maple for Southern gardens. It is native to southern Italy. Growing to 60 ft., it is rather like the Norway maple in form and leaf. No fall color. Zone 7.

A. macrophyllum (mak-roh-*fill*-um). BIGLEAF MAPLE. From the Pacific Northwest and adapted only to almost rain forest conditions, this maple grows to 90 ft. with a huge, spreading crown and three- to five-lobed leaves 8 to 12 in. across. In spring, 6-in. clusters of small, fragrant, yellow flowers. Fall color is yellow to orange. Zone 6 (hardy to 5°, but requires cool, misty conditions).

● **A. mandschuricum** (mand-shoor-*ik*-um). MANCHURIAN MAPLE. An attractive small tree to 30 ft., this grows rapidly, with a very open habit and, unfortunately, shallow, fibrous roots. The three leaflets are joined to a scarlet petiole; autumn color is vivid orange-red. Zone 4.

A. monspessulanum (mon-*spess*-u-lane-um). MONTPELIER MAPLE. From southern Europe and N. Africa and growing to 25 ft., this closely resembles hedge maple, and, like it, has no fall color. Tolerant of city conditions. Zone 5.

UPPER: *Acer palmatum dissectum atropurpureum*, the Japanese maple, is a small hardy species with deeply cut ornate leaves ideal for situations where a specimen foliage plant is needed. LOWER RIGHT: Leaf color, which varies from red to green according to climate, soil and season is most often the reddest in early spring and in late fall. LOWER LEFT: *Acer negundo*, variety *aureo-variegatum*, is a variegated box-elder whose leaves are bordered with broad white margins that make it one of the showiest of variegated trees.

A. negundo (neh-*gun*-doh). BOX-ELDER. A disorderly tree. The trunk usually is misshapen, often hollow. Branches develop in a haphazard fashion, usually with many dead twigs. The compound leaves have leaflets of various forms. Grows very quickly, with wide-spread, shallow roots. Short-lived, generally. Some variegated varieties grow more slowly and have considerable merit where gaudy summer color is needed. *A. n. aureo-variegatum* (aw-*ree*-oh-var-ree-eg-*gay*-tum), leaflets bordered bright yellow, and *variegatum*, leaflets with beautiful, broad white margins, making one of the showiest of all variegated trees. Two tender varieties (Zone 7) are *californicum* (kal-if-*forn*-ik-um) and *texanum* (tex-*ay*-num). The species is hardy to Zone 2.

A. nigrum (*ny*-grum). BLACK MAPLE. A huge, slow-growing tree attaining 120 ft. with time and optimum environment. This often is mistaken for sugar maple but the trunk and branches are blacker and the leaves with three, rarely five, lobes are duller. Native from the Dakotas to Quebec. Zone 3.

● **A. nikoense** (nik-ko-*en*-see). NIKKO MAPLE. With upright, often multiple, trunks, crowning out to a nice vase shape, this maple grows to 25 ft. The three leaflets are 2 to 5 in. long, serrate. Fall color is ruby-red, often smoked with purple. A good ornamental for the small garden. Zone 5.

A. opalus (*oh*-pal-us). ITALIAN MAPLE. A nondescript, smaller European maple, growing to 45 ft. This has an ascending habit and horizontal limbs. The five-lobed leaves are 2½ to 5 in. across. Attractive cluster of yellow flowers in spring. Zone 5.

● **A. palmatum** (pal-*may*-tum). JAPANESE MAPLE. These are the small, to 20 ft., generally red-leaved maples of Japan. In cultivation for centuries, some hundreds of named cultivars are in the Japanese literature and more than 80 variants are grown in the U.S. The trees usually are round-headed, with black, smooth, mature bark and palmately lobed leaves with five to eleven lobes. Zone 5 (hardy to −10°). Donald Wyman, Horticulturist Emeritus, Arnold Arboretum of Harvard University, groups cultivars as follows:

Leaves small, usually with five lobes: *atropurpureum* (at-roh-per-*pew*-ree-um)—red leaves throughout the season, one of the hardiest. 'Burgundy Lace'—cut-leaf, lacy small tree, reddish foliage. *Sanguineum* (san-*gwin*-ee-um)—resembles *atropurpureum* but paler red color. *Scolopendrifolium* (sko-low-pen-dre-*fohl*-ee-um)—leaves cut to center, divisions very narrow and green. *Versicolor* (ver-sik-*kol*-or)—wide leaves green, with white, pink and green variegations. 'Yezo-Nishiki'—dark red leaves with red variegation.

Leaves with seven main lobes: *elegans* (*ell*-eg-anz)—large leaves with a rose-colored margin, at least at first. 'Ohsakazuki'—large leaves, yellow-green, turn-ing flame-red in fall. *Reticulatum* (ret-ik-yew-*lay*-tum)—leaves variegated yellow, white and pale green, with darker green veins.

Leaves dissected, with seven, nine, or eleven lobes: *dissectum* (dis-*sek*-tum), threadleaf Japanese maple, with two variants: *flavescens* (flav-*vess*-enz), with yellowish to bronze-green foliage, and *ornatum* (or-*nay*-tum), with bright- to bronze-red foliage.

● **A. pensylvanicum** (pen-sil-*van*-ik-um). STRIPED MAPLE. MOOSEWOOD. A coarse-leaved, awkward tree to 35 ft., this grows natively in much of northeast N. America. Leaves are three-lobed, 5 to 7 in. long, coloring clear yellow in the fall. Bark is showy, striped white. Zone 3.

A. platanoides (plat-an-*noy*-deez). NORWAY MAPLE. A wide, bulky, upright tree of formal aspect. Densely branched, forming a round head with age, this is a stately tree. Withstands city conditions. Identified by the milky sap that exudes from the broken petiole. Though a tree of considerable presence, this has little to offer as it does not color in the fall, the flowers and fruit are not showy and the tree tends to be surface rooted. Among the most commonly available cultivars are: 'Cleveland'—upright while young, becoming oval. 'Crimson King'—leaves dark red throughout summer; Plant Patent #735. 'Fassen's Black'—similar to the above cultivar but darker. *Erectum* (ee-*rek*-tum)—with short horizontal, lateral branches (to 6 ft.). *Columnare* (kol-um-*nare*)—as the above cultivar but leaves smaller. *Globosum* (gloh-*boh*-sum)—round-headed, dense, to be grafted on a tall whip. 'Harlequin'—with white edge to each leaf; a fine variegated ornamental. 'Schwedleri'—red-leaved in spring, bronze-green through summer and fall. 'Summer Shade'—upright growing with single trunk.

A. pseudoplatanus (soo-doh-*plat*-uh-nus). SYCAMORE MAPLE. This huge European and Asian maple ascends to 90 ft., with great, picturesque, horizontal branches and large, sycamore-like leaves. Much used in western Europe, this seems to thrive only in coastal areas in America. European gardens feature several colored forms not available here. Varieties include: *erectum*—young trees are columnar but become pyramidal with age; *purpureum*—leaves purplish on the underside; *spaethii* (spath-*ee*-eye)—as the above cultivar, but color stronger; *worleei* (war-lee-*ee*)—young leaves rich yellow with red petioles, blades turn green over summer. Zone 5.

A. rubrum (*roob*-rum). RED MAPLE. SWAMP MAPLE. Native to east and central U.S. A fast-growing, silver-barked tree to 120 ft., with three- to five-lobed leaves that are 2½ to 4 in. wide. With showy clusters of red flowers in spring and flame-red fall coloration, this is an ornamental shade tree, but brittle and tends to be surface-rooted on poor soil. Will tolerate a naturally boggy soil. Several wildlings have entered the market recently under various plant patents or copyrighted names, but these do not appear to be better than seedling-grown trees. Zone 3.

A. saccharinum (sak-ar-*rye*-num). SILVER MAPLE. SOFT MAPLE. Native to most of eastern N. America, this tree grows rapidly to as much as 120 ft. high. Though the leaves are handsome, deeply five-lobed and 5 in. or more broad and silver-green below, the tree has little to recommend it save where nothing better will grow. Silver maple has surface roots that invade beds, borders and the lawn. The wood is weak; even young trees sustain ruinous wind damage. The fall color west of the Appalachians is subtle but good; clear, pale yellow, leaves on branch ends often overlaid with smoky purple or dark red or both. Natural varieties include: *laciniatum* (las-in-ee-*ay*-tum), with leaves finely divided and with somewhat pendulous branches (the cultivar 'Wier' is a selection of this); *lutescens* (lut-*tess*-senz), with leaves yellowish, at least early in the season; *pendulum* (*pen*-dew-lum), with drooping branches; and *pyramidale* (pihr-am-*id*-day-lee), narrowly upright. Zone 3.

● **A. saccharum** (*sak*-ar-um). SUGAR MAPLE. HARD MAPLE. A formal-appearing, stately tree with a massive trunk, glossy, dark green leaves to 6 in. across and usually five-lobed. The aspect of a tree grown in the open is oval, dense. Though beautiful, these can be difficult in the garden as the surface roots are invasive and the dense crown shades out grass growing near the trunk. Weed-control chemicals applied to the lawn under the tree frequently cause injury. Most sugar maples color beautifully in the fall. Recommended among the several varieties are: *globosum* (glob-*boh*-sum), dense, ball-shaped, usually grafted to a tall whip to make a globelike, formal tree; 'Newton Sentry,' a narrowly columnar tree with a straight trunk bearing stubby, horizontal branches seldom reaching any more than 6 ft.; 'Temple's Upright,' without a main trunk, but sharply ascending and remaining as narrow as the previous cultivar.

A. spicatum (spye-*kay*-tum). MOUNTAIN MAPLE. This is a North woods species that follows the Appalachian Mts. The tree is small, seldom attaining 25 ft. and sparsely branched. Red fruits, produced in early summer, are attractive and the orange-red fall color is good. A tree for the wild garden, this tolerates considerable shade. Zone 2.

A. tataricum (tat-*tar*-ik-um). TATARIAN MAPLE. An undistinguished small European and Asiatic maple growing to 30 ft. The leaves are simple, broadly ovate, to 4 in. long. The fall color is good, yellow or orange-red. The tree is a narrow oval in silhouette. Zone 4 (hardy to −20°, not suited for hot summers).

A. tschonoskii (tshon-os-*keez*-ee-eye). TSCHONOSKI

Acer pensylvanicum, the striped maple, or moosewood, is a coarse-leaved tree whose foliage turns a solid clear yellow in fall. It is hardy to Zone 3 and flourishes with little attention from the gardener.

MAPLE. From Japan, this maple sometimes grows as a bush, but makes a dense little tree to 20 ft. if kept to one or just a few trunks. The leaves are five-lobed, broadly oval, to 5 in. Fall color is bright yellow. Though recommended as a street tree where low clearance is desirable, this looks better as a background tree in a border. Zone 5.

Aceranthus diphyllus. See *Epimedium diphyllum*.

achene (ak-*keen*). A single-seeded, dry fruit that does not split open when ripe. The seeds of a strawberry are achenes as are sunflower seeds.

ACHILLEA (ak-il-*lee*-uh). YARROW. Composite Family (*Compositae*). Familiar, long-lived perennials with clusters of small, single or double flowers in white, pink or yellow shades. One or more species are native to almost every continent. The taller species are useful in the border and cutting garden, shorter species in rock gardens or as a substitute for grass in sandy, dry areas, especially in sections of Calif. They grow in any well-drained, well-dug garden soil, but ample moisture and full sun will give best results. Divide every two or three years, to avoid a weedy habit of growth. Propagate by seeds, sown early for bloom the first year, or by root division. Only the most important species are listed below; rock-garden enthusiasts cultivate several more. The flat-headed fernleaf yarrow and woolly yarrow are fine for winter bouquets. Cut long stems as heads reach full flower; tie in bunches and hang upside down in a sunless, airy place to dry. The color holds well.

A. clavenae (klav-*veen*-ee). SILVER YARROW. Low, 6 to 10 in. high, with thickly set, deeply lobed, silver-gray leaves and small white flowers. Blooms from July to frost. *A. c. argentea* (ar-*jent*-ee-uh), an even more dwarf variety, to 6 in., is useful in the rock garden and as a ground cover. Zone 6.

A. filipendulina (fil-ip-en-dew-*lye*-nuh). FERNLEAF YARROW. GOLDEN YARROW. Tall, 4 to 5 ft. high, with finely cut, sage-green, threadlike foliage and large flat clusters of small, bright yellow flowers in bloom for several weeks in midsummer. Zone 3.

A. millefolium (mil-ef-*foh*-lee-um). COMMON YARROW. MILFOIL. Wild flower commonly seen along roadsides and in fields. The usual color is white, but there is a rosy pink variety, *rosea* (roh-zee-uh). Several cultivars of this are available. Foliage fragrant when touched. The flower clusters, 1½ to 2 in. across, are made up of tiny florets, ¼ in. across. Culture as above. Zone 2.

A. ptarmica (*tar*-mik-uh). SNEEZEWORT. Single-flowered parent of two double-flowered hybrids, 'The Pearl' and 'Boule de Neige' (*bool duh* nayzsh). They are much grown for their double white flowers, ½ in. across, chrysanthemum-like in form, in loose, attractive clusters. The plants are 1½ to 2½ ft. high, and are useful in the perennial border for their summer bloom, and in the cutting garden. Zone 3.

A. tomentosa (toh-men-*toh*-suh). WOOLLY YARROW. Feathery, semi-evergreen with a carpetlike winter habit, 10 to 20 in. high. Fine for edging border, good at the base of large rocks as a transition to lawn and in the rock garden. Pale yellow flowers in flat heads are produced in early summer. Zone 3.

ACHIMENES (ak-*kim*-in-eez). JAPANESE PANSY. HOT WATER PLANT. KIMONO PLANT. NUT ORCHID. WIDOW'S TEARS. CUPID'S BOWER. MAGIC FLOWER. Gesneriad Family (*Gesneriaceae*). Summer-flowering tender perennials from tropical America, newly rediscovered by 20th-century gardeners, but so popular with the Victorians, they gave them all manner of common names, not to mention the formal naming of every new seedling whose flowers showed the slightest variation from existing varieties. They were probably as widely cultivated in the 1800's as the related African violets (*Saintpaulia*) are today.

Achimenes grow from catkinlike scaly rhizomes. The stems may be upright or trailing, with opposite or whorled leaves 1 to 3 in. long, varying from pale green to reddish bronze. All make showy pot, basket and box plants with tubular, five-lobed or semidouble hose-in-hose flowers from June to Oct. Colors include blue, crimson, lavender, pink, purple, scarlet, violet, white and yellow, some attractively marked with a contrasting hue that appears in the throat of the flowers and may be splashed or dotted.

Achimenes need a minimum nighttime temperature of 55°, but 70° or 80° while seeds or scaly rhizomes are being started. Provide semisun in spring; bright open shade in summer. Plant the scaly rhizomes about 1 in. apart and 1 in. deep from Feb. to April in equal parts garden loam, peat moss, sand

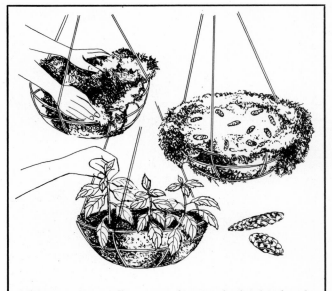

Achimenes grow well in a wire hanging basket lined with sheet moss. Plant rhizomes 1 inch deep. When plants are 2 inches tall, pinch out tips to promote branching.

ABOVE: Achimenes arranged in a bouquet suggest the wide range of colors available in this warm-weather plant that flowers in the shade. For best effect, plant the rhizomes of only one variety in each container or border clump. Achimenes are exceptionally pretty when cultivated in a ceramic strawberry barrel or hanging basket.

ABOVE LEFT: *Achillea millefolium* 'Fire King' is a hybrid of common yarrow or milfoil. It is a completely hardy perennial, especially pleasing near the front of a border. The delicate-appearing flower clusters rise on 18-inch stems from July to October.

LEFT: *Achillea filipendulina* 'Moonshine,' the fernleaf or golden yarrow, has finely cut, silvery-gray leaves. The flowers, on 18- to 24-inch stems, are excellent for cutting, either to use fresh, or to dry for winter bouquets. A superb border plant, especially in a hot, dry, sunny situation.

and leafmold; or in a mixture of equal parts milled sphagnum moss, perlite and vermiculite. Feed every ten days to two weeks through the growing season with a diluted liquid house-plant fertilizer such as fish emulsion. Pinch out the growing tips of young plants to encourage branching. Keep moist from planting time until about Oct. when moisture is withheld until the plants die back. Afterwards set the containers in a dark place with a temperature range of 50°–60° and leave there nearly dry until time to start again. Propagation: Each scaly rhizome multiples into several every year. Achimenes seeds planted in Nov. in warmth and high humidity on moist vermiculite and screened sphagnum moss will provide blooming plants the following summer. Stem cuttings root easily in warmth, moisture, humidity and shade in early summer. Near the end of the flowering season, well-grown achimenes will sprout greenish or reddish rhizomes in the leaf axils. If these propagules are allowed to mature, and then stored over winter in barely moist vermiculite, they will sprout in the spring and may be grown on as mature rhizomes.

Most achimenes in cultivation today are hybrids, derived from breeding species, varieties and cultivars. The most up-to-date records possible are kept by the American Gloxinia and Gesneriad Society, Inc., Eastford, Conn. 06242.

Worthwhile achimenes species grown today by collectors include *A. andrieuxii* (an-*drews*-ee-eye), small violet flowers with purple-dotted white throat; *A. antirrhina* (an-tir-*rin*-uh), scarlet and yellow; *A. candida* (*kan*-did-uh), white inside, buff, cream or reddish outside; *A. ehrenbergii* (air-en-*burg*-ee-eye), orchid with purple-marked white throat; *A. erecta* (ee-*rek*-tuh), formerly A. coccinea, brilliant scarlet; *A. flava* (*flay*-vuh), orange-yellow and *A. patens* (*pay*-tenz), dark violet-purple, yellow-throated. *A. dulcis* (*dull*-siss), white and 'Wetterlow's Triumph,' large-flowered pink, are two lovely achimenes not to be missed. Other named sorts especially recommended for hanging baskets, or to cascade from a shelf, include 'Adelaide,' 'Brilliant,' 'Cattleya,' 'Dentoniana' or 'Giant Pansy,' 'Escheriana' or 'Carmine Queen,' *longiflora* 'Major,' 'Purple King' and 'Royal Purple.'

ACHRAS (*ack*-rass). Sapodilla Family (*Sapotaceae*). Evergreen, broad-leaved tropical trees of Central America occasionally grown in tropical Fla. These take full sun; rich, loamy soil. Propagate by seeds or cuttings. Zone 10.

A. zapota (za-*po*-tah). MARMALADE-PLUM. SAPOTA. This is the only commonly cultivated species. The tree grows to 65 ft. Leaves are up to 16 in. long, glossy. Flowers are white or pinkish. Fruits are russet-brown. The trunk of this tree is tapped for

Acidanthera, the fragrant gladiolus, is grown for its scent and showy blooms. In the North, plant in pots that can be brought indoors to winter over safe from frosts.

the milky sap which is reduced to the chicle used in the manufacture of chewing gum. This tree is also called sapodilla, Sapota achras. Still another incorrect cognomen is calocarpum.

Achyranthes. An obsolete generic name. Plants formerly in this group now are classified as *Alternanthera* and *Iresine*, which see.

ACIDANTHERA (ass-id-*anth*-er-uh). FRAGRANT-GLADIOLUS. DARK-EYE GLADIXIA. Iris Family (*Iridaceae*). Tender, summer-blooming cormaceous perennials from Africa. The conical corms, flattened at the bottom, send up a fan of sword-shaped leaves to a height of 2½ ft. These are very similar to the leaves of gladiolus, but narrower and more graceful. In midsummer flower spikes with three to six blossoms break from the leaf clusters. The white flowers with purple throat resemble gladiolus blooms. In any but the mildest climates, dig the bulbs as soon as the foliage begins to turn yellow and store them in a cool, dry place for the winter. Acidantheras will succeed in any good garden loam but prefer a clay soil. Corms should be planted as soon as danger of frost is past, in holes or trenches 4 to 6 in. deep; deeper in light soils. In cool climates, start them indoors or in the greenhouse. Propagate by bulb offsets or seeds. These force in the warm home greenhouse, treat as gladiolus, but acidanthera requires several more weeks to bloom. Zone 10.

A. bicolor (*bye*-kol-or). Grows about 24 in. high with white flowers with a purple blotch in the center, about 2½ in. across. Flowers, three to six on a stalk, nod gracefully.

A. murieliae (mew-ree-el-*lee*-ee). Sometimes listed incorrectly as Gladiolus murieliae and though similar to *Gladiolus* belongs here. A native of Abyssinia, with leaves about 2 ft. long and 2½ in. wide. Flowers up to 3 in. across, creamy-white shading to pink in the throat, slightly scented.

acidity. The degree of sourness (as contrasted with alkalinity) of soil. The growth of all plants is affected by the degree of soil acidity. Some, such as African violets, blueberries and rhododendrons, grow best in what is considered an acid soil. Others, such as delphiniums, lilacs and sweet peas, prefer a low-acid soil, known as an alkaline soil. Most plants, however, grow best in a neutral soil, or one that is just slightly on the acid side.

Acid soils are found in many parts of the U.S., particularly in humid regions and wooded areas (where decaying leaves produce organic acids). All such soils can be made less acidic by applying lime.

Greater acidity can also be achieved by mixing the soil with a source of humic acids such as peat or by covering it with a layer of oak or beech leaves or pine needles. Another way is to add acidic chemicals as copperas (iron sulfate or aluminum sulfate). See also *soil* and *pH*, *lime* and *acid soil plants*.

acid phosphate. An older name for superphosphate. Rock phosphate is reacted with sulfuric acid to form superphosphates. One hundred pounds of 20 per cent superphosphate contains the following: 20 pounds of calcium, 12 pounds of sulfur and 20 pounds of available phosphoric acid. The calcium and sulfur are combined in oxidized products.

acid soil plants. Soil is acid, neutral or alkaline. Most plants grow in soils that approximate neutrality, but some, notably members of the Heath Family such as heather, azalea, rhododendron and holly do poorly when free lime (calcium salts) are present. These require soil that is acidic. Most garden soils, except those containing limestone chips or those closely underlain by limestone, become acidic through the continued use of organic mulches and various organic manures as these break down to produce humic acids. In this way, tilled soils become acidic, and are suitable for acid soil (lime intolerant) plants. Most acid soil plants also do best in soils rich in organic matter, with or without sand. Peat, dug into the soil, usually gives a sharply acid reaction. Acid soil plants usually grow best when mulched with compost, oak leaves or wood chips or shavings. Never apply lime, bone meal or other alkaline fertilizers to acid soil plants as these

Acidanthera bicolor is creamy white with a purple blotch in the center. It is also called dark-eye gladixia. The small, charming flowers bloom three to six to a stalk and nod gracefully in the slightest breeze.

SHRUBS REQUIRING ACID SOIL

BUXUS	ILEX	PINUS
CALLUNA	ILLICIUM (some)	QUERCUS (most)
CLETHRA	JUNIPERUS (some)	RHODODENDRON
DABOECIA	KALMIA	VACCINIUM
ENKIANTHUS	LEIOPHYLLUM	XANTHORHIZA
ERICA	LEUCOTHOE	ZENOBIA
FIR	LYONIA	
GAULTHERIA	MAGNOLIA (some)	
(some)	MYRICA	

PERENNIALS REQUIRING ACID SOIL

ACTAEA	CYPRIPEDIUM	PRIMULA
ARBUTUS, TRAILING	DICENTRA (some)	SARRACENIA
ARISAEMA	DIGITALIS	TRILLIUM (some)
CHELONE (some)	HYDRANGEA, BLUE	TROLLIUS
CIMICIFUGA	MERTENSIA	

are injurious. Also avoid alkaline spray chemicals such as Bordeaux Mixture.

See also *soils*.

acidus (*ass*-id-us). **-a, -um.** Acid, sour.

ACINETA (ass-in-*nee*-tuh). Orchid Family (*Orchidaceae*). Epiphytic (tree-perching) orchids from Central and S. America. The plant has a thick rhizome with fleshy, brittle roots below and a cluster of stout pseudobulbs with large leaves above. The pendant spike bears many 2- to 4-in. flowers, sometimes fragrant. Grow in orchid rafts, in chopped osmunda or fir bark, with a few tufts of sphagnum and a dusting of rich compost mixed with either. Grow near the glass. Winter minimum temperature is 60°. Harden plants with bright light in the fall and withhold water. Propagate by division. Zone 10.

ACINETA SPECIES IN CULTIVATION		
SPECIES	FLOWER	ORIGIN
A. barkeri	yellow, sometimes crimson blotched; summer	Mexico
A. chrysantha	yellow, tips whitish, fragrant; summer	Mexico
A. densa	yellow, spotted crimson; spring	Central America
A. erythroxantha: A. densa		
A. hrubiana	ivory-white, purple spotted; summer	Colombia
A. humboldtii: A. superba		
A. superba	purplish crimson, lip marked yellow; spring	Colombia

ACOKANTHERA (ah-co-*can*-thu-ruh). Dogbane Family (*Apocynaceae*). Tropical broad-leaved evergreen flowering shrubs; these grow outdoors in tropical Fla. or in large tubs in the intermediate greenhouse. These are very poisonous plants. Pot up in two parts fibrous loam, one part each leafmold, well-rotted barnyard manure or rich compost and sand. Water freely spring and summer, sparingly fall and winter. Propagate by spring cuttings, with bottom heat. Zone 10.

A. spectabilis (spek-*tab*-il-iss). WINTER SWEET. Produces fragrant white flowers in spring, grows 8 to 10 ft. high outdoors. From S. Africa. This species formerly was known as Toxicophloea spectabilis.

Acineta, a tree-perching orchid from Central America, bears its flowers on hanging spikes, many to a cluster. The species *A. densa*, shown here, produces yellow flowers spotted with crimson. Plants will withstand a minimum winter temperature of only 60°, and should be hardened by exposure to bright light in the fall and allowed to dry out sufficiently to create a period of dormancy.

A. venenata (ven-en-*nay*-tuh). BUSHMAN'S POISON. Similar to the preceding species but smaller. Native to S. Africa.

Aconite. See ACONITUM.

Aconite, winter. See ERANTHIS.

ACONITUM (ak-oh-*nye*-tum). MONKSHOOD. ACONITE. Buttercup Family (*Ranunculaceae*). Handsome perennials, chiefly of Europe and Asia, with dark green, deeply divided leaves and showy, helmet-shaped flowers in purple, blue, yellow or white spikes. Important as the source of the several poisonous pharmaceuticals derived from the thick, heavy roots. All parts of the plant are dangerously poisonous in all the species. When grown from seeds, they flower in three years. Aconites are cool-climate plants and prefer a rich moist soil and partial shade. By choosing various species, monkshood may be had in bloom from late June into late autumn. Do not disturb plants unless they become overcrowded to the point where flowering suffers. These are important plants for the perennial border and thrive at the edge of the bog garden. Monkshood, *Aconitum columbianum*, is on the preservation list of Calif. and is protected, that is, is not to be picked or dug up; *uncinatum* is protected in Md.; all native species in N. Mex.; *uncinatum* in N. Car.; all native species (wolfsbane) in Va. (See Bog Plants index in Plant Finder section, Volume 16.) Zone 4 (hardy to −20°), unless otherwise noted.
A. autumnale: *A. henryi.*
● **A. carmichaelii** (kar-mye-*keel*-ee-eye). Sometimes known as A. fischeri. The latest of the monkshoods to bloom. Very tall, to 6 ft., with blue or white flowers in Sept. and Oct. Valuable at a time when good border perennials are hard to come by and especially beautiful as a tall background for chrysanthemums. The variety *wilsonii* (wil-*soh*-nee-eye) is taller, showier and often later and generally handsomer than the species. May need staking. Zone 5 (hardy to −10°).
A. columbianum (kol-lum-bee-*ay*-num). Also called *californicum*, a blue or white species close to *carmichaelii*, and about 3 ft. tall. Zone 5-4.
A. fischeri: *A. carmichaelii.*
A. henryi (*hen*-ree-eye). Sometimes listed in catalogs as A. autumnale. Tall, 4 to 5 ft. high, with very dark blue blossoms with prominent hoods and flowers more openly arranged. There is a white variety. In bloom Aug. and Sept.
A. lycoctonum: *A. vulparia.*
● **A. napellus** (nap-*pell*-us). This European species, blooming in July and Aug., has beautiful, dark blue blossoms on strong stems, 3 to 4 ft. high, sometimes

Aconitum napellus is a European species of monkshood with dark blue blossoms that appear in July and August. Excellent here for the hardy border where it persists for years.

taller. The finely cut leaves add to the decorativeness of the plant. This is one of the great plants of the hardy border; increasing slowly, it persists for years without extra care. There is a white variety, handsome but not as hardy as the type. *A. napellus* is the species commonly grown as the source of the drug, aconite, and it should be remembered that its roots are dangerously poisonous.
A. uncinatum (un-si-*nay*-tum). WILD MONKSHOOD. A good wild flower that is native to the eastern U.S., this climbing or trailing plant grows up to 5 ft. The blue flowers, blooming in summer and autumn, make a fine show in the wild garden.
A. vulparia (vul-*pay*-ree-uh). WOLFSBANE. Formerly A. lycoctonum. Grows 4 to 5 ft. tall, with narrow, yellow or cream blossoms in graceful spires. Large, deeply divided leaves. Blooms in midsummer.

acorn. The fruit of oaks. Without its cap, the acorn, technically, is a true nut.

ACORUS (*ak*-or-us). Arum Family (*Araceae*). Hardy perennials, growing in marshy places of the Northern Hemisphere. Slender, irislike leaves and small, long-lasting, greenish-yellow flowers in short spikes. The stout, aromatic rootstock has been used commercially in making perfume. All parts of the plant are fragrant. These plants grow easily in full sun and boggy locations. Propagate by division.
A. calamus (*kal*-am-us). SWEET FLAG. Grows 3 to 6 ft. high, with irislike leaves. The spikes of small, greenish flowers appear in June. Although not a particu-

larly decorative plant, its delicious lemon fragrance recommends its use in the bog garden, wild garden or herb garden. *A. c. variegatus* (var-ree-eg-*gay*-tus) has green leaves with cream stripes. Zone 3.

A. gramineus (gram-*min*-ee-us). A 12-in.-high Japanese species with grasslike foliage; practically a miniature of sweet flag. Varieties are *variegatus*, as the species but with cream-striped leaves and *pusillus* (pew-*sill*-us) a 3-in. miniature. Zone 5.

acre. An area containing 43,560 sq. ft. (4,840 sq. yds.). The equivalent of a square having sides of approximately 209 ft. It takes 640 acres to make a square mile. When used as a descriptive noun, as *Sedum acre,* the term means "of the tilled land."

acris (*ay*-kriss), **-e.** Sharp, pungent.

Acroclinium. See *Helipterum roseum.*

ACROCOMIA (ak-ro-*coh*-mee-uh). Gru-gru (a palm). Palm Family (*Palmae*). Very tender palms of tropical America suitable for growing in frost-free areas where the soil is sandy and fairly moist. Species are somewhat undetermined but those in current horticultural literature include *A. aculeata, A. armentalis* and *A. totai.*

ACROSTICHUM (a-*cross*-ti-cum). Fern Family (*Polypodiaceae*). Evergreen ferns from tropical swamps. Except in Zone 10 grow these tubbed in the warm greenhouse or plant room. In early spring divide and pot in equal parts loam, sand, peat, leafmold and natural charcoal chips. Water freely through warm weather; moderately at other times. High humidity and light shade are essential. Propagate by division and by spores (early summer). Zone 10.

A. aureum (*aw*-ree-um). Fern with leathery, evergreen fronds 1 to 2 ft. high while young but growing taller after several years.

A. daneaefolium (dan-ee-*foh*-lee-um). Fern with leaflets resembling foliage of the shrub danae; dark green, lustrous. To 6 ft. and more under tropical rain forest conditions.

ACTAEA (ak-*tee*-uh). Baneberry. Cohosh. Buttercup Family (*Ranunculaceae*). Long-lived, sturdy perennials with deeply cut leaves and showy clusters of small white flowers, followed by shiny, red or white berries (poisonous) in late summer. They are easily grown in a moist woodsy soil and partial shade. Useful in the shady border, the rock garden or the wild garden. Propagate by seeds sown early in spring or by root division. Baneberry, *Actaea rubra* and

pachypoda, are on the preservation list of Conn.; all native species are protected in Washington, D.C.; *rubra* and *pachypoda* in Iowa; *pachypoda* in Ohio.
A. alba: *A. pachypoda.*

A. pachypoda (pack-ee-*pohd*-uh). White baneberry. A native plant found in the woodlands of eastern N. America. Grows to 1½ ft. Conspicuous white or pinkish berries, each with a dark blue eye, follow the fluffy white flower clusters that bloom in May. There is a variety with red berries, *rubrocarpa* (roo-broh-*kar*-puh). Zone 3.

A. rubra (*roob*-ruh). Red baneberry. Red cohosh. From Labrador south to the Middle Atlantic states and westward to the Dakotas, red baneberry is a common plant of the shady woodlands. It grows to 2 ft., with showy clusters of small white flowers followed by poisonous red berries. The root of this plant is a violent purgative and emetic. Zone 3.

A. spicata (spye-*kay*-tuh). Black baneberry. Herb

Above: *Actaea alba,* white baneberry, is also called doll's eye for its conspicuous white or pink berries, each with a dark blue eye. Berries follow fluffy white flowers that bloom in May.
Right: *Acorus calamus,* sweet flag, is a plant that grows in bog gardens. Greenish flowers are borne on small spikes in June. Flowers aren't particularly decorative, but many plant sweet flag for its lovely lemony scent. Generally hardy throughout Zone 3 and in all regions south.

UPPER: *Actinidia arguta*, which is called bower actinidia and also tara vine, is a fast-growing deciduous climber that bears sweet yellow fruit often used for preserves.
LOWER: Chinese actinidia, with showier leaves, is less hardy.

CHRISTOPHER. A plant from Europe and Japan, growing 2½ ft. Blooms in April with white flowers and blue-black berries that are extremely poisonous. Zone 5.

acti-dione. An antibiotic fungicide for controlling various plant diseases. See *fungicide*.

ACTINEA (ak-*tin*-ee-uh). Composite Family (*Compositae*). Alpine and alkaline High Plains perennials, 1 to 10 in. high. From specialized habitats, these are difficult in cultivation out of their native range. The daisylike yellow flowers are produced in early summer, later at higher altitudes. Some species are poisonous to range livestock. Zone 4.

A. acaulis (uk-*kaw*-liss). WOOLLY ACTINEA. A 1- to 6-in.-high plant of the alpine ridges, this bears yellow, gaillardia-like flower heads 1 to 3 in. across. The entire leaves are densely clothed with feltlike white hairs. The variety *caespitosa* (ses-pit-*toe*-suh) is smaller in all its parts.

A. argentea (ar-*jen*-tee-uh). PERKY SUE. A 3- to 6-in.-high plant with 1-in. yellow daisylike flowers of the southern Rocky Mts., this species grows thickly, coating the foothills with golden yellow through April and after summer rains. Often it flowers into Oct.

A. grandiflora (gran-di-*floh*-ruh). GRAYLOCKS ACTINEA. RYDBERGIA. This small Rocky Mt. alpine perennial grows 1 to 6 in. high. The dissected leaves and upright, stout stems are covered with soft, loose white hairs. Clear yellow flower heads, 2 to 4 in. across, top the tiny plants in midsummer. A difficult species to cultivate.

A. simplex (*sim*-plex). In rocky, subalpine meadows this perennial composite grows to 10 in. high. With more slender stems than the above species, and usually with entire leaves, this plant is covered with silvery-white down. The flowers, similar to those of *A. grandiflora* but somewhat smaller, are produced singly from early to late summer.

ACTINIDIA (ak-tin-*nid*-ee-uh). Dillenia Family (*Dilleniaceae*). Deciduous, twining, Asiatic vines of vigorous growth, with handsome, dense foliage. Male and female flowers borne on separate plants. They are satisfactory for covering arbors and trellises where there is plenty of room. Easily grown in ordinary garden soil in full sun or partial shade. At least six species are in cultivation. Propagate by stratified seeds sown in spring; softwood and hardwood cuttings root easily.

A. arguta (ar-*gew*-tuh). BOWER ACTINIDIA. TARA VINE. A fast-growing, deciduous vine to 20 ft. or more. Lustrous, oval, dark green leaves to 6 in. long and finely toothed. They make an interesting contrast with the short red petioles. Small clusters of insignificant white flowers in summer are followed by sweet, yellow fruit for eating out of hand or for preserving. Plants having male flowers do not bear fruit. Zone 4.

A. chinensis (chin-*nen*-siss). CHINESE ACTINIDIA. YANGTAO. Grows up to 30 ft. long, with heart-shaped leaves to 5 in. long, white-velvety beneath. When young, the branches and twigs are covered with shaggy, reddish hairs. Insignificant white flowers are produced on year-old wood. The edible fruit, similar to gooseberries in taste, is useful for preserves. Handsomer than *A. arguta*, it is less hardy. Zone 7.

A. kolomikta (ko-lo-*mik*-ta). KOLOMIKTA ACTINIDIA. The male vine is the most ornamental of all actinidias, the foliage variegated with white and pink blotches. A lime-craving species. The female Kolomikta actinidia bears green leaves; flowers and fruit are insignificant. This makes a good tub vine for the home greenhouse. Zone 4.

A. polygama (pol-*lig*-am-uh). SILVER VINE. As the above species, the male plants of this bear silver-variegated foliage, leaves 3 to 5 in. long, while female plant leaves are solid green. Flowers and fruit are of little value. The scent of the vine attracts cats (outdoors and in the greenhouse) which quickly shred it. Zone 4.

ACTINOPHLOEUS (ak-tin-oh-*flee*-us). Palm Family (*Palmae*). An Australian palm genus, only one species commonly cultivated. Propagate by seed. Zone 10.

A. macarthuri (mac-*ar*-thur-eye). CLUSTER PALM. A small palm, to 10 ft., growing in clusters, and with feathery leaves. Plant outdoors in tropical Fla. in part shade. This is a good tub palm; the soil mix is Basic Potting Mixture. Apply liquid fertilizer spring and summer, water freely April to Sept.; moderately other times.

aculeatus (ak-kew-lee-*ay*-tus), **-a, -um.** Prickly.

acuminatus (ak-kew-min-*nay*-tus), **-a, -um.** Long-pointed, tapering; acuminate.

acuti- (ak-yew-tih). Prefix meaning sharp.

acutus (ak-*kew*-tus), **-a, -um.** Acute; sharp-pointed. Combining prefix: acuti.

ADA (*ah*-dah). Orchid Family (*Orchidaceae*). Small group of epiphytic orchids mostly from Colombia. Pot in equal parts coarse peat or chopped osmunda fiber and fresh sphagnum moss. Water freely while in active growth, moderately otherwise. For the cool greenhouse only; from March to Sept. 55°–60°, Sept. to March 50° night, 55° day. These need shade the

year round. Propagate by seed (sterile flask) or divide as new growth begins.

A. aurantiaca (aw-*ran*-tye-ak-uh). Small plant with odontoglossum-like orange flowers on delicate spikes in Jan. Cool tropics.

A. lehmannii (*lay*-man-ee-eye). Similar to the above in form, but leaves gray-marked. Flowers cinnamon-orange with pale to whitish labellum. Blooms in early summer. Cool tropics.

Adam-and-Eve. See APLECTRUM.

Adam's laburnum. See x *Laburnocytisus adamii*.

Adam's needle. See *Yucca filamentosa*.

Adder's-tongue. See *Erythronium; Ophioglossum*.

Adder's-tongue Family (*Ophioglossaceae*). A small family of ferns, native in the U.S. and Eurasia. Quite small in size, they are grown occasionally in rock or wild gardens. *Botrychium* and *Ophioglossum* are the two genera included in this encyclopedia.

Adder's-tongue fern. See *Ophioglossum vulgatum*.

ADENANTHERA (ad-en-*anth*-er-uh). BEAD TREE. Pea Family (*Leguminosae*). Tropical, evergreen trees and shrubs allied to mimosa. With yellow flowers, these bloom in midsummer. Where frosts occur grow tubbed and keep pruned to reasonable size; move into warm home greenhouse over winter. Repot occasionally in March, equal parts garden loam, brown peat and fine sand. Water freely spring and summer, moderately fall and winter. In the tropics grow as tall background shrubs or small flowering trees. Propagate by seed or heel cuttings in April. Zone 10.

A. bicolor (*bye*-kol-or). RED SANDALWOOD TREE. Small spreading or wide shrub, with sprays of yellow flowers in July. From Ceylon.

A. pavonina (pav-on-*nye*-nuh). PEACOCK FLOWER FENCE. Bushy shrub or small tree, yellow and white flowers in tufts, in July. From China.

adeno-. Prefix meaning sticky.

ADENOPHORA (ad-en-*off*-o-ruh). LADY BELL. Bellflower Family (*Campanulaceae*). Perennials, native to mountain regions of the Far East. Very similar to campanula. Rich, well-drained loam and full, or nearly full, sun. When once established, they should not be disturbed. Propagate by seeds, cuttings or division.

Among species grown are Farrer's Lady bell, *A. conusa*, dark blue inch-long flowers, Lilyleaf

Lady bell, *A. lilifolia*, whose flowers are fragrant and bluish. A species seen in European gardens is *A. coelestis*.

A. potaninii (poh-tan-*nee*-nee-eye). The best of the species, this summer-flowering plant grows to 3 ft., with violet-blue, bell-shaped, drooping blossoms, 1 in. across, in graceful sprays. Valuable for July and Aug. bloom. Good in the perennial border. There is a fine white variety, *alba* (*al*-buh). Zone 3.

ADHATODA (ad-*hay*-to-dah). Acanthus Family (*Acanthaceae*). A group of 25 tender shrubs rather like *Justicia* but with anthers that have fewer spurs. It is considered by some authorities as a member of the *Justicia* genus, which are primarily greenhouse plants grown for showy spikes. Propagate by cuttings in late winter or spring rooted in sand. These will flower the following season. After flowering, plants are headed back, or discarded excepting those to be kept to supply cuttings for a new crop. Zone 10.

A. cydoniaefolia (sye-do-nee-ay-*fo*-lee-uh). BRAZILIAN BOWER PLANT. A native of Brazil, this is one of the very few species of *Adhatoda* found on this continent. Generally grown in Calif.

ADIANTUM (ad-ee-*an*-tum). MAIDENHAIR FERN. Common-fern Family (*Polypodiaceae*). A large genus, native mostly to S. America, but a few species are found in the U.S. Handsome, shade-loving ferns with delicate fronds on slender stems. Many are favorites for the shaded portion of the intermediate greenhouse; our native species are easily grown in gardens if their natural habitat of high-humus woods soil and shade are duplicated. In the greenhouse use Basic Potting Mixture with doubled peat. They require high humidity. Propagate by division or spores. Maidenhair fern, *Adiantum pedatum*, is on the preservation list of Conn., Maine, Md., N.J. and Va.; *capillus-veneris* is protected in N. Mex.; *pedatum* in N. Car.

A. capillus-veneris (*kap*-il-us-*ven*-er-iss). SOUTHERN MAIDENHAIR FERN. VENUS-HAIR. The slender, erect, black leaf stalk rises about 1½ ft. high. Compound leaves, more or less fan shaped. Primarily a greenhouse subject, it can be grown outdoors in warm, moist regions. Zone 9.

A. cuneatum (kew-nee-*ay*-tum). DELTA MAIDENHAIR FERN. This native of Brazil is widely grown in greenhouses for house decoration and ornament. It is the species commonly used by florists. Beautiful, feathery fronds, 15 in. long and 9 in. wide, on polished, brownish-black stems. Several cultivars of this fern have been named by commercial growers, such as 'Elegantissimum,' 'Gracillimum,' 'Grande' and 'Pocottii.' Zone 10.

A. hispidulum (hiss-*pid*-yew-lum). ROSY MAIDENHAIR

UPPER: *Adenophora potaninii*, a hardy species of lady bell, produces violet-blue blossoms in July and August.
LOWER: *Adonis amurensis*, pheasant-eye, has bright yellow flowers in late winter. Both are hardy in Zone 3.

FERN. A tropical fern from Eastern Hemisphere rain forests. Grows 10–12 in. tall and tolerates pot culture. An excellent greenhouse plant. Zone 10.

A. pedatum (ped-*day*-tum). AMERICAN MAIDENHAIR FERN. A hardy species, common in rocky woods of N. America. Wiry, black-purple leaf stalk, about 1 ft. high, forked at the top. Large, feathery fronds to 1½ ft. across, with bluish-green leaflets. A handsome species, easily grown in cool, high-humus soil and shade in the wild garden. Zone 2.

A. tenerum (*ten*-er-um). BRITTLE MAIDENHAIR FERN. A sturdy erect species, growing up to 3 ft. Common in the tropics, it is occasionally found in Fla. An excellent greenhouse plant, with deeply notched fronds on shining, brownish-black stems. The attractive variety x *farleyense* (far-lee-*en*-see) has slightly larger fronds, to 3 ft. long, of a more delicate green than the type. Zone 10.

ADINA (ah-*dee*-nuh). Madder Family (*Rubiaceae*). Deciduous Chinese shrubs with opposite leaves and terminal globe-shaped flower clusters with attractively extruded pistils. The flowers are white or pinkish lavender and fragrant.

The cultivated species, *A. rubella* (rue-*bell*-uh), takes full sun, well-drained, moderately rich soil, preferably gritty or somewhat sandy. Flowers are produced over several weeks in midsummer. Zone 6.

ADLUMIA (ad-*loo*-mee-uh). ALLEGHENY VINE. MOUNTAIN FRINGE. Fumitory Family (*Fumariaceae*). There is only one species, a delicate, biennial vine, native to eastern N. America. Sow seeds in early spring where plants are wanted. Shade part of the day, rich garden loam, plenty of moisture and protection from wind are needed. Where these requirements are met, it thrives and self-sows, insuring long-blossoming vines each year. Mountain fringe, *Adlumia fungosa*, is on the preservation list of Conn. and Mass. and is protected, that is, is not to be picked or dug up. Zone 3.

A. fungosa (fun-*goh*-suh). Light, airy, three-part leaves and white or purplish-pink flowers, ¾ in. long in drooping clusters, similar to the blooms of the bleeding-heart. Grows to 15 ft. in its second year, after a low, shrubby growth the first year from seeds.

Adobe-lily. See *Fritillaria pluriflora*.

adobe soil. A heavy, highly mineralized clay soil that compacts tightly. Found commonly in desert regions in the U.S., largely limited to arid portions of the Southwest. Alkaline soil-tolerant plants such as rabbit brush, greasewood, mesquite, some yuccas and some cacti will grow in adobe. To make garden soil of it, dress with gypsum (land-plaster), 50 to 100 pounds

Adiantum is the lovely maidenhair fern. The species here, *A. cuneatum*, flourishes in the warm reaches of Zone 10 and in greenhouse culture farther north. It is the species florists use to add green to bouquets of cut flowers.

per 100 square ft., and turn in as deeply as possible. Crop with rape (*Brassica napus*) or other cabbage-family species, and turn under for green manure. When the top layer approaches friability, double dig, incorporating gypsum and organic debris in the lower layer as it is broken. By free addition of organic manures, and a minimal use of fertilizer containing sodium salts, chloride salts, or many soluble trace elements (other than iron), adobe can be converted to good garden soil in a few seasons.

ADONIDIA (ad-doh-*nid*-ee-uh). Palm Family (*Palmae*). A South Pacific palm genus with a single species in cultivation.

A. merrillii (mer-*rill*-ee-eye). MANILA PALM. A slender-trunked palm to 25 ft., with a feathery crown of pinnately compound leaves to 5 ft. or more. Named after Dr. E. D. Merrill, a U.S. botanist who worked extensively on Philippine flora. Propagates easily by seeds from the beautiful red fruits grown in large clusters. Zone 10.

ADONIS (ad-*doh*-niss). PHEASANT-EYE. Buttercup Family (*Ranunculaceae*). Hardy annuals and herbaceous perennials from Europe and Asia, with feathery foliage and pretty, yellow or red flowers, usually daisylike in form. Easily grown in almost any rich garden soil, in full sun or partial shade. Propagate by seeds for annuals and perennials, the latter also by root division.

A. aestivalis (ess-tiv-*vay*-liss). SUMMER ADONIS. An annual species from central Europe, with finely divided foliage and crimson 1½-in.-wide flowers in early summer. To 1 ft. Variety *citrina* (sit-*rye*-nuh) has yellow flowers.

A. aleppica (ah-*lep*-ih-ca). ALEPPO ADONIS. From Syria, this annual species is similar to the above; with dark red flowers 2 in. across in early summer.

A. amurensis (am-moor-*ren*-siss). Perennial, from Asia, with large, bright yellow-cupped flowers, 2 in. across, blooming in late winter and early spring. This species grows 1 to 1½ ft. high, with fernlike, finely cut foliage. Needs rich soil to grow well. Fine in the spring border with early bulbs and for cutting. There is a double-flowered variety, 'Fukiju Kai.' Zone 3.

A. annua (*an*-yew-uh). AUTUMN ADONIS. RED-CHAMOMILE. Annual, from Great Britain, with dark scarlet flowers less than 1 in. across, each with a very dark eye. Blooms in May to Sept. Grows 1 to 2 ft. high; these plants are useful in the border and the cutting garden.

A. brevistyla (brev-ih-*sty*-la). A rare perennial species from Tibet and western China. Foliage finely divided, midsummer flowers white, backs of petals blue. The plant grows 9 to 12 in. high. Zone 3.

A. chrysocyathis (cry-so-sigh-*ay*-this). A 9- to 12-in.-high, summer-blooming perennial species from Kashmir. Showy flowers, bright golden yellow. Zone 4.

A. davidii: *A. brevistyla.*

A. pyrenaica (pye-ren-*nay*-ik-uh). PYRENEES ADONIS. A July-blooming perennial species from the Pyrenees Mts. With finely divided foliage to 1 ft., flowers yellow. A rock-garden species. Zone 4.

A. vernalis (ver-*nay*-liss). SPRING ADONIS. This perennial species from southern Europe grows to 1 ft. or higher, with large, bright yellow flowers, 3 in. across. Blooms from April to June; with dense whorls of finely cut leaves. Useful in the rock garden or the spring border. A white variety and a double form are available. Zone 3.

adpressus (ad-*press*-us), **-a, -um.** Pressed against or together.

ADROMISCHUS (ad-roh-*misk*-us). Stonecrop Family (*Crassulaceae*). Perennial succulents from S. Africa, once included under *Cotyledon*, but having smaller flowers that are erect rather than pendulous. Only a few in. high, they are valued for the thick,

alternate leaves that are often interestingly shaped and colored. Fine pot plants for the home or greenhouse. Easily grown in sun in Basic Potting Mixture with doubled sand. Give them plenty of water during the summer, very little in winter. Propagate by leaf cuttings. Zone 10.

A. cooperi (*coo*-per-eye). The crisp foliage is red and greenish (bright light gives improved color). Flowers are unimportant. Grows to 1 ft. From S. Africa.

A. cristatus (kris-*tay*-tus). A slow-growing species, 4 to 10 in. high. Short, reddish stems with hairlike aerial roots. Wedge-shaped, velvety, crested leaves to 1 in. long form a rosette. Inconspicuous greenish flowers to ½ in. long.

A. hemisphaericus (hem-iss-*feer*-ik-us). With frosted, olive-green leaves that are thickened, half-round. Spikes of tubular greenish flowers. To 14 in.; from S. Africa.

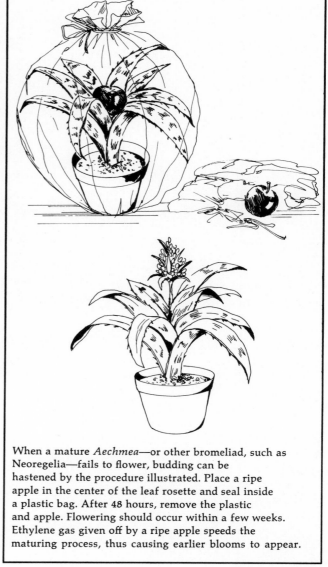

LEFT: *Adonis vernalis*, spring adonis, is a perennial from
Europe well suited to the hardy rock garden or
the herbaceous border in Zone 3. Plant stands
to 12 inches high and produces large yellow
flowers from April to June.
ABOVE: The species *Adonis aestivalis*, summer adonis, is
an annual that may be sown out-of-doors in September
or in March. Plants bloom in June and July. Adonis foliage
is feathery and the plants, perennial or annual,
grow readily in almost any rich garden loam in either
full sun or partial shade. Red chamomile is an autumn
adonis with dark scarlet flowers and is useful
both in the perennial border and for the cutting garden.

When a mature *Aechmea*—or other bromeliad, such as
Neoregelia—fails to flower, budding can be
hastened by the procedure illustrated. Place a ripe
apple in the center of the leaf rosette and seal inside
a plastic bag. After 48 hours, remove the plastic
and apple. Flowering should occur within a few weeks.
Ethylene gas given off by a ripe apple speeds the
maturing process, thus causing earlier blooms to appear.

A. maculatus (mac-yew-*lay*-tus). A low, spreading
species from S. Africa, with handsome foliage. The
glossy, gray-green fleshy leaves are splotched with
reddish-purple markings.

A. rhombifolius (rom-bif-*foh*-lee-us). An undistinguished species; irregular, gray stems, greenish flowers and scalelike, gray-green leaves.

adsurgens (ad-*ser*-jenz). Ascending.

adventitious. Term describing buds or roots that arise
at an unusual or abnormal location on a plant. For
example, under certain conditions a cut begonia leaf
may grow adventitious roots along its veins or pedi-
cel; adventitious buds (not in leaf axils, as normal)

may develop when a plant has been severely pruned
or damaged.

advenus (ad-*veen*-us), **-a, -um.** Newly arrived, recent.

AECHMEA (*eek*-mee-uh). Bromelia Family (*Bromeliaceae*). Drought-resistant, ornamental relatives of the
pineapple, these plants are known as air plants or
bromeliads. They make fine and easy house plants or
greenhouse subjects with their bold foliage and colorful flower clusters with conspicuous bracts. From
S. America, these plants are usually epiphytic (tree-
perching) in their native habitat. The stiff leaves form
a dense rosette at the base, out of which rise the
flower stalks, bearing blooms at almost any season

the plant reaches maturity. They will grow in either sun or shade in a warm room. Use Basic Potting Mixture with doubled sand and vermiculite. Do not overwater (water in the leaf funnel is all that is really necessary). Propagate by suckers or offsets removed from the base of the old plants. Zone 10.

AEGLE (*ee*-glee). BAEL FRUIT. Rue Family (*Rutaceae*). A monotypic genus.
A. marmelos (*mar*-mel-los). A small tree of tropical India with white flowers in April and hard greenish-yellow fruits, pulp of which is used in preparing drinks and in medicine. Requires sharp drainage and fertile soil. Propagate by seeds. Zone 10.

Aechmeas are air plants, or bromeliads, native to tropical America, and they make handsome indoor or hothouse plants. They require abundant water during the summer months but should be allowed to dry out slightly in winter. Some shade from strong summer sun is desirable. The species here, *Aechmea fulgens*, is from Brazil, and produces showy clusters of red florets tipped with blue.

ORNAMENTAL AECHMEAS IN CULTIVATION

SPECIES	PLANT	FLOWERS	ORIGIN
A. amazonica	Tubular rosette to 3 ft., flared at top. Leaves green, purple beneath, cross-banded silver; blackish marginal spines.	Mealy white stalk, red bracts, orange flowers.	Brazil, Peru, Colombia
A. angustifolia	Heavy rosette to 2½ ft. Leaves 2½ in. wide, gray with brown scales, short spines at margins.	Red spike, red bracts, yellow flowers, then blue fruit.	Costa Rica, Brazil, Peru, Colombia
A. chantinii	Open rosette. Leaves hard, olive-green, with bold pinkish cross bandings.	Branched spike, green, red bracts tipped yellow.	Venezuela, Brazil, Peru
A. distichantha	Cylindrical rosette, dense. Leaves stiff, gray.	Sturdy spike with pale rose-pink bracts and purplish-blue flowers.	Brazil
A. fasciata	Heavy rosette of leathery green leaves frosted with gray scales and mottled silver-white. Blackish marginal spines.	Heavy spike with flattened globose head of rose-pink bracts. Flowers blue.	Brazil
A. fulgens	Loose rosette; leaves stiff, with gray bloom.	Tall, showy panicle of clustered red florets, each tipped blue.	Brazil
A. lasseri	Star-shaped rosette. Leaves broad, green, with bloom, sometimes reddening.	Pendulous spike, white-scaled, and with greenish-white flowers.	Venezuela
A. marmorata	Tall, very formal cylindrical rosette. Leaves recurved, bluish, mottled green and maroon.	Pendant spike, bracts rose-pink, flowers blue.	Brazil
A. racinea	Rosette to 18 in., leaves shiny, green, straplike.	Spike pendant, orange-red receptacles support yellow and blue-black flowers.	Brazil
A. zebrina	Broad, urn-shaped rosette. Leaves wide, rounded at tip, olive-green, cross-banded white, spiny margins.	Branched, spreading spikes. Red bracts at branches. Flowers yellow, subtended by boat-shaped yellow bracts.	Colombia

These represent a sample of the more than 50 *Aechmea* species. Many have handsome varieties, and hybridizers have created several fine cultivars. See Graf's *Exotica* for a more complete listing.

LEFT: *Aechmea fasciata* 'Silver King' has handsome green leaves mottled and striped with silver. It produces pink bracts with rose-pink and blue flowers. This species is from Brazil, and cultural requirements are similar to those for *A. fulgens*, opposite.

RIGHT: Ground cover *Aegopodium podograria* is bishop's weed, a sturdy perennial hardy to Zone 3. It spreads by means of slender creeping root stocks choking out most other plantings in its path. An excellent cover for naturalized areas and as a transition planting between rocks and lawn. It will succeed in partial shade and is often used to hold the soil on shady slopes where few other ground covers would succeed.

AEGOPODIUM (ee-go-*poh*-dee-um). GOUTWEED. Carrot Family (*Umbelliferae*). A small genus of sturdy perennials from Europe and Asia. The species described below grows about 1 ft. high and spreads by slender, creeping rootstocks. Bold, divided foliage. Useful for edging perennial or shrubbery borders. Partial shade and ordinary garden soil, well turned to a spade's depth. Propagate by seed or division. (Many plants suitable for use as edgings may be found in the index, Plant Finder section, Volume 16.)

A. podagraria (pod-ah-*gray*-ree-uh). BISHOP'S-WEED. Usually grown in the green-and-white-leaved variety, *variegatum* (var-ee-eg-*gay*-tum), this plant is found almost throughout the U.S. Its lively foliage sets off other familiar and equally sturdy garden perennials. The flowers are small, greenish white, and inconspicuous, growing in 3- to 4-in. flat clusters. An excellent plant for the base of large rocks as a transition to lawn, for edging the herb garden and for a ground cover on shady slopes, as well as for the perennial border. As a ground cover, it needs thinning every two or three years; otherwise it will spread away, trying to escape its own tangled stems. The green-and-white foliage is effective when cut for arrangements. Zone 3.

AEONIUM (ee-*oh*-nee-um). Stonecrop Family (*Crassulaceae*). Once included under *Sempervivum*, these fast-growing succulents from the Madeira and Canary Islands are low, shrubby perennials. The fleshy leaves grow in rosettes on the ends of woody stems. Large clusters of yellow, red or white flowers appear above the leaves in late winter or early spring, after which the plant may die if offsets have not been produced. Usually, however, the branches begin new growth. The species below are representative of the many plants to be found in this genus. All are easily grown in the sunny greenhouse or on window sills in the house; use Basic Potting Mixture with double sand. The plants add distinction to outdoor gardens in southern Calif. and similar frost-free regions. Water well in summer, but lightly in winter when the plants usually are dormant. Pots may be plunged outdoors or displayed on shelves or other staging during the summer. Propagate by seeds or cuttings. Zone 10.

A. arboreum (ar-*boh*-ree-um). Probably the best-known species, this is a much-branched shrub up to 3 ft. high. The rosettes of spoon-shaped green leaves are edged with fine hairs. Conical clusters of golden-yellow flowers ¾ in. across. There is a variety with striking, dark purple leaves.

A. caespitosum (seess-pit-*toh*-sum). A pretty, small plant forming clumps of woody stems up to 6 in. high. Narrow, lance-shaped leaves in dense rosettes. Forked clusters of yellow flowers in early spring.

A. canariense (kan-ar-ee-*en*-see). One of the larger species, growing to 1½ ft. or more. The broad, spoon-shaped leaves form a flattened rosette up to 20 in. across. Clusters of white or yellow flowers.

A. decorum (*dek*-or-um). Small, bushy shrub up to 1 ft. high, with thick, lance-shaped, glossy green leaves tinged with coppery red. Pink flowers with white petals.

A. haworthii (hay-*worth*-ee-eye). Shrubby, woody-stemmed species 1 to 2 ft. high and much branched at the base. Ovalish, sharp-pointed, bluish-green leaves in rosettes to 3 in. across. White flowers, often rose-tinted, appear in early spring.

A. nobile (*noh*-bil-ee). A striking species with thick, broad, green leaves to 1 ft. long in large rosettes, topped by a huge, dense cluster of dark red flowers.

aequinoctialis (eek-wee-nok-tee-*ay*-liss), **-e.** Pertaining to the equinox.

aeration. Refers to manipulating a growing medium (natural soil, *in situ* or in a container or a growing mixture) to provide roots with sufficient oxygen for their needs. Without oxygen in the soil, plants cannot take up or use water or the minerals necessary for growth. Hence the need to take steps to see that the soil receives as much oxygen as possible. These often are relatively simple:

In heavy soils, add organic matter and sand to lighten the texture so that air can enter more easily.

Cultivate horticultural soils frequently; spade beds and hoe them, fork borders, perforate the lawn. This not only allows oxygen to penetrate, but also eliminates weeds that compete with good plants for the available oxygen.

On lawns, avoid using heavy rollers and tampers, except when there is no other way to level the surface. Go over the turf once or twice annually (or more often if the lawn is used as a playground) with a small spiked aerator. For best results, rent a power aerator that removes small plugs of soil to a depth of 3 or 4 in.

Drain low spots in which water stands; otherwise plants will be drowned (deprived of oxygen). See *tiling.*

Keep the soil for pot plants stirred on the surface, and be sure to use containers with bottom drainage holes. Common red clay pots are particularly recommended because they supply bottom drainage and because the clay itself is porous enough to permit a small amount of oxygen to seep into the soil.

aerial root. A root produced above-ground, sometimes functioning as a true root (as of epiphytes), sometimes used for attachment (as on ivy and other vines) and sometimes serving to prop up the plant, as banyan or screw-pine.

AERIDES (ay-*ehr*-id-eez). Orchid Family (*Orchidaceae*). Epiphytic (tree-perching) orchids from the East Indian region. The thick leaves grow in two ranks along a single stem. The flower stems grow from the leaf axils and produce a profusion of showy flowers in erect or in gracefully drooping clusters. These orchids need a warm, humid greenhouse and plenty of moisture at their roots. Use fir bark or osmunda fiber for

ORNAMENTAL AERIDES CULTIVATED BY ORCHID GROWERS			
NAME	FLOWER COLOR	TIME OF BLOOM	ORIGIN
A. crassifolium	amethyst-purple	summer	Burma
A. crispum	white-pink, lip rose-purple	summer	Bombay area
A. falcatum	creamy white, lip with purple stripe	late summer	Burma-India
A. fieldingii	white, rose-purple mottles, lip rose purple	summer	Assam
A. japonicum	greenish white, marked red, lip with purple spots	summer	Japan
A. lawrenceae	white, waxy, marked crimson-purple	autumn	Philippines
A. lobbii	white, rose-flushed, lip purple tinged	summer	Burma
A. maculosum	rose, purple-spotted, lip rose-purple	summer	Bombay
A. multiflorum	amethyst (variable)	summer	India
A. odoratum	(see above)		
A. quinquevulnerum	white, purple-spotted lip with amethyst streak	late summer	Philippines
A. vandarum	white (leaves terete)	fall-winter	India

the potting medium. Good light also necessary. Fertilize when growth is active. Propagate by air layering.

Horticulturists list twelve or more species for this genus, but classification is confused, due to localized forms of species and to naturally occurring or artificially induced hybrids. All may be divided into two groups, one exemplified by *A. odoratum* a species with hornlike, spur-shaped labellum, and the other by *A. multiflorum* (mull-tif-*floh*-rum), with a flat labellum.

A. odoratum (oh-dor-*ray*-tum). Strap-shaped leaves to 7 in. long and 2 in. wide. Delightfully fragrant flowers 1 in. across bloom in late summer or fall. The flowers are mostly white but are spotted with lavender and red. The clusters of these showy flowers are up to 15 in. long. The stems of this plant may grow from 2 to 4 ft. high. Aerial roots usually develop from the upper part of the stem. Zone 10.

x **AERIDOVANDA** (ay-*err*-id-o-*van*-da). Orchid Family (*Orchidaceae*). The "x" preceding this generic name indicates these result from crossing species of two different genera, in this case *Aerides* x *Vanda*. Bigeneric and trigeneric crosses commonly are created by orchid growers. The resulting plants should be given only cultivar names.

aero-. Prefix meaning of or in the air.

aerobic. Commonly referring to bacteria that live only when oxygen is present. Aerobic bacteria are the principal agents of decomposition in a compost heap.

AESCHYNANTHUS (esk-in-*anth*-us). BLUSHWORT. LOBB'S BASKET VINE. BUGLE PLANT. Gesneria Family (*Gesneriaceae*). (Formerly listed as *Trichosporum*, and still so called in many books and catalogs.) Trailers and climbers from tropical Asia with opposite or whorled leaves. Showy tubular, scarlet to yellow flowers, some greenish, usually from spring through fall, but some nearly everblooming. The fruit is in the shape of long capsules. Beautiful basket plants for any bright location in the house or greenhouse that receives a half-day of sun in winter. Fine plants to hang outdoors in warm weather, protected from hot, dry winds and direct sun. Aeschynanthus may also be trained upright on tree-fern trunks or moss-covered blocks. Young basket or upright forms grow well in a fluorescent-lighted garden. A potting mixture of equal parts sphagnum moss and osmunda with a little charcoal added will give excellent results. The Cornell Peat-Lite mix (which see) is also recommended. Propagate by cuttings or seeds, preferably from late winter to summer, in a warm, shaded, moist place. Zone 10.

A. lobbianus (lob-ee-*ay*-nus). LIPSTICK VINE. A trailing plant with slender stems 2 ft. or more long. Fleshy leaves about 2 in. long, usually in pairs on short, hairy stems. The bright red, tubular flowers are twice the length of the shimmering black-red calyx cups from which they thrust. As the plush-covered red buds begin to emerge from the calyx, but before the lips furl back, they appear to be a lipstick inside a tube, hence the popular name. Seed capsules to 14 in. long.

A. marmoratus (mar-moh-*ray*-tus). ZEBRA BASKET VINE. Waxy, dark green leaves, marked with a contrasting netting of yellow, maroon beneath, to 4 in. long. The inch-long green or reddish flowers appear in the leaf axils almost constantly. Easily cultivated, but at best tending to coarseness. Breeders are working to combine the vigor of this species with the beauty of the others. 'Black Pagoda' (*A. marmoratus* x *A. speciosus*) is an outstanding example. It has the hand-

x *Aeridovanda*, a cross between *Aerides* and *Vanda* orchids, is a striking hybrid that flowers in summer and is evergreen. It grows best in a warm, humid greenhouse and requires plenty of moisture, conditions resembling those in its native setting.

some variegated leaves, with prettier green and yellow, brown-marked flowers in the terminals and the axils—at the same time easily grown, and often in flower.

A. pulcher (*pull*-ker). ROYAL RED BUGLER. Similar to *A. lobbianus*. The stems and flowers are smooth except for a fringe of fine hairs along the edge of the flower lobes. Scarlet flowers 2½ in. long with yellow throats. The ovate leaves, about 2 in. long, are waxy, as in other aeschynanthus, and quite unlike the typical fuzzy-leaved gesneriad. 'Pullobbia' is a hybrid of *A. pulcher* and *A. lobbianus*, and best of the three. It is easier to grow, blooms more and the calyxes change from green to dark purple as the flowers open.

A. speciosus (spee-see-*oh*-sus). Sometimes called Trichosporum splendens. Wiry stems, to 2 ft., set with waxy green, lanceolate leaves to 4 in. long. While the plant tends to appear straggly, the terminal clusters of 4-in. flowers, fiery-orange and yellow, are really stunning.

x **splendidus** (*splend*-id-us). A hybrid of *A. parasiticus* and *A. speciosus*, this basket planting is like a

Aesculus x *carnea*, the red horse-chestnut, variety *briottii*, is a handsome shade tree to Zone 3. It grows to a height of 75 feet and produces showy pink to red flowers in spring, its period of bloom.

burst of fireworks when it blooms, the clusters of upright, tubular flowers vivid orange-red with dark maroon blotches.

AESCULUS (*ess*-kew-lus). HORSE-CHESTNUT. BUCKEYE. Horse-chestnut Family (*Hippocastanaceae*). One of the most widely planted groups of shade trees and shrubs of the North Temperate Zone. Large, deciduous leaves with three to nine leaflets arranged in fingerlike fashion. Showy flowers are borne in large, many-flowered clusters, mostly in spring. The fruit consists of large, smooth or spiny capsules, usually containing one big seed. They thrive in ordinary soil that is not too dry. One, *A. parviflora*, is a handsome shrub for rigorous climates. Most species are tough and durable. The larger ones are suited only for park planting or for large, open landscapes. All horse-chestnuts are messy, shedding twigs, leaves, bark, fruit hulls or fruit. None color in the fall. All are subject to various obscure leaf diseases and insect damage but seldom require spraying. Propagate by seeds sown when they are ripe, or by grafting. Buckeye, *Aesculus glabra*, was declared the official tree of Ohio in 1953.

A. californica (kal-if-*forn*-ik-uh). CALIFORNIA BUCKEYE. Grows about 25 ft. high in a rounded form. The fragrant, white flowers bloom in narrow spikes to 8 in. long. The fruit is rough but not spiny. Zone 8.

A. x carnea (*karr*-nee-uh). RED HORSE-CHESTNUT. Hybrid of *A. hippocastanum* and *A. pavia*. It grows to 75 ft., with leathery leaflets to 6 in. long and prickly fruit. The winter buds are resinous. Flesh-colored to red flowers appear in panicles (clusters) to 8 in. long. Two varieties of the red horse-chestnut are better than the parent hybrid. *Briotii* (bry-*ott*-ee-eye), ruby horse-chestnut, flowers larger, darker pink to red, with yellow throat, and *plantierensis* (plan-*ti*-er-en-sis), damask horse-chestnut, tight, light pink flowers with red or yellow throat. Zone 3.

A. chinensis (chin-*nen*-siss). CHINESE HORSE-CHESTNUT. A white-flowering, ragged species from northern China that blooms in May or June. Grows 80 to 90 ft. Zone 4.

A. discolor (dis-*kol*-or). WOOLLY BUCKEYE. Shrub or small tree to 30 ft. Bright green leaflets to 7 in. long with whitish, woolly hairs beneath. Smooth fruit. Zone 5.

A. glabra (*glay*-bruh). OHIO BUCKEYE. Grows to 30 ft. The five leaflets, to 5 in. long, turn yellow in the fall. The greenish-yellow flowers bloom in clusters, to 6 in. long. The fruit is prickly. Zone 3.

A. hippocastanum (hip-poh-*kast*-an-um). COMMON HORSE-CHESTNUT. A large and handsome tree to 100 ft. or more, with very resinous buds. Leaflets to 10 in. long; white flowers with a reddish tinge, blooming in

UPPER: *Aesculus parviflora* is a low-growing flowering form of horse-chestnut that makes attractive informal hedges.
LOWER: *Aesculus hippocastanum*, the common horse-chestnut, grows to 100 feet and is hardier than the hybrid shown opposite. Flowers are candle shaped and white with a pinkish cast, and very decorative.

clusters to 12 in. long. Prickly fruit. One of the showiest of all flowering trees, but suited for planting only in spacious, open locations, where the fine proportions and handsome flowering may be appreciated. Varieties include: *Baumannii* (bow-*man*-ee-eye), Baumann's horse-chestnut. Double white flowers with red streaks in tight clusters on 9-in. spikes. *Pyramidalis* (peer-ah-mid-*day*-liss), pyramidal horse-chestnut. Obscure varieties in European collections include: *memmingeri* (mem-*min*-jer-eye), *luteo-variegata* (lew-*tee*-oh-vay-ree-eg-*gay*-tuh), *laciniata* (las-in-*nay*-tuh), *pumila* (*pew*-mil-uh) and others. Zone 2.
A. indica (*inn*-dik-uh). A rare, Himalayan species to 100 ft. with white flowers, blotched yellow and rose.
A. x mutabilis (mew-*tab*-il-iss). A hybrid species, quite variable, usually a small tree bearing, in June, open spikes of bright yellow and red flowers. The variety *harbisonii* (har-*biss*-on-ee-eye) has long spikes of red flowers; *induta* (in-*dew*-ta) is a shrubby

Leaf bud of the horse-chestnut shown in the process of opening. Stems and young leaves are just visible. Leaves develop in early spring and are followed by showy flowers borne in many-flowered clusters.

cultivar with coppery-pink flowers that appear in spring and are quite decorative.

A. neglecta (neg-*lek*-tuh). From N.C., a 60-ft. sparsely branched native species; flowers pale yellow, veined red, in spring. Variety *georgiana* (jor-gee-*ay*-nuh) is shrubby with yellow and red flowers. Zone 6.

A. octandra (ok-*tand*-ruh). YELLOW BUCKEYE. Rarely to 60 ft., usually smaller or shrubby, this May-blooming species is common in river bottoms through central and southeastern U.S. Chartreuse-yellow flowers marked orange. Fruits are poisonous. Zone 3.

● **A. parviflora** (par-vif-*floh*-ruh). DWARF HORSE-CHESTNUT. A wide-spreading shrub that may grow to 12 ft. Leaflets 8 in. long; white flowers in narrow clusters, and smooth fruit. Zone 4.

A. pavia (*pay*-vee-uh). RED BUCKEYE. Small tree to 20 ft. or sprawling, open shrub native to Mississippi River Valley south of the Missouri River. Bears, in June, tubular bright scarlet flowers widely spaced on 4- to 8-in. spikes. Zone 4.

A. splendens (*splen*-denz). An attractive shrub that

grows to 12 ft. Leaflets are white and hairy underneath. Its only real distinction lies in the bright red flowers in showy clusters to 8 in. long. Zone 7.

A. turbinata (tur-bin-*nay*-tuh). JAPANESE HORSE-CHESTNUT. Creamy-white flowers on short spikes. Attains 100 ft. with age. Zone 6.

aestivalis (ess-tiv-*vay*-liss), **-e.** Pertaining to summer.

aestivation. The disposition or method of arrangement of floral parts on a bud.

aestivus (ess-*tye*-vus), **-a, -um.** Pertaining to summer.

Hanging Gardens

Plastic bulb pans or azalea pots, with three evenly spaced holes melted in their rims for hanging chains or wires (use an ordinary soldering gun), will make neat, relatively drip-free (less watering) containers for all manner of bushy and trailing plants. *R.B.* 🌷

AETHIONEMA (eeth-ee-oh-*nee*-muh). STONE-CRESS. Mustard Family (*Cruciferae*). Masses of candytuft-like rose, magenta, or lilac flowers smother these low, shrubby perennials from the Mediterranean region. Usually grown in the rock garden or rock wall, they are also useful in the spring border, when adequate drainage can be provided. They require full sun, a sandy, coarse soil with lime added, and a dry location. Prune back after flowering. Propagate by seeds sown in early spring, or by cuttings in summer.

A. coridifolium (kor-id-if-*foh*-lee-um). LEBANON STONE-CRESS. Sometimes listed in catalogs as Iberis jucunda. Low-growing, shrubby, compact plant, 6 to 10 in. high, with small, creamy white to rose-lilac flowers in thick, short clusters in June. Best in the rock garden or dry wall. Zone 5.

A. grandiflorum (gran-di-*floh*-rum). PERSIAN STONE-CRESS (sometimes listed as A. pulchellum). Similar to the above but with bluish foliage. Small, pink or rose flowers, ¼ in. across, in upright heads cover the entire plant. A choice plant in the border, the rock garden, or the dry wall. The cultivar 'Warley Rose' is dense, with rose flowers and blue leaves; 'Warley Ruber' with dark rose flowers. Zone 6.

A. iberideum (ib-er-id-*ee*-um). SPANISH STONE-CRESS. An early blooming gray-leaved cushion plant with white flowers in short clusters. For high in the rock garden or in the dry wall. Zone 6.

affinis (af-*fye*-niss), **-e.** Related, as to another species.

Afghan lily. See *Lilium polyphyllum.*

African daisy. See *Arctotis stoechadifolia.* See also *Dimorphotheca,* cape-marigold; *Gerbera,* Transvaal daisy; *Lonas; Ursinia* and *Venidium.*

African hemp. See SPARMANNIA.

African lily. See *Agapanthus africanus.*

African marigold. See *Tagetes erecta.*

African milkbush. See SYNADENIUM.

African tulip-tree. See *Spathodea campanulata.*

africanus (af-rik-*kay*-nus), **-a, -um.** From Africa.

African violet. See SAINTPAULIA.

AGAPANTHUS (ag-ap-*panth*-us). LILY-OF-THE-NILE. Lily Family (*Liliaceae*). Tender, moisture-loving, evergreen perennials of Africa, widely grown for their showy flowers. The fleshy, tuberous roots send up clusters of long, narrow, thick, dark green leaves. Many-flowered clusters of blue or white, funnel-shaped flowers bloom at the tops of stiff, fleshy, bare stalks, somewhat taller than the leaves. Grown outdoors in frost-free regions, they need rich, moist soil and plenty of room for the roots. In colder climates, they are best grown in large pots or tubs in which the roots can remain undisturbed for several years. Use Basic Potting Mixture with doubled peat. When moved indoors for the winter, give enough light and moisture to keep the leaves from dying, then give more light, heat and fertilizer to encourage new growth in the spring, after which flowers will appear for a long period in the summer. Plants need to become well-rooted before flowering and kept constantly moist during the growing season; in fact, they do their best if partially submerged at the edge of a pool. Propagate by root division. Zone 10.

● **A. africanus** (af-rik-*kay*-nus). AFRICAN LILY. Incorrectly listed as A. umbellatus and A. umbellatus minor. Grows up to 3 ft., with leaves up to 2 ft. long and 1 to 1½ in. wide. Circular clusters, 4 to 8 in. across, of beautiful sky-blue flowers. Grows best in

UPPER: *Agapanthus campanulatus,* lily-of-the-Nile, is a tender, moisture-loving evergreen perennial native to Africa. Excellent for damp places in gardens in frost-free regions. In cooler regions, plant in containers and move indoors for winter.
LOWER: *Aethionema grandiflorum,* stone-cress, is a small perennial suited to the rock garden in Zone 6, or farther south.

Agapanthus orientalis, a showy species of lily-of-the-Nile, bears many flowers in each cluster. The variety here is *albus*. There are many others, some with striped leaves, some cross-banded with yellow. Hardy into Zone 6 when mulched for winter and protected from wind.

full sun but will tolerate some shade. A white variety is available.

A. campanulatus (kam-pan-yew-*lay*-tus). In the trade as A. moorianus or A. umbellatus 'Mooreanus.' Scapes to 18 in. with heads of sky-blue flowers all summer. This species is hardy in Zone 5 when mulched over winter.

A. caulescens (kaw-*less*-senz). Tall, to 24 in., with narrow leaves and violet-blue flowers; not as ornamental as others. Blooms in June.

A. inapertus (in-*a*-pert-us). To 4 ft. but usually lower, with drooping mid-blue flowers rising from a massive rootstock. This species from N. Africa and Asia Minor is hardy into Zone 6 when mulched over winter every year.

A. orientalis (or-ee-en-*tay*-liss). More tender than *A. africanus*, but otherwise different only in being somewhat larger, with many more flowers in each cluster. Varieties of *orientalis* include: *albus* (*al*-bus) with white flowers, *aurivittatus* (aw-riv-it-*tay*-tus) with lengthwise yellow stripes on the leaves, *flore-pleno* (floh-ree-*plee*-noh) with extra petals in each flower, *giganteus* (jye-*gan*-tee-us) much larger in all its parts, *leichtlinii* (lysht-*linn*-ee-eye), with deep blue flowers, *maximus* (*max*-im-us) with larger leaves and

flowers, *maximus albus* as the preceding but with white flowers, *monstrosus* (mon-*stroh*-sus) with large, massive leaves and scapes and blooms of heavy quality, *pallidus* (*pal*-id-us) with pale blue flowers and *variegatus* (var-ree-eg-*gay*-tus) with cross-bands of yellow on the leaves. Probably the two dwarf agapanthus cultivars belong with this species; 'Peter Pan,' 18 in., blue, and 'Rancho,' 24 in., white.

A. pendulus (*pen*-dew-lus). A 2½ ft. high, tender species, rare, with clusters of drooping purple-blue tubular flowers. Blooms all summer.

AGAPETES (ag-ah-*pete*-eez). Heath Family (*Ericaceae*). A small, broadleaf evergreen shrub from subtropical India. Only one genus in cultivation.

A. buxifolia (bux-if-*foh*-lee-uh). In frost-free climates grow in peaty soil, full sun and keep moist. In the North grow as a small greenhouse plant as follows: in late summer root small cuttings in perlite and peat under mist. Pinch when rooted, and pot up; the compost is Basic Potting Mixture with double peat. Grow cool over winter and water moderately. In spring syringe frequently, keep quite moist, fertilize regularly and give full sun. Soon showy, red, tubular flowers will develop on all the ascending branches. After blooming, clip back, move to a slightly larger pot and grow on. Zone 10.

Agaricus campestris (ag-*gay*-rik-us kam-*pest*-riss). See *mushroom*.

Agarita. See Algerita.

Agastache. See BRITTONASTRUM.

Agathaea. See FELICIA.

AGATHIS (*ag*-ath-iss). Dammar-pine. Monkey Puzzle Tree Family (*Araucariaceae*). Tall evergreen trees, to 100 ft., from Australia and Malaya, with fine, needlelike foliage. These are all very fast-growing, with weak wood, subject to wind breakage. These are grown in subtropical and tropical parts of southern Calif. and southern Fla. Propagate by seeds. Zone 10.

Species commonly encountered are *alba* (*al*-buh), the white dammar-pine, and *robusta* (ro-*bust*-uh), the queensland kauri.

AGATHOSMA (ag-a-*thos*-ma). Rue Family (*Rutaceae*). These are seldom-encountered low, broadleaf evergreen shrubs from S. Africa. Grow outdoors in frost-free climates. They also are suitable as tub plants in the cold greenhouse. Pot up in Basic Potting Mixture, reduce the loam to one-half. Keep moderately damp. Propagate with half-ripe summer cut-

LEFT: *Agapanthus africanus*, the African lily, grows
up to 3 feet and has beautiful sky-blue flowers.
RIGHT: *Agave*, a native of Mexico, is grown outdoors for
its arresting foliage, but also makes a dramatic house plant.

tings. Zone 10, intolerant of hot, windy, dry weather
in exposed situations.

Cultivated sorts include: *A. ventenatiana*, white,
lilac or purple, and the more common *A. villosa*, light
purple.

AGATI (ah-*gah*-tee). Pea Family (*Leguminosae*). An
Asiatic tree growing to 40 ft., with attractive foliage
and habit. One species is cultivated. Propagate by
seeds. Zone 10.

A. grandiflora (gran-di-*floh*-ruh). White, pink or red
blossoms followed by glossy pods. Natives sometimes
eat young foliage, flowers and immature pods.

AGAVE (ag-*gay*-vee). Amaryllis Family (*Amaryllidaceae*). A very large genus of decorative, succulent
perennials native mostly to Mexico, where some are
important economically as a source of fiber or for
juice which is fermented. The species described below are representative of the many plants in this
genus. All have stiff, fleshy leaves in rosettes, leaves
often armed with needlelike spines at the tips and
along the margins. Leaves usually are basal but sometimes appear on the tops of the stems when these are
present. Small, mostly yellow, clustered flowers on
long, upright stems above the foliage appear only
after many years. The plants may then die, but so
many offsets are produced that it is easy to start new
plants. Grown primarily for the striking foliage,
agaves are easily raised in the cool greenhouse or outdoors in frost-free regions. They make satisfactory
but large house plants and may be set outside during
the summer. Use Basic Potting Mixture with doubled
sand. They need sun, good drainage and adequate
moisture (more than for most succulents), although
they need to be kept fairly dry during the winter. The
only agave found naturally in the U.S. is *A. virginica*
(vir-*jin*-ik-uh), a small, fleshy sort producing a naked
scape with fragrant, greenish-yellow flowers. Ranges
from Fla. and Tex. to S.C. and Mo. growing in dry
woods and open glades. Propagate by seeds or offsets.
Most agaves are not frost-hardy. Century plants,
Agave lechequilla, *palmeri*, *parryi* and *schottii* are on
the preservation list of N. Mex. and are protected,
that is, are not to be picked or dug up. Zone 7.

● **A. americana** (am-eh-rik-*kay*-nuh). CENTURY PLANT.
In public conservatories, a plant that takes 10 to 50
years to develop its maximum height of about 40 ft.
In big tubs, the lance-shaped, grayish-green leaves
may reach a length of 6 ft. The yellowish-green flow-

ers are produced after many years on a stalk that rises from the center of the plant. The variety *marginata* (mar-jin-*nay*-tuh) has yellow-edged leaves. *A. a. medio-picta* (mee-dee-oh-*pik*-tuh) has yellow stripes along the center of the leaves. For small pots, one of gardening's most uncomplaining house plants. Zone 7.

A. attenuata (at-ten-yew-*ay*-tuh). Spineless species with a trunk (sometimes prostrate) that may reach 5 ft. in height. Rosettes of grayish-green leaves to 2½ ft. long. Greenish-yellow flowers, 2 in. long, in large spikelike clusters on an arching stalk up to 10 ft.

A. filifera (fye-*lif*-er-uh). A trunkless species with spine-tipped leaves 1 to 2 ft. long in a dense rosette. Grows to 15 ft., but is much smaller in greenhouses. Each leaf has curled, threadlike filaments along its edge. Maroon-purple flowers 2 in. or more long.

A. lechequilla (lech-a-*keya*). Grows to 18 in. and is used for potting by many gardeners. Blue-green leaves, white flowers. Foliage is poisonous to goats and sheep. Native to Mexico. Zone 10.

A. palmeri (pal-*may*-ree). Leaves to 30 in. long, yellow flowers. Grows in Ariz. and N. Mex.

A. parryi (*par*-ee-eye). Prickly, with creamy-yellow flowers. Grows in Mexico, N. Mex. and Ariz.

A. schottii (*shot*-ee-eye). Leaves to 12 in. long and spiny. Flowers are yellow. Southern Ariz. and N. Mex.

A. stricta (*strikt*-uh). HEDGEHOG AGAVE. Stemless species with many narrow leaves to 1 ft. long in a spiny rosette to 2 ft. across. Flowering stalk may eventually reach 12 ft. Easily grown as a pot plant.

A. victoriae-reginae (vik-*toh*-ree-ee-rej-*jye*-nee). One of the smaller species suited to indoor pot culture. Dark green leaves up to 6 in. long and 2 in. wide with gray edges. The flowers are greenish and 1¼ in. long, appearing after many years on a 12-ft. stalk.

AGERATUM (aj-er-*ray*-tum). Composite Family (*Compositae*). These tender annuals, native to tropical America, range in size from 6 in. to 2 ft. The small blue flowers (occasionally, pink or white) are each only ½ in. across, but they are clustered in attractive, fluffy heads and bloom all summer and autumn until frost. Much hybridization with these plants has produced many dwarf and compact varieties, as well as a wider color range. The dwarf varieties are excellent for edgings. For early bloom in the garden, start seeds indoors in March and plant out in ordinary garden soil in either full sun or partial shade. These versatile small plants also grow well as pot speci-

LEFT: *Ageratum* is one of the most useful of the low-growing annuals. It blooms from early summer to autumn and is ideal for use as an edging in the flower border. For early bloom start seeds indoors in late winter.

Agave attenuata is a spineless species with rosettes of grayish-green leaves and greenish-yellow flowers. It grows to a height of about 5 feet and is related to the century plant, *A. americana*, which is a much larger specimen.

mens in the home or cool greenhouse. For use indoors, either dig up plants in the fall (they should be cut back) or plant seeds in Sept., using Basic Potting Mixture. Young wood cuttings root easily if a special color is to be kept on. Propagate by cuttings or seeds. (For border uses of ageratum, see Annuals lists index, Plant Finder section, Volume 16.)

● **A. houstonianum** (hoos-ton-ee-*ay*-num). This widely grown species, with many attractive hybrids, grows 6 to 8 in. high (sometimes higher). The lavender-blue flowers make an attractive addition in beds and borders, as well as being excellent for cutting. Blooms until hard frost. Plants should be sheared back for repeated bloom.

Ageratum, hardy. See EUPATORIUM.

aggregate. For information on the use of aggregate in garden structures, see article, Paths, Walks, Walls listed under *construction*.

aggregatus (ag-reg-*gay*-tus), **-a, -um.** Grouped, clumped.

AGLAONEMA (ag-lay-oh-*nee*-muh). Arum Family (*Araceae*). Vigorous, tropical plants from Asia and Africa. Grown indoors and in greenhouses for the ornamental foliage, they are practically indestructible and tolerate light shade, making them ideal for city apartments. The large oblong leaves are often interestingly variegated. The tiny flowers are inconspicuous and often do not appear on cultivated plants. When they do, the showy, but not edible, berries that follow persist for several months. Use Basic Potting Mixture. Propagate by cuttings or division. Zone 10.

A. commutatum (kom-mew-*tay*-tum). About 2 ft. high with oblongish, deep green leaves to 6 in. long and 2 in. across.

A. costatum (kos-*tay*-tum). A low species, not over 8 in. tall. Broad, bright green leaves spotted with white.

A. modestum (mod-*dest*-um). CHINESE EVERGREEN. About 1½ ft. high, with shiny, pointed, dark green leaves to 18 in. long and 5 in. across.

A. picta (*pik*-tuh). Leaves to 6 in. long and 2 in. across, spotted white. The variety *tricolor* (*trye*-kol-or), has leaves with golden-yellow spots. Zone 10.

A. simplex (*sim*-plex). CHINESE EVERGREEN. About 3 ft. high. Leaves to 12 in. long. This species can be grown in water and in poorly lighted places. Its durability knows no bounds.

agrarius (ag-*ray*-ree-us), **-a, -um.** Of the fields.

agrestis (ag-*rest*-tiss), **-e.** Of the fields.

Agriculture, U.S. Department of.

At the present time, the U.S.D.A. is in a period of reorganization and change. Hopefully, home gardeners will be included in future programs as they have been in the past.

For years, the Department maintained plant collectors abroad, particularly in undeveloped areas. While their chief goal was to ship home plants with real or potential economic value, many ornamental species were included. Through various Research Stations, and, particularly, through the National Arboretum, and the Glenn Dale Station, these have been released to nurserymen for distribution to America's gardeners. The systematic introduction of plants by the U.S.D.A. has dwindled to a trickle; still, some fine ornamental kinds continue to come into the country, often from foreign Botanic Gardens and private plant breeders.

The U.S.D.A. has a plant breeding program of its own; specialists seek to improve native and exotic species and to originate new cultivars of ornamental flowers, shrubs and trees as well as fruits, nuts and vegetables.

Garden chemicals have, traditionally, come under the scrutiny of the U.S.D.A. All fertilizers, weed-control chemicals, insecticides, fungicides and similar products had to be examined and cleared by U.S.D.A. before marketing. Apparently a new, environment-oriented agency will soon assume this responsibility, or part of it. Meanwhile, the U.S.D.A. continues to check all products and their labels.

The Government has been in the printing business for a long time and the U.S.D.A. has provided its share of material. Write to U.S.D.A., Washington, D.C. 20250, for a list of all home and garden bulletins or specifically for List #5, which is "Popular Publications for the Farmer, Suburbanite, Homemaker and Consumer." This pamphlet includes an order blank which allows you to select ten publications without cost. Publications are seldom more than twenty-five cents. From annual flowerbed care and asparagus production to zizyphus (Chinese-date) culture—the handy booklets and pamphlets help home gardeners with problems and projects. A recent departure is departmental research on growth, involving studies on light, nutrition, growing media and so on. Pamphlets are already in preparation.

AGRIMONIA (ag-rim-*moh*-nee-uh). AGRIMONY. COCKLEBUR. HARVEST-LICE. Rose Family (*Rosaceae*). Most of these are coarse, persistent weeds found on ground once cultivated, then abandoned. Gray's *Manual of Botany* lists seven species. Of some interest is *A. eupatoria*, brought to this country from Europe and now naturalized. The harsh, alternate leaves are pinnately compound. Leafy stems to 3 ft. bear small, nondescript yellow flowers. Once the plant was an important source of yellow dye for home-woven fabric. All propagate readily from seed. Zone 3–4.

Agrimony. See AGRIMONIA.

AGROSTEMMA (ag-*ros*-stem-uh). CORN COCKLE. PURPLE COCKLE. Pink Family (*Caryophyllaceae*). An annual (biennial, South) from Europe, now naturalized in eastern U.S. This has small, linear leaves sparsely produced along 3-ft.-high, occasionally branched stems. Stems and leaves densely matted with short, silver-white down. Five-petaled blossoms, 1 to 2 inches across, are brilliant fuchsia (rose-purple) with a few tiny black dots. This blooms all summer and deserves a spot in the sunny border. Propagate by seed sown in place, late fall or early spring.

A. githago (gith-*ay*-go). This is the only species in cultivation. Grow as bachelor's-buttons (*Centaurea cyanus*). About 3 ft. tall and blooms May, June and July. The pod contains purple-black poisonous seeds.

AGROSTIS (ag-*ross*-tiss). BENTGRASS. Grass Family (*Gramineae*). A large genus of annual and perennial

LEFT: *Aglaonema* is grown indoors and in greenhouses for its ornamental foliage. Practically indestructible and tolerant of light shade, it is a good plant for apartment dwellers.
RIGHT: *Agrostemma*, corn cockle, blooms all summer, and is especially useful in the front of borders when planted in masses.

grasses, a few of which are widely used in lawns. Forming dense, rich green tufts, these are low plants with many narrow leaves and diffuse panicles (clusters) of small flower spikelets. All grow best in cool regions and need a well-drained loamy soil. For best results, these grasses should not be neglected, but given fertilizer, adequate watering and good disease control if necessary. Propagate by division, stolons or seeds. Zone 5 (hardy to −15°). (For other perennial grasses, see Plant Finder section, Volume 16.)

A. alba (*al*-buh). REDTOP. Native to Europe, this perennial species is widely naturalized in N. America. Though much used as a "nurse-grass" in lawn mixtures, it is seldom necessary and may become a persistent weed in lawns where better grasses are desired. Coarser in texture than most of the other species. Up to 3 ft. high with narrow leaves to 8 in. long and green or reddish flower clusters up to 1 ft. long. Tolerates heat and some shade.

A. canina (kan-*nye*-nuh). BROWN BENTGRASS. VELVET BENT. A useful lawn grass native in the U.S., this perennial grass grows up to 18 in. high with leaves 2 in. long and ½ in. wide.

A. nebulosa (neb-yew-*loh*-suh). CLOUDGRASS. Native to Spain, this is a delicate, ornamental annual with short, narrow leaves and clusters of tiny spikelets borne on many branches. Good for dry bouquets.

Propagation is by seeds sown in mid-April in a sunny location in well-drained loamy soil.

A. palustris (pal-*lust*-riss). CREEPING BENT. Creeping perennial species up to 1 ft. high. Short, narrow leaves to 3½ in. long and dense panicles to 4 in. long. Native to the shores of Europe and eastern N. America, this is resistant to salt spray and is widely used on golf courses, as well as in high-maintenance lawns. 'Cocoos' bent and 'Washington' bent are but two of the trade names used for this grass.

A. tenuis (*ten*-yew-iss). COLONIAL BENTGRASS. Similar to *A. alba*, but smaller. Native in Europe, it has naturalized in N. America, where it is used as pasture and lawn grass. Spreading by stolons, it soon turns into a bright green carpet of soft grass. Does best in moist conditions and full sun. Of the many improved strains, 'Astoria' and 'Colonial' are good creeping forms. Among non-creeping forms are 'New Zealand' and 'Prince Edward Island' bent.

Ahuwhuete. Local name for *Taxodium mucronatum*.

AICHRYSON (ay-ee-*cry*-son). Crassula Family (*Crassulaceae*). Tender, succulent plants mostly from the Canary Islands. Related to *Sedum* and *Sempervivum*, these are fleshy-leaved and slow-growing. After a period of one to three years they produce a head of yellow flowers, then die. Grow in Basic Potting Mixture, sunny window or warm greenhouse. Water freely during warm weather, sparingly other times. Propagate by seeds or cuttings. Zone 10.

A. dichotomum (dy-*kot*-oh-mum). A biennial. Sow seed in early summer for flowering plants the following May. The foliage is attractive, the yellow flowers are pleasing. Other species rarely obtainable include: *A. domesticum*, *A. tortuosum* and *A. palmense*.

AILANTHUS (ay-*lanth*-us). Quassia Family (*Simarubaceae*). Large deciduous trees of Asia and northern Australia, sometimes grown in cities for their smog-tolerant and insect-resistant foliage, but not worth growing elsewhere. Propagate by seeds or root cuttings.

A. altissima (al-*tiss*-im-uh). TREE-OF-HEAVEN. (Also the tree "that grows in Brooklyn.") A coarse, brittle, fast-growing tree to 60 ft. or more. Alternate leaves, to 5 in. long, each with 13 to 20 leaflets. The small, greenish flowers bloom in large terminal clusters; male and female flowers usually on separate trees. Male plants have an unpleasant odor. The papery fruit is showy when mature. The variety *erythrocarpa* (ehr-ith-roh-*karp*-uh) has darker green leaves, more glaucous beneath, and showier, bright red fruit. Zone 5.

AIRA (*eye*-rah). HAIRGRASS. Grass Family (*Gramineae*). A frost-hardy winter annual grass from southern Europe. Seed germinates in fall to produce finely foliaged tufts that overwinter. These fruit with pretty, very fine, open sprays of flowers in late winter or early spring. Or sow seed in April for early, temporary lawns. Propagate by seeds. Zone 6.
A. caerulea: See *Molinia caerulea*.
A. elegans (*ell*-eg-anz). Sometimes in the trade as A. capillaris, grows 12 to 18 in., with long-awned florets. The variety *pulchella* (pul-*kell*-uh) is more fragile and refined. Sometimes this grass is grown in pots, cool greenhouse, for winter decoration.

air layering. A method of developing roots on a plant stem to propagate a new plant. See *propagation*.

Airplane plant. See CHLOROPHYTUM.

air plant. A plant that may reproduce itself on and from the leaf of an older plant (*Kalanchoe*, for example). Also a plant that has roots living in the air, rather than in the ground. See *epiphyte*.

Air plant. See *Kalanchoe pinnata*.

Air-potato yam. See *Dioscorea bulbifera*.

Aizoaceae. See Carpetweed Family.

Ajuga sweeps a blue carpet through the late spring garden and persists in bloom for several weeks. An excellent ground cover, the leaves make a heavy mat of foliage.
GARDEN OF MR. AND MRS. FRED WIEDEMANN

AJUGA (aj-*yew*-guh). BUGLEWEED. Mint Family (*Labiatae*). Low-growing, modest, European perennials, extremely useful for ground covers or edgings in shady places. Ajuga grows into a heavy mat of foliage and is very hardy. These need rich soil for best results, but will grow under almost any conditions, in sun (North, only) or shade. Propagate by seeds or division of roots or rooted runners. Zone 3. (For other ground covers, see Ground Cover Plants index, Plant Finder section, Volume 16.)

A. alpina: *A. genevensis.*

A. genevensis (jen-ev-*ven*-siss). GENEVA BUGLEWEED. ALPINE BUGLEWEED. Sometimes listed in catalogs as A. alpina. Blue spikes of bloom, 8 to 10 in. high, on this hardy, creeping ground cover that is nontrailing. Useful at the base of large rocks, at the foot of trees as a transition to lawn, in the rock garden, and as an edging. Plants set 8 in. apart form a solid mat of growth in one season.

● **A. reptans** (*repp*-tanz). BUGLEWEED. CARPET BUGLE. Often seen naturalized in fields and along roadsides in the eastern U.S., this trailing species has bluish-purple flowers and a matlike carpet of foliage. Varieties include *alba* (*al*-buh), white flowered; *variegata* (var-ee-eg-*gay*-tuh), with white-spotted leaves, sometimes with pink blotches; and *rubra* (*roob*-ruh), with purple leaves, *atropurpurea* (at-roh-per-*pew*-ree-uh) with bronze leaves and blue flowers, *metallica crispa* (met-*tal*-ik-uh *kriss*-puh) with curled, metallic leaves, blue flowers. The last two may be hybrid forms. Recently several cultivars have been marketed; 'Burgundy Lace' is a choice one. The dark leaves of the purple and bronze varieties make a heavy mat, giving a strong color accent when used as an edging or in

Leggy Plants

Too often shrubs develop, with age, ungainly legs. They need what gardener's jargon terms "facing down" with other plants that are big enough to conceal ungainly underpinnings behind them but not screen decorative flowers and foliage at higher levels. Where existing plants follow a vertical habit of growth in addition to being leggy, face them down with plants of moundlike or spreading form. Where broad and massive background plants are a problem, set erect small plants in front of them.   *R.B.* ❦

the rock garden. The stems root freely to form new plants.

AKEBIA (ak-*kee*-bee-uh). Akebia Family (*Lardizabalaceae*). Deciduous or semi-evergreen woody vines

from Asia. The best-known species are described below. Among the most useful of all porch or trellis vines, these also climb over stumps and rocks, cover banks and tolerate heavier shade than almost any other vine of comparable quality. Any well-drained garden soil and sun. Propagate by freshly gathered seeds, cuttings, or root division. Zone 5.

A. quinata (kwin-*nay*-tuh). A slender vine, climbing to 30 ft. or more with beautiful, airy foliage, evergreen in mild climates. The delicate leaves are 3 in. long with five leaflets on each leaf. The small flowers produced in spring are dark purple and fragrant. Separate male and female florets are in the same cluster, the female larger and darker in color. The grayish-purple fruits are 3 to 5 in. long, but are seldom seen in cultivation.

A. trifoliata (try-fohl-ee-*ay*-ta). Sometimes in the trade as A. lobata. A vigorous climber to 35 ft. Foliage three-part, deciduous. Purple flowers in summer followed by pale violet-colored fruits.

Alabama snow-wreath. See *Neviusia alabamensis.*

Alaska goldthread. See *Coptis trifolia.*

alatus (al-*lay*-tus), **-a, -um.** Winged (usually with reference to bark or seeds).

albidus (*al*-bid-us), **-a, -um.** White.

ALBIZIA (al-*biz*-ee-uh). Pea Family (*Leguminosae*). Deciduous trees and shrubs, usually of tropical and subtropical regions. The trees are spreading, umbrellalike, the wood is very weak. Propagate by seeds, budding or grafting. Formerly albizzia. Zone 5.

A. julibrissin (ju-*lib*-riss-in). SILK-TREE. Often incorrectly called mimosa. Much planted in the South, this grows to 40 ft. or more under ideal conditions. Further north it is likely to be lower, very wide-spreading, and often with much dead wood. The alternate leaves are pinnately compound with 40 to 60 leaflets. Feathery, fragrant flower heads bloom in late May and intermittently afterwards. Flowers range from white to dark rose-pink. Brown seeds, flat, 1/8 x 3/8 in., are produced in 6-in.-long flat pods. These trees are subject to damage from the mimosa webworms and occasionally are parasitized by clay colored beetles. When these pests appear, spray with Dylox, Sevin or Diazinon. A fungus wilt frequently attacks trees in the South, quickly killing them. Cultivars 'Charlotte' and 'Tryon' are said to be fungus-resistant. In Zone 5 and parts of Zone 6, winter injury results in serious trunk decay problems. Prompt tree surgery may save a damaged specimen. The variety *rosea* (roh-zee-uh), sometimes known as 'Ernest

ABOVE: *Akebia quinata* has lovely, airy foliage and dark purple flowers that make it one of the most attractive of evergreen vines. It tolerates more shade than almost any other climber of comparable quality.

UPPER LEFT: A view of the same vine as a mature plant. It climbs readily over porches, trellises or old stumps and will cover banks. The plant looks best when kept free of any long loose shoots. Propagation is simple and layering is the easiest method: fasten the ends of shoots in the ground with wooden pegs in autumn. Cuttings can also be rooted in pots in sandy soil during July and August.

LOWER LEFT: *Akebia quinata* loses its leaves in cold climates but is evergreen in the South. Flowers are fragrant; the male blooms pale purple and small, female blooms dark purple and 1½ inches across. Akebias produce edible, sausage-shaped fruits 2 to 3 inches long.

Albizia julibrissin, the silk tree, is a member of
the Pea Family, and is often mistakenly called mimosa.
Much planted in the South, it grows to 40 feet
or more in ideal conditions. Feathery, fragrant flower
heads bloom in late May and sporadically thereafter. Flowers
range from white to dark rosy-pink. The variety here,
rosea, is considered one of the best and is one of the hardiest.

Wilson' (from Korea) is hardier, and has the best
dark pink flowers.

Other, more tender and infrequently grown species
are:

A. kalkora (cal-*core*-uh). From India, poor, drooping
flowers, tree very similar to *A. julibrissin*. Zone 10.

A. lebbek (*leb*-bek). WOMAN'S-TONGUE-TREE. From
tropical Asia and naturalized in the West Indies. This
grows to 50 ft. Flowers are small but with elongated,
greenish-yellow stamens; flowers are clustered into
balls, like powder puffs. Foot-long seed pods are
decorative and give the tree its common name.
Zone 10.

A. lophantha (loh-*fanth*-uh). PLUME ALBIZIA. A small,
shrubby tree to 20 ft. from Australia, now naturalized
in the South. Leaves twice pinnate with 14 to 24
pinnae, each with 40 to 60 leaflets. Small, yellow
flowers in 2-in.-long, upright spikes in spring. This
makes a nice tub plant for the intermediate greenhouse. Zone 9.

albo-. Prefix meaning white. Also sometimes *albi-* or
alba-.

Albrecht azalea. See *Rhododendron albrechtii*.

ALBUCA (al-*bew*-kuh). Lily Family (*Liliaceae*). Tender, bulbous perennials of Africa. Each bulb sends up
a cluster of bright green leaves, from the center of
which appear long spikes of white or yellow, fragrant
flowers. Suitable for outdoor planting in warm climates only, but they do well in pots in the cool greenhouse. Use Basic Potting Mixture. Propagate by offsets. Zone 10.

A. major (*may*-jor). Grows up to 3 ft., with leaves up
to 1½ ft. long. Pale yellow flowers, about 1 in. across,
with a green streak in the center of each petal.

A. minor (*mye*-nor). Leaves up to 1 ft. long. Yellow
flowers, ¾ in. across, with a broad green band
through the center of each petal, bloom on stalks up
to 1½ ft. high.

albulus (*al*-bew-lus), **-a, -um.** Whitish.

albus (*al*-bus), **-a, -um.** White.

ALCHEMILLA (al-kem-*mill*-uh). Rose Family (*Rosaceae*). Gray-leaved European perennials and annuals of strong, almost weedy growth, whose principal attraction is their silvery foliage. The species
listed are useful in borders and rock gardens. Small,
yellow-green flowers in loose heads are negligible.
Full sun and ordinary, well-drained garden soil. Propagate by seeds or root division. Zone 3.

A. alpina (al-*pye*-nuh). MOUNTAIN LADY'S MANTLE.
With green leaves, silvery beneath, divided into five
to seven leaflets. A rock garden plant.

A. vulgaris (vul-*gay*-riss). LADY'S MANTLE. The large
leaves, 5 in. wide, in velvety gray clusters, make this
perennial an effective accent plant in the border. Although the flower stalk grows to 1 ft., the plant can
be placed toward the front of the border since the
heavy leaf clusters make it a low accent. This species
appears in the earliest herbals and is much used in
old-fashioned gardens and in herb gardens. In early
morning when dewdrops glisten on the lobe tips of
the leaves the effect is beautiful.

Alder. See ALNUS.

Alder, black. See *Alnus glutinosa; Ilex verticillata* is
also sometimes called black alder.

Alder buckthorn. See *Rhamnus frangula*.

Alder, white. See *Alnus rhombifolia;* CLETHRA.

Aleppo adonis. See *Adonis aleppica*.

Aleppo iris. See *Iris sindjarensis*.

ALETRIS (*al*-et-riss). STARGRASS. Lily Family (*Liliaceae*). A small genus of perennials, native to N. America, with grasslike leaves and slender, erect stalks of white or yellow flowers. Easily grown in full sun and moist, rich acid soil, they are useful for colonizing in the wild garden. Propagate by seeds or division. (For other wild garden plants, see Wildflowers index, Plant Finder section, Volume 16.)

A. farinosa (fa-rin-*noh*-suh). This species grows about 3 ft. high, with yellowish-green leaves to 6 in. long, clustered at the base of the plant. The bell-shaped, white flowers bloom in May, June, and July. Zone 4.

ALEURITES (al-yew-*ree*-teez). Spurge Family (*Euphorbiaceae*). Small to larger deciduous trees with variously shaped alternate leaves, from the Asian tropics. Not especially attractive, the plants are seldom used for ornamental plantings. But the nuts of several species are rich in useful oils, particularly drying oils essential to fine-quality paints, and these are grown commercially. Propagate by spring-sown seed which germinates in two months or less.

A. cordata (kor-*day*-tuh). JAPAN WOOD-OIL-TREE. Similar to the above tree. Oil yield is poor. Zone 8.

A. fordii (*for*-dee-eye). TUNG-OIL-TREE. Small trees to 25 ft. Leaves three-lobed; terminal sprays of russet-streaked white flowers of little ornamental value. Two- to 3-in. diameter fruits contain nuts rich in oil.

Alchemilla vulgaris, lady's mantle, growing around a bird bath. It makes a very effective accent plant in a border. The leaves are almost 5 inches wide and velvety gray. It was a favorite in old-fashioned herb gardens of the past.

Thousands of acres of these are grown commercially in the Deep South and in Tex. Zone 9.

A. moluccana (moll-loo-*cay*-nuh). CANDLENUT-TREE. A larger tree, to 60 ft., with leaves variously lobed. Flowers are insignificant. The round, greenish nuts are rich in oil and Pacific Island natives string them for use as torches. Zone 10.

A. montana (mon-*tay*-nuh). Of fairly recent introduction. Similar to *A. fordii,* and selected, high-oil-producing strains are now planted with the tung-oil tree.

Alexandrian-laurel. See *Danae racemosa*.

Alfalfa. See *Medicago sativa*.

alga (*al*-guh). A plant generally water-dwelling and characterized by very simple structure. It contains chlorophyll and reproduces without seeds.

Some algae (*al*-jee) are the microscopic, one-celled plants that make the slimy green coating on rocks in water and on the insides of vases. Some are larger—even up to several hundred feet long (kelp is an alga). In ponds and streams algae are important because they are eaten by the small aquatic animals on which fish feed. But in a clear reflecting pool or a fountain, algae can be an unsightly nuisance. Copper sulfate or patent compounds sold as algae-control preparations (used according to directions) will kill them. An ounce of copper sulfate will control the algae in approximately 10,000 cubic ft. of water (50 ft. by 20 ft. by 10 ft.) without necessarily harming other plants or fish. Excess soluble copper salts sterilize (and poison) water and adjacent soil.

Algae also flourish in fish tanks and containers for indoor water plants, but can be controlled by excluding the light. Growth can also be checked by the introduction of fresh-water snails. A combination of less light and a few snails generally keeps water clear.

Algerian iris. See *Iris unguicularis*.

Algerian ivy. See *Hedera canariensis*.

Algerita. See *Mahonia trifoliata*.

Alismaceae. See Water-plantain Family.

alkaline soil plants. Where rainfall is scanty, as in desert regions, various basic (alkaline) minerals remain in the upper layers of soil. In fact, these minerals often increase each year, making the soil increasingly alkaline. While many plants tolerate moderate alkalinity, only a few will grow well on soil that is very much more alkaline than the neutral point.

Allamanda is a handsome tropical vine called golden trumpet or yellow bell. It grows easily outdoors or in greenhouses in the North. The large funnel-shaped flowers are yellow or purple and bloom profusely in the summer.

Members of the cabbage family, bluegrass, lilacs, baby's-breath, delphinium and mesquite are examples of plants that will grow on fairly alkaline soils. Natural pools with pipewort growing at the margin and with the harsh alga *Chara* growing in the water are sure to be alkaline. Where alkalinity is due to excessive lime, numerous plants will survive, many will thrive. The alkalinity of desert soils often is due to certain sodium salts toxic to most plants. See *soil*.

alkalinity. The degree to which a soil or other substance contains alkalis beyond the point of neutrality. Any soil with a pH above 7 is said to be alkaline. Some plants, such as delphiniums and lilacs, prefer an alkaline soil, but most plants do better in a neutral or slightly acid soil. See *acidity* and *soil*.

Alkanet. See ANCHUSA.

Alkekengi. See PHYSALIS.

ALLAMANDA (al-lam-*mand*-uh). GOLDEN TRUMPET. Dogbane Family (*Apocynaceae*). Rapid-growing, vigorous, tropical vines with handsome flowers and opposite or whorled leaves. The large, funnel-shaped, yellow or purplish flowers, reminiscent of waxy petunias, bloom profusely in summer. Easily grown in intermediate-to-warm greenhouses or outdoors in mild climates. Tubbed, with a small trellis for support, these make fine plants for the terrace; in the greenhouse over winter, they bloom almost continu-

ously. Light, rich, well-drained soil and sun are needed when grown outdoors; in greenhouse use Basic Potting Mixture. Easy to propagate by soft cuttings.

A. cathartica (kath-*art*-ik-uh). A tall evergreen climber from Brazil, with thick stems and large leathery leaves, usually in fours, to 6 in. long. Tubular, golden-yellow flowers to 3 in. across. Can be clipped to make a formal hedge, but needs sturdy support. Will grow up to 40 ft., climbing by twining stems. Easy to train when young, all become brittle with age. A very popular variety is *hendersonii* (hender-*soh*-nee-eye) with larger and more profuse blooms; *williamsii* (will-*yams*-ee-eye) is a double.

A. neriifolia (neer-ee-if-*foh*-lee-uh). OLEANDER ALLAMANDA. A bushy, rarely climbing Brazilian species. Small flowers brilliant yellow, rust-striped inside.

A. violacea (vye-ol-*lay*-see-uh). VIOLET ALLAMANDA. Climbing vine with bell-like flowers a rose-violet.

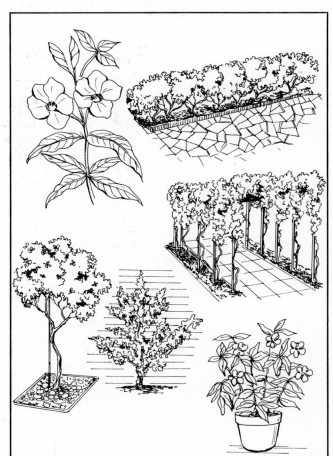

Allamandas usually grow as vines, but they may be readily tailored to fit special needs. Here they are shown as a clipped hedge, trained on an arbor, pruned to small tree shape (*A. neriifolia* is suggested), an informal fan-shaped espalier (the violet allamanda, *A. violacea*, is choice for this) and as a pot or tub plant for the patio.

An allée is not only an attractive means of leading
the stroller to some special, private retreat
in the landscape, but may also block an unattractive
view. Above: An allée of birches frames a Chinese
figure. Upper right: Various classic espalier
patterns suggested as an allée leading to
an arbor. Middle right: Slender-branched trees
in a pleached allée with formal hedge. Lower right:
Dense evergreens clipped in the manner of
topiary for an allée leading to a splashing fountain.

All America Selections. A commercial seedsmen's arrangement for promoting new cultivars of flowers
and vegetables grown from seed. The originator of a
new cultivar sends seeds to the All America Selections agent who is financed by various seed producers' organizations. The seed is forwarded to trial
growers scattered around the country at some 34 locations. Many of the "test" plots are located at the
grounds of major seed producers though a few are
located at universities; one is at a Canadian Botanic
Garden and one has been in a private garden. Un-
doubtedly there is benefit to the amateur grower from
this program. As seeds are labeled under numbers
(rather than fully identified as to source), and are
grown in widely varying environmental conditions,
the award "All America Selection" should indicate a
superior cultivar. The programs would carry considerably more validity, however, if the testing were
carried out by noted horticulturists at a large number
of Botanic Gardens, with predetermined criteria, thus
establishing a more scientific basis for the award.

allée. A garden walk or way bordered on both sides
by trees set in a formal pattern, often pruned or
trained to stylized forms. The allée reached its height

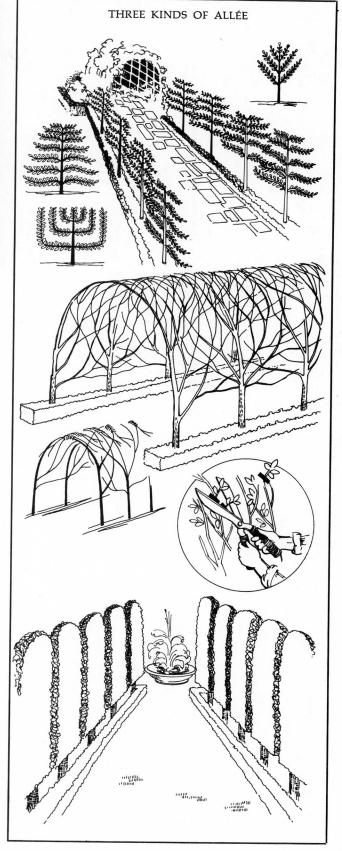

THREE KINDS OF ALLÉE

of formal development in the 18th and 19th centuries. There is a spectacularly pruned allée of mature trees in the *Jardin des Plantes* in Paris, to name but one example.

Allegheny spurge. See *Pachysandra procumbens.*

Allegheny vine. See ADLUMIA.

Alligator-apple. *Annona palustris.*

Alligator-juniper. See *Juniperus pachyphlaea.*

Alligator-pear. See *Persea americana.*

ALLIUM (*al*-lee-um). Lily Family (*Liliaceae*). Alliums are often known as "the onions," although the edible onion is only one of the many species in this genus, some of which bear strikingly handsome flowers. Native to many parts of the Northern Hemisphere; they are almost all hardy perennials. However, those whose bulbs are harvested, as are the eating onion and garlic, will not grow again. Bulb-forming, they have elongated leaves springing directly from the bulb, which in several American species grows on, or very close to, the surface of the ground. Others grow deep in the soil. The tufts of dark green foliage are practically pest-free and do not give off the typical onion odor unless crushed. Leaves are flat, straplike or hollow and round (terete). Various species are good subjects for the herbaceous border, the rock garden, the wild garden and the cutting garden, especially since the attractive flower heads are freely borne and, in some species, sweet-scented. Globular clusters of white, yellow, pink, red, blue or purple flowers are borne on bare stalks that rise somewhat higher than the leaves. Easily grown, the ornamental species are useful in borders, rock gardens, or wild gardens. Alliums succeed in sandy, well-drained, ordinary garden soil and some can stand partial shade, although full sun is best. Propagate by seeds or bulbils.

Organic gardeners plant *Allium* species including chives, garlic and onions, with roses and other ornamentals as deterrents to insects.

● **A. albopilosum** (al-boh-pye-*loh*-sum). For the flower border, this species grows 1 to 1½ ft. high,

UPPER: The onion that is a flavor staple in most lands is an *Allium*, a genus that includes prized ornamental plants. Edible onions produce small seed heads that resemble the flowers of the ornamental species.
LOWER: 'Golden Garlic' is the Allium species *moly*, an ornamental that grows to 12 inches, has gray-green leaves and loose heads of yellow flowers in spring.

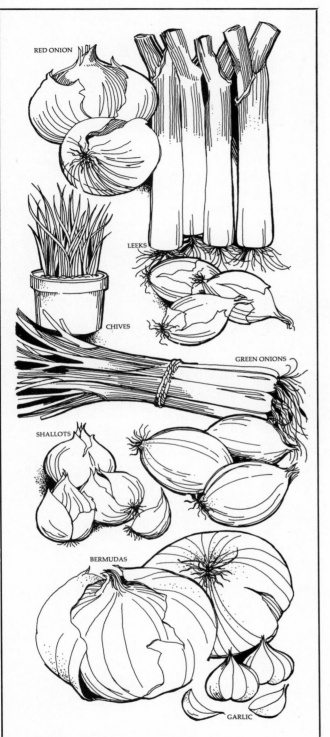

RED ONION

LEEKS

CHIVES

GREEN ONIONS

SHALLOTS

BERMUDAS

GARLIC

These familiar herbs, the leeks, green onions, chives, shallots, garlic, are all alliums, and like the big yellow and red onions, are the bulbs of one or another species of *Allium*. They are all hardy perennials that can be planted in cold ground in early spring and will be ready to harvest in summer. If unharvested and left in the ground through winter they will produce larger plants the following year.

with gracefully arching leaves up to 1½ ft. long and 1¾ in. across, whitish on the undersides. Bright lilac-purple flowers in clusters that may be as much as 8 in. across. Zone 5.

A. azureum: *A. caeruleum.*

A. caeruleum (see-*rew*-lee-um). Sometimes listed in catalogs as A. azureum. An ornamental species, growing up to 3 ft., with narrow, cylindrical leaves up to 2 ft. long, forming a rushlike clump. Dense heads of bright blue flowers in late spring. This is an extremely variable species. Should have full sun and perfect drainage, particularly in winter. Zone 5.

A. cepa (*see*-puh). ONION. This species includes the common onion for table use. The various green or bunching onions and the shallot, which has a flavor that is a cross between an onion and garlic. (The true shallot, *ascalonicum*, is rarely grown here.) Multiplier onions, sometimes called potato onions, are a form in which the ripened bulb divides into separable parts and each is planted the following spring (autumn in the South) as are onion "sets" (see below). Another variety of *cepa*, *viviparum* produces a small bulbil that appears in the flower cluster in the place of blossoms, and these are also handled as "sets," and planted the following season. Multiplier and top onions are grown primarily for use as small green early bunch onions, also called scallions. Bermuda, or Spanish onions, are slow-maturing mild onions. "Green onion," "shallot" and "scallion" seem to be used interchangeably, and are also applied to different races in different regions.

The familiar red, white or yellow kitchen onions are raised from "sets," which look like very small onions or shallots. To grow "sets" a field is very thickly planted with onion seed, and the bulbs are harvested and dried while still small. The following season, they are planted, and onions mature more quickly than had they been started from seed. In the North it is the custom to grow onions from "sets." These are offered at garden-supply centers and in catalogs. The big Bermuda and Spanish onion are usually bought as started seedlings, since they require a long growing season. Bunching onions are also generally started as seedlings, though some are available as "sets."

Onions are heavy feeders. Add 1 lb. of 4-8-4 with extra humus to every 20-ft. row. Onions require plenty of moisture and do not succeed in soils short of humus, which bake dry during the summer.

When frost is barely out of the ground, plant onion "sets" and shallots (which will grow from those purchased at the grocery store), pointed tip up, in holes 1 in. deep and about 8 in. apart. Cover with ½ in. soil. Tamp firmly, as night crawlers sometimes dislodge the small plants. To grow "sets" plant onion seeds early in furrows ½ in. deep, cover with ¼ in. soil, tamp. When they reach scallion size, they can be harvested as needed for kitchen use, and a few weeks later harvested for "sets." Onions grow tall, tubular stems which eventually carry a rounded seed head: bend all the stems when a few have fallen over of themselves, so that less effort will go into the production of seed, and more into maturing the bulb which is the edible root of the allium.

Pull onions, or dig, on a sunny day when a stretch of dry weather is expected, and leave in the fields until tops dry out or until rain threatens. When dry, rub away soil, and braid stems in bunches of eight. Or pull away dried tops and store in a cool dry place. They will keep until the following spring. Shallots are harvested as onions, but are smaller, and ready earlier in the season. The perennial bunching onions can be harvested as needed.

A. cyaneum (sye-*an*-nee-um). An ornamental species, growing up to 10 in. high. Grasslike leaves form a dense clump. Clusters of bright blue, gracefully nodding flowers. A choice rock garden plant that should not be completely sunbaked in summer. Zone 5.

A. flavum (*flay*-vum). YELLOW ONION. An ornamental that grows about 2½ ft. high. Loose clusters of yellow flowers in summer. Zone 6.

A. giganteum (jye-*gan*-tee-um). GIANT ONION. An ornamental with bluish-green leaves up to 2½ in. wide and 18 in. long. Dense heads of bright blue flowers on stalks that may grow as high as 5 ft. Zone 5.

● **A. karataviense** (kar-at-av-ee-*en*-see). TURKESTAN ONION. Especially valued for its two broad, flat leaves, 10 in. long and 2 to 5 in. wide, that make a handsome show on bare ground among other early-flowering bulbs. White flower clusters in May or June. Often dried for use in arrangements. Zone 5.

● **A. moly** (*moh*-lee). GOLDEN GARLIC. A pretty species, usually about 1 ft. tall, with gray-green leaves 1 in. wide and about 1 ft. long. Loose heads of yellow flowers in spring. A useful border or rock garden subject, it naturalizes easily, thrives in shade. Zone 3.

● **A neapolitanum** (nee-ap-ol-it-*tay*-num). NAPLES ONION. A particularly decorative species, growing about 14 in. high, with leaves that are 1 in. wide and up to 1 ft. long. Heads of fragrant, clear white flowers bloom in early spring. Useful for cut flowers when grown in boxes or under glass in cold frame or cold

UPPER: *Allium giganteum*, the giant onion, is a handsome ornamental species with bluish-green leaves up to 2½ inches wide and dense heads of bright lavender-blue flowers on stalks that grow as tall as 5 feet.
LOWER: *Allium ostrowskianum* is a species from Turkestan that produces pink-to-maroon flowers with shapely, spiky petals. Very handsome in the border.

greenhouse. The variety *grandiflorum* (gran-di-*floh*-rum) has larger flowers. Zone 7.

A. ostrowskianum (awstro-skee-*ay*-num). OSTROWSKY ONION. Also called *A. oreophilum ostrowskianum* though its bloom is soft pink rather than the maroon of *oreophilum*. It grows to 12 in. tall, and bears flowers on 6-in. stems, which makes it well suited to the rock garden. A species grown from seed, it has complicated dormancy problems. Seeds planted in the open garden may take two years to germinate. Allow seeds to mature fully, then dry, mix with a little moist peat moss, tie into a plastic bag and store at room temperature for six months. Store in a refrigerator three months more before sowing. Zone 3.

A. porrum (*pore*-um). LEEK. Hardy onionlike vegetable with a distinct, but milder taste than onions. Both the bulb and the leaves may be cooked and eaten. Sow seeds indoors in Feb. and plant out when ground is warm for a late autumn crop. Thin to stand 4 to 6 in. apart in rows 2 to 3 ft. apart. Very rich soil with plenty of moisture during the growing season gives best results. The lower part of the plants is often blanched by hilling up the soil around it. Leeks may be left in the ground until the soil freezes. In European gardens, leeks are sown as seed, transplanted when seedlings are 2 in. high. When tops are long and plump they are again transplanted to trenches 12 in. deep, set 12 in. apart. Mound to blanch bottoms.

A. sativum (sat-*tye*-vum). GARLIC. Onionlike plant to 2 ft., with flat leaves to 1 in. wide and a thinly covered bulb that breaks up into separate parts or "cloves." Plant bulblets as onion sets (see *A. cepa* above), in good garden soil in early spring 6 in. apart. Culture is as *A. cepa*, but garlic matures sooner. When fresh, it resembles a leek and has a very mild, delicious flavor.

A. schoenoprasum (skee-noh-*pray*-sum). CHIVES. Dense clusters of dark green, terete leaves 6 to 12 in. long. The lilac flowers, in dense heads, appear in early summer on stems that are 9 to 10 in. high. The leaves are commonly used as a pot herb for their delicate onion flavor. Tops may be snipped as needed, and should be kept from forming seed heads if the plant is used as an herb. Aside from its culinary use, this species makes an excellent edging plant for flower borders, thriving in any reasonably good soil any place except in deep shade. Zone 3. See special article on chives, beginning page 103.

A. triquetrum (trye-*kwet*-rum). Grows to 1½ ft., with slender, three-cornered leaves up to 1 ft. long. White flowers, with a green streak down the center of each petal, appear in early spring. Zone 7.

A. tuberosum (too-ber-*roh*-sum). CHINESE CHIVES. A decorative species, growing up to 18 in. high, with slender leaves in spreading clusters. White flowers with a green midrib bloom in late summer. Zone 5.

UPPER: *Allium flavum* in a close-up shows shapely heads with loose clusters of bulbous spikelets. Flowers are yellow and bloom in summer. Hardy only to Zone 6.

LOWER: *Allium karataviense* is the Turkestan onion, and is especially valued for the two broad leaves, 10 inches long and 2 to 5 inches wide, that make a handsome show on bare ground among the early-flowering bulbs. The flower clusters are white and appear in early May or June. This species is often used for dried arrangements. It is hardy to Zone 5. Many other Alliums are offered in garden catalogs and the best of the many species have been hybridized. Most species give off a faint onion scent when stems are broken.

Chives

By LILLIAN ILLIG

What could be more satisfying than picking fresh chives from a back-door garden? Their bright green succulent leaves, finely cut, add zest and color to almost any dish. The early Dutch settlers liked the taste of chives so much they planted them in their pastures so the cows would give chive-flavored milk.

The chive (*Allium schoenoprasum*) is a member of the onion family and like all its cousins has an onion flavor. But unlike onions, it is smaller in size, milder in taste, less odorous and kinder to weak stomachs. The chive is about one-fourth the size of the shallot, but unlike the shallot, its white narrow bulb root is not eaten. It is left in the earth to produce leaves. Only the tender, cylindrical leaves are eaten. They are cut near the root and are quickly replaced by new leaves that grow from the cut end. These leaves are taken garden-fresh into the kitchen to cut up.

To grow your own, buy a pot of chive seedlings from your garden-supply center or grocer and transplant to a garden where it can spread out, multiply and supply you all season. In the South, these pots are found any time of year except in June, when the winter garden has dried up, and in September, when the summer chives have dried up. Plant outside any month in the South, since chives are hardy and can withstand most climates if they are well mulched. In a very cold climate where chives would freeze, plant them in a sunny window box in the greenhouse for the winter.

You can grow chives in the house for many months if no greenhouse is available. Dig a clump before frosts, pot in garden soil, moisten well, keep shaded for a few days, then set in a sunny window in a cool room. Harvest at will once they have started to grow and keep trimmed to encourage production.

The leaves of *Allium schoenoprasum* are commonly called chives and are used to add a delicate onion flavor to such culinary delicacies as vichyssoise.
A perennial, it puts up dense clusters of
dark green leaves from early spring until it dies
back in late autumn. The charming lilac flowers growing
in tight, round heads make it an attractive edging plant
for the vegetable or the herb garden. The tops may be snipped
for use as needed and should be kept from forming
seed heads if the plant is used as an herb. Chives can
be brought indoors and grown in a pot on a sunny
window sill when the summer season is over, or they
can be picked and dried or frozen for later use in cooking.

To Transplant

To transplant, choose a spot near your back door, handy to the kitchen. A plot 2 ft. by 3 ft. will give ample chives for a family of five. The soil should be well drained, and receive as much sun as possible. The author has a banana tree near her chive garden which cuts off the morning sun. This is harmful only in September when the banana tree is in full leaf. The chives are shaded so much then that six weeks are needed for them to mature; in June, only a week or two is necessary.

You can transplant chives from a pot almost any time of year in the South, or in spring and summer in the North. Remove them from the pot, separate their pods, and then divide each pod into its component cloves. Plant each clove separately in shallow holes the size of the clove. Plant even those with no green leaves, since leaves will appear soon. The cloves should be planted 3 or 4 in. apart to give them room to expand. This they do readily; when the garden dries up and you dig them up again, each pod will be thick with new cloves. Around those that have green shoots, pull the dirt up so tightly they will stand up straight. Sprinkle with mulch to hold in moisture and keep out the cold; feed with very little organic fertilizer, and then wait. If they have enough sunshine, they will fairly jump out of the earth. They thrive even in the cool of early spring.

As they mature and grow (the average height is 9 in. but they can grow as tall as 16 in.), they will bend over from their weight, since they are hollow. So cut the bent-over ones first to keep the garden looking trim. When you cut the leaves, be careful not to cut the new shoots.

If, after trimming your crop of all its bent-over leaves, you see that you have more than you need, do one of two things. First, wash them lightly and dry by patting with a paper towel. Then, either keep them for three or four days in the hydrator or freeze them.

To Freeze

To freeze chives: It is simpler to freeze chives than most other vegetables. Others have to be blanched to stop enzymatic action that leads to spoilage. Luckily, chives are immune to this. Simply wash them lightly so as not to bruise leaves or otherwise disturb their volatile oils; it is these oils that preserve chives in the freezing process. Chop by cutting with scissors. Hold the bunch evenly in one hand, the scissors in the other. Cut into 1/16-in. pieces, letting these fall into a small plastic box. Fasten tightly; put into freezer.

These are spoken of as "chopped chives." Cutting

makes them ready for salads and garnishes, but if you are going to use them only for seasoning in soups and stews, they may be frozen whole. To do so, place in plastic containers with lids, in glass jars with screw lids or in plastic envelopes sealed with a hot iron. The main point in freezing anything is to retain the original moisture. A whole chive will retain more moisture and flavor than a chopped one, because the latter tends to "bleed" and thus lose its moisture. It is not feasible to chop chives after they have been frozen, because they are too limp. But freezing both whole and chopped in separate containers prepares chives for either kind of future use.

To use frozen chopped chives, remove container from freezer, quickly dig out as many spoonfuls as you need; then replace the lid, and return container to freezer. To use whole chives, take out of jar or bag and put right into the soup or stew. No thawing is necessary, since this occurs immediately.

What is the result of freezing? Chives retain their blue-green coloring but lose their crisp texture and flavor, the chopped ones more so than the whole ones. The flavor is excellent.

To Dry Chives

In summing up, the best procedure is to grow your own chives either in a garden, a cold frame or indoors in a window box. Second-best is to use frozen chives from your freezer or from the supermarket. Third choice is to use dried chives. The very essence of chives, their volatile oils, is altered in drying. Their texture is changed to a powder, their color is changed to a gray-green and their taste is one of strong oils. But chives that you dry yourself seem to have something special.

To dry, hang a bunch of chives in a paper bag so they do not touch the paper (the paper is to exclude dust). Keep in the bag for several weeks until dry; then finish their drying in the oven at 100° for only a minute, and seal in tight jars.

Growing your own chives from seeds is easy. It takes more time, but you will have a much larger garden if all the seeds come up.

Any good nurseryman or seed store sells herb seeds in packages. A 35-cent packet of chive seeds will plant a 25-ft. row. The time to plant seeds depends upon your location: in the North, May and June; in the Midwest, April to June; in the South, March to October; in the Gulf section and southern California, September to May.

To plant chive seeds, use a bed similar to the one used for transplanting the bulbs from the pot. Sow the seeds ¼-in. deep in rows about 18 in. apart. When the seedlings are about 3 in. high (they will look like grass but will have two blades in the shape of a "Y"), thin to rows about 6 in. apart. Thinning is necessary so that the bulbs will form and have space to expand.

Whether to plant the seeds in a cold frame or not depends upon the coldness of the weather and the planting time as indicated on the package. It might be easier to start your seedlings in a soil-filled shallow box. This will save bending down to a garden row. When you transplant to an outdoor garden, mulch the soil well. In a few weeks the chives will be waving their tender green shoots skyward ready to be cut whenever the cook needs them.

Uses of Chives

Since chives have been known to cooks for hundreds of years, it would be impossible to give all the interesting uses of this versatile and flavorsome herb. We are content to list a few, knowing that other ideas will come to any cook tantalized by the availability of his or her own chive patch.

Summer soups: Garnish frozen cream of tomato, asparagus, mushroom or vichyssoise with sour cream; sprinkle with chopped chives. Garnish jellied soups with thin slices of avocado and chopped chives.

Salads: Add chives to any fresh cucumber-and-dill combination; or garnish cucumber "boats" stuffed with a mixture of cottage cheese, chopped chives and dill with red caviar, with more chives added for color.

Vegetables: To curried green beans (cooked), add butter seasoned with more curry powder and chopped chives.

Bundle canned white asparagus into pepper rings and garnish with mayonnaise sprinkled with chopped chives.

Baked potatoes: Slit open while hot and insert red caviar sprinkled generously with chopped chives.

Hot chive bread: Season a whole French or Italian loaf just as you would for making garlic bread, replacing the garlic in the butter with chopped chives. Wrap in foil and heat in oven.

Hot herbed biscuit: Mix two tablespoons chopped chives into dry biscuit ingredients (for a batch of 12) just before milk is added.

Chive-covered croutons: Pour melted butter and sprinkle chopped chives over cubes of crisp bread. Scatter upon a cream soup or add to a salad.

Green butter: Mash chives into a paste with a mortar and pestle and use twice their weight in butter. Use to garnish grilled meats.

Chive mayonnaise: Mix ¼ cup of chopped chives into a cup of mayonnaise and use as a dressing for salad, a sauce for meats.

Herbed chicken: To herb a chicken or other fowl,

Smaller than a teacup is the charming little Mexican foxglove, *Allophyton mexicanum*. It makes an excellent house plant and thrives in an east window or a terrarium with plants requiring similar cultural conditions.

mix with butter one part each of chopped fresh chives, parsley and tarragon. Insert into openings large enough to get fingers between skin and flesh around the neck of the chicken. Sew openings closed before roasting.

Smoked salmon roll: Lay on thin slices of salmon a mixture of sour cream, chopped chives, dill and a dash of paprika, and roll salmon firmly; secure with toothpicks.

There are hundreds of others you can try. As much fun as growing your own chives will be the pleasure of using them in such rewarding variety, and, perhaps, discovering new ways to capture the zest, flavor and appetizing green color of this lovely herb.

ALLOPHYTON (al-low-*phy*-ton). Figwort Family (*Scrophulariaceae*). A genus of tender perennials from Mexico and Guatemala. Only one species is in cultivation.
A. mexicanum (mex-i-*cane*-um). MEXICAN FOXGLOVE. A small, dark green plant with simple leaves and spikes of violet or purple flowers similar to small *Digitalis* blossoms. Sow seed in late winter for summer bedding plants (high shade, woodsy soil) or sow seed in spring, raise young plants in a shaded bed, pinch once and pot up singly. Use Basic Potting Mixture but add one part compost or leafmold. Grow for winter flowering, ideal night temperature of 55° to 60°, although it will prosper in the average window garden with morning sun.

ALLOPLECTUS (al-o-*plek*-tus). Gesneria Family (*Gesneriaceae*). Fibrous-rooted relatives of the florists' gloxinia (*Sinningia*) and African violet (*Saintpaulia*), some upright to 3 ft., others trailing as the related *Columnea*. Approximately 80 species are found in the West Indies, tropical South and Central America. As ornamentals for a warm, moist, bright but shaded place in the house or greenhouse, they are most noteworthy for decorative foliage and clusters of colorful calyxes, which last long after the flowers fade. They are not easy plants to cultivate, but if you have succeeded with the more common gesneriads, try the alloplectus as your next adventure into this large, rewarding family of pot plants. Use a growing medium composed of equal parts by volume of peat moss, vermiculite and perlite. Feed every two weeks with a liquid house-plant fertilizer, diluted according to directions on the container. Nip out the growing tips to encourage branching, especially of the vinelike species. The upright kinds may be grown to one stem, without branching, but with age may require staking. Propagate, preferably from late winter to summer, from cuttings or seeds; provide gentle bottom heat, and evenly moist growing medium such as milled sphagnum moss or vermiculite, and high humidity.
A. ambiguus (am-*big*-yeu-us). Vinelike plant with yellow flowers set in red or green calyxes. Showy as a hanging basket plant, or may be trained upright on a small trellis.
A. capitatus (cap-ih-*tay*-tus). VELVET ALLOPLECTUS. The squared, fleshy stems of this upright species, to 3 ft., are covered in plush red down. Ovate leaves, to 8 in. long, are olive above, maroon beneath. In autumn dense clusters of yellow flowers are borne from dark red calyxes.
A. schlimii (*schlim*-ee-eye). With age the upright green stems of this species become woody. They are set with showy, broad-lanceolate leaves, 4 in. long, light green above, flushed purple beneath. The crimson-streaked, golden flowers appear in the leaf axils.
A. vittatus (vit-*tay*-tus). STRIPED ALLOPLECTUS. Ovate, crenate, quilted leaves of bronze-green, to 6 in. long, frosted with white hair and feathered with silver along the midrib and lateral veins. The leaf undersides glow a rich burgundy color. Red bracts and orange-red calyxes form a beautiful setting for the yellow flowers. A jewel among tropical foliage plants for a warm, humid, bright place—with showy flowers as an added bonus.

Allspice. See *Pimenta officinalis*.

Almond. See *Prunus amygdalus*.

Almond, earth. See *Cyperus esculentus*.

Almond, flowering. See *Prunus triloba; Prunus glandulosa albiplena; Prunus sinensis.*

Almond, Indian. See *Terminalia catappa.*

Almond, Russian. See *Prunus tenella.*

Almond-scented mugwort. See *Artemisia lactiflora.*

Almond, tropical. See *Terminalia catappa.*

ALNUS (*al*-nus). ALDER. Birch Family (*Betulaceae*). A large group of deciduous trees and shrubs native to the Northern Hemisphere and the Andes. Alternate, generally coarse-toothed leaves that fall in autumn usually while still green. The flowers are in the form of catkins, which appear in early spring before the leaves. Of limited garden use, alders are recommended chiefly because they grow well in moist or wet soils where many of the more ornamental trees would not thrive. Sometimes attacked by tent caterpillars. Spray with Sevin, Diazinon or malathion for these and other insect pests. Propagate by cuttings, suckers or seeds.

A. cordata (kor-*day*-tuh). ITALIAN ALDER. Round-headed tree, 30 to 50 ft. high, with handsome, glossy green, ovoid leaves to 4 in. long. Considered by many to be the best alder for ornamental use. Zone 5.

A. glutinosa (glew-tin-*noh*-suh). BLACK ALDER. Sometimes listed in catalogs as A. vulgaris. A mature tree may grow to 70 ft. or more. Dark green, coarsely toothed leaves to 4 in. long. When unfolding, the leaves are sticky. The catkins appear in March. Has become naturalized in some parts of eastern N. America. There is a yellow- and a cut-leaved variety. Zone 3.

A. hirsuta (herss-*yew*-tuh). MANCHURIAN ALDER. To 60 ft. A hardy, vigorous tree with large leaves, from Japan and Manchuria. Tending to be densely pyramidal, this is one of the handsomest alders. Zone 4.

A. incana (in-*kay*-nuh). SPECKLED ALDER. Shrub or tree to 75 ft. Yellow catkins in March, followed by the ovoid leaves, which are bluish-gray beneath. Varieties include: *Aurea* (*aw*-ree-uh), young shoots yellow-green; *coccinea* (kok-*sin*-ee-uh), leaves yellowish, young twigs reddish; *pendula* (*pen*-dew-luh), with drooping branches; and *pinnata* (pin-*nay*-tuh), with small leaves, deeply lobed. Zone 2.

A. rhombifolia (rom-bif-*foh*-lee-uh). WHITE ALDER. A native of the Pacific Coast, where it is widely grown. A fast-growing tree to 90 ft. or more. Whitish bark and dense foliage characterize this species. Zone 5.

Hoary catkins of the speckled alder, *Alnus incana*, are yellow and bloom in March. The genus includes species that are shrubs and others that grow into trees 75 feet tall. It is hardy and will succeed in Zone 2.

A. rugosa (roo-*goh*-suh). HAZEL ALDER. Branching, coarse shrub or small tree found along streams, bordering ponds and in swamps, Me. to Tex. Usually not over 15 to 25 ft. Zone 4.

A. serrulata (ser-rew-*lay*-tuh). SMOOTH ALDER. Shrubby tree (or treelike shrub) seldom over 25 ft. tall. Grayish, finely toothed (serrate) leaves, downy on the undersides. Native east of the Ozarks, from Me. to Fla. Zone 5.

A. vulgaris: *A. glutinosa.*

ALOCASIA (al-oh-*kay*-zee-uh). Arum Family (*Araceae*). Handsome foliage plants from tropical Asia. The arrow- or heart-shaped leaves are large and usually attractively variegated. Grown outdoors only in tropical and subtropical regions, they are often grown in warm humid greenhouses for their foliage. They need plenty of water (especially during active growth, March to Jan.) and a warm house with a night temperature of at least 60°. High humidity and protection from direct sunlight are also essential. Use Basic Potting Mixture with doubled peat. Propagate by suckers, root cuttings or seeds. These are not suited for average house culture. All Zone 10. (See House Plants index, Plant Finder section, Volume 16.)

ABOVE: *Alocasia* x *sedenii* is a handsome hybrid of this genus of showy foliage plants. Alocasias are grown outdoors only in tropical or semitropical situations but will flourish in a humid greenhouse. Not suited to house culture. This species has leaves of dark metallic green, purple beneath, with gray margins and raised veins.
UPPER RIGHT: The giant leaves of *Alocasia indica.*
LOWER RIGHT: The very large leaf of *A. watsoniana* is bluish green, purple below and white-margined.

ALOCASIAS OF NOTE TO THE GARDENER, AND PRESENTLY IN

NAME	ORIGIN	DESCRIPTION	NAME	ORIGIN	DESCRIPTION
A. x amazonica	(A sanderiana x A. lowii grandis)	Bushy, leaves dark green, white irregular margin; veins white.	A. lindenii	New Guinea	Stems white; elongate leaves glossy green with creamy-white veins.
A. x argyraea	(A. longiloba x A. pucciana)	Large, arrow-head leaves overlaid with silver sheen.	A. longiloba	Java	Broad, bluish-green arrow-head leaves with silvery-gray margins and veins.
A. cadierei	Annam	Broad dark green arrow-head leaves, wavy margin; gray-green veins.	A. longiloba x A. sanderiana	Cultivar	Bluish-green leaves with bloom; silver veins and margins.
A. x chantrieri	(A. indica metallica x A. sanderiana)	Bushy, leathery olive-green leaves with white, wavy margins, opalescent veins.	A. lowii	Malaya	Leathery leaves broad arrow-head shaped, metallic blue-green; with gray-green veins.
A. chelsonii	(A. longiloba x A. cuprea)	Leaves waxy, bronze to olive-green. Wavy margins and veins silvery gray.	A. lowii grandis	Malaya	Leaves larger than the species and bronze-green, veins with silver sheen.
A. cucullata	Bengal, Burma	Smaller, cupped, arrow-head leaves, deep green with prominent veins.	A. lowii veitchii	Java	Stems green, variegated pink. Leaves as the species but all veins whitish, giving a marbled effect.
A. cuprea	Borneo	Leaves dark, metallic green, purple below; with deeply depressed veins.	A. macrorhiza	Malaya, Ceylon	Plant to 15 ft., with large, broad arrow-head leaves, waxy, medium green, with wavy margins.
A. cuprea x A. longiloba	Mauro (natural hybrid)	Stem pink, brown striped, elongate arrow-head leaves gray-green, purple beneath, with raised silver-gray viens and wavy margin.	A. macrorhiza variegata	East Indies	As the species but leaves blotched and mottled white.
A. cuprea x A. lowii grandis	Mauro (natural hybrid)	Similar to preceding hybrid, but leaves olive, with gray sheen.	A. micholitziana	Philippines	Leaves narrow, arrow-head shaped, bright green with white mid-rib; pale green petioles marked purple.
A. 'Hilo Beauty'	Cultivar, parentage unrecorded	Small overall, stems bluish-black with grape-like bloom; leaves green, papery, with translucent chartreuse blotches.	A. 'New Guinea'	Cultivar	Leathery leaves ovate, deep green, with silver mid-rib.
A. indica	Malaya	Large; arrow-head leaves rich dark green, with raised veins.	A. odorata	Philippines, Formosa	Large light green, arrow-head leaves fleshy, with prominent veins; petioles marked purple. Flowers fragrant.
A. indica metallica	Malaya	As preceding species but leaves olive-green with purplish sheen, purple below.	A. princeps	Borneo	Small plant with arrow-head leaves, olive-green, with wavy margins and purple-green veins.
A. indica variegata	Malaya	As the species, but with many white blotches on the foliage.	A. putzeysii	Java	Very handsome plant. Leathery ovate arrow-head leaves crinkled and wavy edged, purple below. Leaves dark green, veins silver-white.
A. korthalsii	Borneo	Stiff, upright plant, leaves gray-green with yellowish tinge, purple below; with silvery veins.			

HORTICULTURAL COLLECTIONS

NAME	ORIGIN	DESCRIPTION
A. regina	Borneo	Waxy, thick arrow-head leaves with long basal lobes and wavy margins, leaves dark olive-green with metallic bloom, below gray-maroon, with maroon veins.
A. sanderiana	Philippines	Arrow-head leaves shiny metallic green with white margins deeply lobed; veins silver-white.
A. sanderiana 'Van Houtte'	Cultivar	Dwarfer than the species, with broader leaves with gray-white margins, shallow-lobed and gray-white blotching along the mid-rib.
A. x sedenii	(*A. cuprea* x *A. lowii*)	Stocky plant. Leaves elongate, deep metallic green, gray margin wavy, purple beneath with raised veins.
A. 'Spotted Papua'	Unidentified New Guinea species	Flaring arrow-head leaves, leathery, copper-green with irregular yellow spots, purple below.
A. van-houtteana	East Indies	Large, leathery leaves elongate, shiny mid-green, puckered and with veins and margins white. Purple below.
A. wat-soniana	Sumatra	Leaves large, crinkled, bluish-green, purple below; with silver-white veins and margins.
A. wavrin-iana	Celebes	Arrow-head leaves long and narrow, metallic green with raised mid-rib and wavy margins; purple below.
A. wentii	New Guinea	Leaves waxy, emerald green, with prominent raised veins and shallowly wavy margins.
A. zebrina	Philippines	Large, mid-green arrow-head leaves carried on slender pale green petioles, banded brown.

ALOE (al-*loh*-ee). Lily Family (*Liliaceae*). A very large genus of handsome, perennial succulents ranging in size from small bushy shrubs to giant treelike plants. A representative list of species is offered below. Mostly from S. Africa, all have thick, stiff, fleshy leaves in rosettes and branching spikes of showy flowers in midwinter, a time when brilliant color is needed in home, greenhouse or garden. They are admirably suited to pots or tubs, which may be put outdoors in summer either in the garden or as a distinctive addition to the terrace. Outdoors, they can only be grown in frost-free regions. Indoors, use Basic Potting Mixture with doubled sand. They need sun, plenty of moisture during the late spring and summer and good drainage. Propagate by seeds, division or cuttings. Zone 10.

A. africana (af-rik-*kay*-nuh). Quick-growing, treelike species to 10 ft. The stout trunk is topped by a dense rosette of sword-shaped, pointed leaves 1½ to 2 ft. long and edged with brown prickles. Dense clusters of yellow or orange bell-like flowers cover the tall flower stalks in early spring.

● **A. arborescens** (ar-bor-*ress*-senz). One of the most popular of the larger species, this is a tall, shrubby

Aloe variegata has triangular dark green leaves marbled with white and produces showy scarlet flowers that bloom in midwinter. It makes a good house plant and grows best in partial shade or in a north window.

plant with a rosette of gracefully arching leaves to 2 ft. long. From the center of the plant rise the 6- to 10-ft. stems covered with narrow clusters of brilliant, fiery red flowers to 1 in. long in midwinter.

● **A. aristata** (ar-riss-*tay*-tuh). A dwarf species excellent for pot planting. Very thin, stemless leaves to 3 in. long and ½ in. wide form a dense rosette about 6 in. high. Reddish-yellow flowers to 1 in. long. The attractive foliage is grayish green, spotted with white and edged with hairlike white teeth.

A. brevifolia (brev-if-*foh*-lee-uh). A small, short-stemmed plant that forms clumps of dense rosettes. The leaves are grayish green. Spikes of red flowers on 9- to 15-in. stalks.

A. ciliaris (sil-ee-*ay*-riss). The stems are weak and either sprawl or climb 2 to 3 ft. Linear, lance-shaped leaves to 5 in. long and bright red flowers in long-stalked clusters 6 to 8 in. high. Useful in hanging baskets. Widely grown outdoors in southern Calif.

UPPER FAR LEFT: *Leontopodium alpinum* is edelweiss, the best known of this collection of alpine plants.
UPPER CENTER: *Saxifraga caesia*, alpine saxifrage.
UPPER RIGHT: *Gentiana acaulis* has the intense color of other gentians and grows wild in European mountains.
LOWER LEFT: *Eryngium alpinum* thrives in poor dry soil.
LOWER RIGHT: *Papaver pyrenaicum* is the wild mountain poppy of the Pyrenees. As a group the alpines are charming small plants suited to the alpine garden and to use in massed plantings in the rock garden.

A. ferox (*fee*-rox). Stately, treelike aloe 9 to 15 ft. high. The thick trunk is topped by a broad rosette of very thorny, green leaves. Showy red flowers.

A. mitriformis (mye-trif-*for*-mis). Grows 3 to 4 ft. high, with thick, triangular, green leaves to 6 in. long and curved inwards. The plant is crowned by dense clusters of bright red flowers.

A. nobilis (*noh*-bil-iss). Stems are 2 to 3 ft. long, often prostrate, and bear toothed leaves to 6 in. long and red flowers in clusters.

A. striata (strye-*ay*-tuh). Triangular, spineless leaves form a wide rosette, out of which rise branching stems that bear numerous coral-red flowers.

● **A. variegata** (var-ree-eg-*gay*-tuh). A fine house plant with triangular, dark green leaves marbled with white, shaped in a rosette 1 ft. high. Scarlet flowers. This species grows best in partial shade.

A. vera (*vee*-rah). BARBADOS ALOE. UNGUENTINE PLANT. Thick fleshy leaves grow in a fan shape from the base of the plant, and have soft spines on the leaf margins. They exude a gluey gelatinous substance when cut and are used medicinally on burns and cuts. Propagate by rooting offshoots. Red or yellow bell-shaped flowers on a leafless stem. Sometimes grown indoors but rarely flowers. Probably a native of India. A smaller variety, *chinensis*, has reddish flowers.

ALONSOA (al-*lon*-zoh-uh). MASK FLOWER. Figwort Family (*Scrophulariaceae*). Small shrubs from tropical America, grown as summer annuals in the garden or indoors for the pretty flowers, which bloom in terminal clusters. The flowers are red and turned upside down, due to the twisting of each flower stalk. These plants are easily grown in ordinary garden soil and full sun. For winter bloom indoors in a cool greenhouse, use Basic Potting Mixture. Propagate by seeds sown 1/16 in. deep in March (indoors) or cuttings. Zone 10.

A. acutifolia (ak-kew-tif-*foh*-lee-uh). From Mexico, grows 2 to 3 ft. high, with scarlet flowers, and variety *alba* (*al*-buh) with white flowers.

A. compacta: *A. warscewiczii*.

A. grandiflora: *A. warscewiczii*.

A. incisifolia (in-sye-sif-*foh*-lee-uh). From Peru; to 18 in. high, with scarlet flowers in midsummer.

A. linearis (lyn-ee-*ay*-riss). From Peru; 1 to 2 ft. high, with scarlet flowers in summer.

A. liniflora: *A. linearis*.

A. meridionalis (meh-rid-ee-oh-*nay*-liss). From Peru; 1 to 2 ft. high, with salmon-pink flowers in summer.

A. mutisii: *A. meridionalis*.

A. myrtifolia. *A. acutifolia*.

A. warscewiczii (var-shuh-*vitz*-ee-eye). Often listed in catalogs as A. compacta or A. grandiflora. A bushy plant to 3 ft., with ovalish to lance-shaped opposite leaves that have toothed margins. Loose clusters of scarlet-red flowers, each with two irregular petals.

Aloysia. See LIPPIA.

alpestris (al-*pest*-riss), **-e.** Alpine (or nearly so).

alpine. A term indicating the portion of a mountain

Aloe africana, a quick-growing treelike species that reaches 10 feet in height, produces a rosette of sword-shaped leaves edged with brown prickles. Dense clusters of yellow, or orange, bell-like flowers appear in early spring.

high above timberline; also the plants from the Alpine Zone. All native alpines are on the preservation lists of Colo., Mass., and Vt. and are protected.

Alpine anemone. See *Anemone alpina*.

Alpine azalea. See *Loiseleuria procumbens*.

Alpine bugleweed. See AJUGA.

Alpine chickweed. See *Cerastium alpinum*.

Alpine flax. See *Linum alpinum*.

alpine garden. A specially constructed rock garden for growing plants from the Alpine Zone of high mountains. Often the retaining stones are of granite, sandstone and limestone or dolomite, to provide varying density and acidity. The pockets, too, are variously constructed, with different blends of stone chips of the three kinds of stone, with peat, some soil and, perhaps, other ingredients. Little fertilizer is used. The advanced grower of alpine plants will want a scree or a moraine. A scree in nature is the deep, loose layer of rock chips and debris that collects below the face of a mountain cliff. A moraine is the accumulation of small stones and grit pushed up by a glacier. Each has its own characteristic, highly specialized, flora. The moraine is constructed so it can be watered from below (to simulate the melting glacier) while the scree depends on surface water.

alpine house. A cool or unheated, generally low-roofed greenhouse given over to the culture of container-grown alpine and rock-garden plants. Usually plants are set in clay pots or pans of carefully blended rock-garden soil, and the surface is covered with stone chips or larger stones. The pots usually are plunged rim-deep in the gravel or coarse sand that fills the benches. Careful management permits perfect flowering of difficult mountain species where these could not be grown well in the open garden.

Alpine poppy. See *Papaver alpinum.*

Alpine rose. Translation of the German term *alpenrose* which refers to one of two European mountain rhododendrons, *R. ferrugineum* and *R. hirsutum.* A third species, *R. chamaecistus,* is called *zwergalpenrose,* dwarf alpine rose. *Alpen heckenrose* (alpine hedge rose) is *Rosa alpina: R. pendulina.*

Alpine sea-holly. See *Eryngium alpinum.*

Alpine strawberry. This refers to a small fruited, sweet, wild strawberry from the European mountains. See FRAGARIA.

Alpine toadflax. See *Linaria alpina.*

ALPINIA (al-*pin*-ee-uh). Ginger Family (*Zingiberaceae*). A large genus of Asian perennials, a few of which are cultivated for the attractive foliage and showy flowers. The leafy stems bear variegated, long, narrow leaves. The curious little orchidlike flowers bloom in terminal clusters, eventually nodding gracefully. Outdoors in frost-free regions, they need good rich soil, plenty of moisture and partial shade. Indoors in a greenhouse the temperature should not go below 60°. Basic Potting Mixture with doubled peat, good humidity and abundant watering give best results. Propagate by division. Zone 10.

A. nutans: *A. speciosa.*

A. purpurata (pur-pew-*ray*-tuh). RED SHELLFLOWER. An East Indies plant with cornlike leaves growing to 8 ft. outdoors, much less in a container. Everblooming in the tropics or humid, warm greenhouse, this species bears 1 ft. spikes of showy red bracts that enclose the small, white flowers. Small, leafy plantlets form on the aged spike; these root easily.

A. sanderae (*san*-der-ee). BANDED GALANGAL. A handsome foliage plant growing to 6 ft. in the open but

UPPER: *Alsophila,* a tree fern, from the warm steamy forests of Asia, can be grown in America in a moist greenhouse.
LOWER: *Alpinia speciosa* is another tropical for use as a greenhouse plant. It is known as the shellflower.

seldom over 1½ ft. high in containers; rarely flowering under cultivation. The pale green leaves, to 8 in. long and 1 in. wide, are attractively banded with pure white.

A. speciosa (spee-see-*oh*-suh). SHELLFLOWER. Often listed in catalogs as A. nutans. A majestic plant forming dense clumps of leafy stems up to 10 ft. tall. The leathery leaves, 1 to 2 ft. long and up to 5 in. wide, are not variegated in this species. Fragrant, bell-shaped, white flowers flushed with pink bloom in dense clusters up to 1 ft. long. The crinkled yellow edges of the flowers are colored with red and brown.

alpinus (al-*pye*-nus), **-a, -um.** Alpine; growing above the timber line.

Alsine. See ARENARIA; STELLARIA.

ALSOPHILA (al-*soff*-il-uh). Tree fern Family (*Cyatheaceae*). Ferns with woody trunks to 20 ft. from the warm, steamy, tropical rain forests of Asia, Tasmania and Australia. These are fair subjects for the large conservatory provided sufficient humidity is maintained. In tubs, begin with a 2-in.-deep layer of shards for drainage. The potting compost is equal parts loam, peat and leafmold, with one-half part each of sand and chipped charcoal. Keep damp in summer, barely moist in winter. Grow in full shade and syringe the fronds daily. Propagate by spores, a tedious, slow process. Zone 10 (hardy to 45°, requiring warm moist air).

The commonly cultivated species, with fresh green fronds to 6 ft. or more, is *A. australis.*

ALSTONIA (all-*stow*-nee-uh). Dogbane Family (*Apocynaceae*). *A. scholaris* (sko-*lare*-iss) is a tender tall-growing tree for Fla. and Calif. tropical regions. The leaves are leathery, 4 to 8 in. long. Flowers are small, insignificant. The tree is one of a genus of latex-yielding species that supply some small amount of caoutchouc. Most alstonias are from Southeast Asia. Another species, *A. macrophylla,* also is grown in the U.S. Progagate by seeds. Zone 10.

ALSTROEMERIA (al-strem-*meer*-ee-uh). Amaryllis Family (*Amaryllidaceae*). Tender, tuberous-rooted perennials of S. America. The slender, leafy stems form a fine tangle from a clump of established roots, each stem ending in a cluster of showy, lilylike flowers, resembling half-furled umbrellas, in the brilliant colors we associate with Spanish shawls—orange, red, yellow, purple and brown. Outdoors in frost-free regions, they succeed in moderately rich, humusy soil with good drainage but ample moisture, and full sun to partial shade. Further north, lift after light

Alstroemeria, the named variety 'Walter Fleming.' In frost-free regions it succeeds out of doors in moist humusy soil. In the North it is brought indoors for winter.

frost, dry for ten days, trim off foliage and store in barely damp sand in a cool place. Propagate by freshly gathered seeds or root division.

A. aurantiaca (aw-ran-*tye*-ak-uh). YELLOW ALSTROEMERIA. This is the hardiest species, growing 2 to 3 ft. high, with pointed leaves 3 to 4 in. long. Clusters of yellow flowers, about 1½ in. across, with a brown spot at the tip of each petal. The variety *major* (*may*-jor) is larger than the species, with orange flowers. Two cultivars that probably derive from *A. aurantiaca* are 'Doves Orange,' with orange-red flowers, growing to 3 ft. and *lutea* (*lew*-tee-uh), bright yellow, growing to 2½ ft. Hardy to Zone 6 with winter protection.

A. chilensis (chil-*len*-siss). CHILEAN ALSTROEMERIA. A thick stem, 2 to 4 ft. high, with bluish-green, fringe-edged leaves. Rose-colored or red flowers. Zone 8.

A. litgu (*leet*-gew). From Chile, and nearly as hardy as *A. aurantiaca,* this species bears flowers that are pale pink, pale lilac or off-white, trumpet-shaped, to 2 in. long. The plant grows to 4 ft. Zone 6 (hardy to 0°) with protection.

A. Litgu Hybrids. This strain, apparently from *A. litgu* x *A. haemantha* (an obscure species) is best for

Alstroemeria litgu hybrid is a species from
Chile and hardy to 0° with protection.
The flowers are pale pink, pale lilac or off-white.

general garden growing. The vigorous stems, to 4 ft.,
bear large open sprays of 2- to 3-inch trumpet flowers
in pink, salmon, flame, orange and yellow shades.
Zone 6 (hardy to 0°) with protection.

A. pelegrina (pell-uh-*gree*-nuh). INCA-LILY ALSTROEME-
RIA. Another Chilean species. Flowers lilac, spotted
red and purple. This species often is grown as a warm
greenhouse plant. Pot up in fall in Basic Potting Mixture with double sand, water lightly until growth is
vigorous, then generously. Give bright light; set outdoors in late spring. Zone 10.

A. pulchella (pull-*kell*-uh). PARROT ALSTROEMERIA.
Grows 2 to 3 ft. high, with scattered leaves up to 3
in. long. Some of the stems do not have flowers, and
these are shorter, with clustered leaves. Dark red
flowers with green-tipped petals and brown specks.
Zone 8.

altaclarensis (al-ta-klar-*en*-siss), **-e.** A latinized play
on the name Highclere, a horticulturally notable es-
tate in Wales.

Altai columbine. See *Aquilegia glandulosa.*

altaicus (al-*tay*-ik-us), **-a, -um.** From the Altai Mountains.

ALTERNANTHERA (al-ter-*nanth*-er-uh). Amaranth
Family (*Amaranthaceae*). Low compact plants of
tropical America, once popular for summer bedding,
and though now somewhat out-of-fashion, as useful
as ever. Their richly variegated foliage may still be
enjoyed if you are willing to give them the care they
need. They do not tolerate frost, except in Zone 10,
must be kept indoors or in a warm greenhouse during
the winter. Outdoors give them well-drained, un-
fertilized garden soil and full sun; indoors, use Basic
Potting Mixture. Propagate by spring cuttings from
large plants saved from the preceding year or from
bedding plants in late summer. Fill a broad bowl with
cuttings in the fall and grow in water all winter near
a window.

A. amoena (am-*meen*-uh). Usually not over 4 in.
high, this bushy species has small, opposite, lance-
shaped leaves blotched with red and orange. There
are many forms and varieties of this and of the following species that offer a wide choice in size and
leaf coloring.

A. bettzickiana (bet-zik-ee-*ay*-nuh). Low, clustering
plant, growing about 15 in. high, but it may easily be
kept under 6 in. by shearing back. The narrow,
twisted leaves are colored in shades of cream-yellow
and red.

alternate. Referring to the way twigs, branches, or,
especially, leaves have their point of attachment or
emergence at different levels, not opposite one another, on stem or trunk. Technically, one leaf at
each node (joint) of a stem. Compare *opposite* and
whorled.

alternate host. A plant on which a parasite or disease
organism lives during part of its life cycle. For example, the red-cedar is the home (host) of cedar-apple
rust fungus. But during part of the year, the rust may

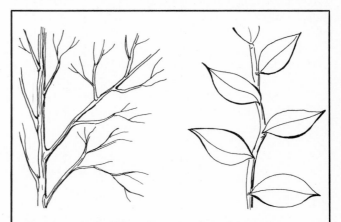

These branches and leaves appear along the stems in an
alternate fashion, one at each node instead of two or more.

attack nearby apple trees, which then become its alternate host. Since the life of a parasite of this type depends on both host plants, the surest way to control it is to separate the hosts widely or to eliminate one of them.

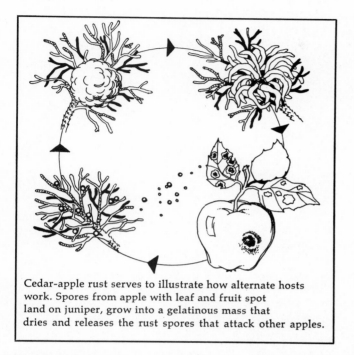

Cedar-apple rust serves to illustrate how alternate hosts work. Spores from apple with leaf and fruit spot land on juniper, grow into a gelatinous mass that dries and releases the rust spores that attack other apples.

alternifolius (al-ter-nif-*foh*-lee-us), **-a, -um.** With alternate leaves.

ALTHAEA (al-*thee*-uh). Hollyhock. Mallow Family (*Malvaceae*). Favorites in old gardens, equally effective in new, hollyhocks give architectural dignity to the simplest planting, with their tall, sturdy spikes of bloom, 3 to 7 ft. high, in summer. There are white and yellow and red flowers in every shade and blend. Flowers may be single or double. Full sun and rich, well-drained garden soil, well turned to a spade's depth. It may be necessary to spray with Aramite or malathion if mites (red spiders) are a problem. In some areas, hollyhocks are much disfigured by rust on the leaves, but even with rust they are still satisfactory and hardy. Spraying new plants with ferbam may prevent rust. Hollyhocks are effective at the back of borders, as a foundation planting and, although all originated in Europe or Asia, in clumps in the wild garden. Propagate by seeds or root division. Zone 4. The shrubby althaea of gardens, incorrectly A. frutex (rose-of-Sharon) is *Hibiscus syriacus*, which see.

A. ficifolia (fye-sif-*foh*-lee-uh). Fig-leaved hollyhock. This biennial, often grown as an annual, grows up to 6 ft. tall, with white, pale yellow or apricot-colored flowers, 2 in. across. Deeply cut leaves. Annual garden strains such as Indian Spring, Triumph

Supreme and Madcap are bred largely from this species.

A. officinalis (off-iss-in-*nay*-liss). Marsh-mallow. A European perennial, naturalized in marshes of the eastern U.S. The pink flowers, 1 in. across, bloom in July and Aug. on stems up to 4 ft. high. An attractive plant for the wild garden or for cultivating in sunny, wet places.

A. rosea (roh-*zee*-uh). Garden hollyhock. This biennial, 5 to 8 ft. tall, is a stately plant, with flowers in many shades of pink to garnet and white to dark yellow. Some varieties have frilled or double flowers, many with white centers. All are handsome. Though strictly biennials, the plants self-sow and may be treated as perennials.

Althaea, shrub. See *Hibiscus syriacus*.

alti-. Prefix meaning tall.

altissimus (al-*tiss*-im-us), **-a, -um.** Tallest, very tall.

altus (*al*-tus), **-a, -um.** Tall.

Aluminum plant. See *Pilea cadierii*.

aluminum sulfate. A compound sometimes used to increase soil acidity but not recommended over sulfur, which, in powdered form, does the same job more cheaply and with less risk of harming plants than aluminum. See also *copperas* and *iron sulfate*.

Alum root. See HEUCHERA.

ALYSSUM (al-*liss*-um). Madwort. Mustard Family (*Cruciferae*). Perennials from Europe and Asia, indispensable in spring for the rock garden, the rock wall or the border edging. Excellent when used with spring bulbs. The abundant white, pale yellow or bright gold clusters of bloom make a fine show in any sunny location with ordinary garden soil, well turned to a spade's depth. Easy propagation by seeds or root division. For other plants suitable for rock gardens see index, Plant Finder section, Volume 16.

The plant known as sweet-alyssum, the annual, is *Lobularia*, which see.

A. alpestre (al-*pest*-ree). Silver madwort. Low-growing plant, 3 to 4 in. high, with silvery-gray leaves and yellow blossoms in small clusters. A source of

OVERLEAF: *Althaea rosea* 'Powderpuff' is the breeder's answer to what a modern hollyhock should be. Available in rose, apricot, lavender, pink, white or yellow. Although perennial, early-started seeds may bloom first year. They are most effective massed at the back of the flower border.

bright color in the rock garden in early summer, when color is much needed. Zone 4.

A. argenteum: *A. murale.*

A. condensatum (con-den-*say*-tum). A Syrian alyssum growing to 5 in. and with limp, trailing stems. Leaves small, silver, hairy. Flowers yellow, in late spring. Best grown in the rock garden or the dry wall. Zone 5.

A. idaeum (ee-*dee*-um). From Crete, this requires a rocky pocket or dry wall position. Stems short, rising, with creamy white to pale yellow flower heads to 5 in. Leaves very small, downy gray. Zone 6.

A. moellendorfianum (moel-en-dorf-ee-*ay*-num). MoELLENDORF ALYSSUM. An early spring blooming species from the Balkans. Cushionlike plant with limp stems; requires rocky bed or dry wall position. The tight heads of small yellow flowers stand 6 in. above the mat of small, silvery-fuzzy leaves. Zone 5.

A. montanum (mon-*tay*-num). Fragrant, gray-leaved, low-growing plant with yellow flowers in late spring. Carpetlike habit, 6 to 8 in. high.

A. murale (mew-*ray*-lee). YELLOW-TUFT ALYSSUM. About 12 in. high, with dark yellow flowers in clusters above leaves that are silvery white underneath. Blooms all summer, from early May.

A. saxatile: See *Aurinia saxatilis.*

A. serpyllifolium (sir-*pile*-if-*fohl*-ee-um). A subshrub, often with bushy, upright shoots to 12 in., though sometimes spreading. From the Pyrenees and southward. Pale yellow flowers on flattish heads, late spring through midsummer. Leaves with fine silver or white pubescence on both surfaces. Zone 4.

A. spinosum (spye-*noh*-sum). SPINY ALYSSUM. A cushion-form, shrubby sort from southwest Europe, to 3 ft. though usually much less. With showy, silverwhite, ribbonlike leaves. White flowers (fragrant) in tight heads, spring through summer. The variety *roseum* (roh-*zee*-um) is much smaller, with purplish flowers that fade to pink. Zone 6.

Rock garden specialists also cultivate *A. atlanticum, A. bertolonii, A. paetreum, A. pyrenaicum, A. repens, A. scandicum, A. tortuosum* and *A. wulfenianum.*

Alwoodii Pink. A hybrid group of dianthus pinks created by Montague Allwood of England who crossed *D. plumarius* with *D. caryophyllus* to obtain *D. x allwoodii,* which see.

UPPER LEFT: *Amaranthus caudatus* is called love-lies-bleeding and the tassel flower. It makes a showy subject for the border. LOWER LEFT: *Amaranthus tricolor,* cultivar 'Molten Fire,' has dark maroon leaves and bright pink bracts. RIGHT: *Amaranthus tricolor,* in another form, showing the three colors from which it derives its name. Amaranthus grows well outdoors in full sun or in pots indoors. Poor soil improves the foliage color.

amabilis (am-*mab*-il-iss), **-e.** Lovely.

Amaranth. See AMARANTHUS.

Amaranthaceae. See Amaranth Family.

Amaranth Family (*Amaranthaceae*). Many genera, some weedy and some very ornamental, comprise this family of plants found in all parts of the world. Alternate or opposite leaves (often highly colored) and small flowers, showy when massed. *Alternanthera, Amaranthus, Celosia, Gomphrena* and *Iresine* are the genera included in this encyclopedia. *Alternanthera* and *Amaranthus* are in this volume.

Amaranth, globe. See *Gomphrena globosa.*

AMARANTHUS (am-ar-*ranth*-us). AMARANTH. Amaranth Family (*Amaranthaceae*). A large genus of coarse, weedy annuals native to many parts of the world. Pigweed is a member of this family. There are a few species, however, that deserve a place in the garden. Alternate leaves, sometimes riotously colored in cultivated forms. Showy clusters of small flowers bloom in summer. Outdoors, full sun and a relatively poor but cultivated soil are needed to maintain the variegated colors of the leaves. These plants may also be grown indoors in home or greenhouse, where they

need plenty of sun and Basic Potting Mixture. Propagate by seeds.

A. caudatus (kaw-*day*-tus). LOVE-LIES-BLEEDING. TASSEL-FLOWER. Grows 3 to 5 ft. high, with white, pink or red flowers and colored leaves. Transplants easily when small. A showy plant for the border. The long, slender, drooping spikes of bloom are excellent for cutting, to use fresh or dried.

A. hybridus (*hib*-rid-us). This is a common weed of the tropics, but it is often grown elsewhere as an annual in the attractive variety *hypochondriacus* (hye-poh-kon-*dry*-ak-us). Called prince's-feather, this plant grows about 4 to 5 ft. high and bears upright spikes of crimson flowers.

A. tricolor (*trye*-kol-or). JOSEPH'S-COAT. A native of China and India, this species is a dramatic foliage plant. The greenish leaves are spotted with patches of red, violet and yellow. Growing 1 to 4 ft. high, it is assertive but sometimes useful at the back of borders and in formal beds. Seedsmen offer cultivars of this under such names as A. *salicifolius,* 'Aurora,' 'Early Splendor,' 'Molten Fire,' 'Joseph's Coat' and others.

Amarcrinum howardii. See *Crinodonna howardii.*

amari-. Prefix meaning bitter.

Amaryllidaceae. See Amaryllis Family.

AMARYLLIS (am-ar-*rill*-iss). NAKED LADS. NAKED LADIES. Amaryllis Family (*Amaryllidaceae*). A genus with the single species below. It is a large, bulbous plant from S. Africa, closely related to and confused with *Hippeastrum.* The pinkish, lilylike flowers appear in the summer. It is grown indoors or out like *Hippeastrum.* Zone 5.

A. belladonna (bel-luh-*don*-nuh). BELLADONNA-LILY. Long strap-shaped blue-green leaves from spring until early summer, followed by fragrant rose-pink flowers, two to four in a cluster, usually blooming in late summer on hollow flower stems 1½ to 3 ft. high. This is a variable species with several forms marketed including *elata* (ee-*lay*-tah) with rosy flowers, and *major* (*may*-jor), larger in all its parts.

Amaryllis, blue. See *Griffinia hyacinthina.* For other blue flowers see Plant Finder section, Volume 16.

Amaryllis Family (*Amaryllidaceae*). Mostly tropical, bulbous plants with alternate or basal leaves and lilylike flowers (in most genera). *Agave, Alstroemeria, Amaryllis, Crinodonna, Crinum, Galanthus, Habranthus, Haemanthus, Leucojum, Lycoris, Nerine, Narcissus, Sternbergia* and *Zephyranthes* are among the genera included in this encyclopedia. These are

Amelanchier canadensis is one of the hardiest of the shadbush species and one of the most decorative. It grows wild in forests in cooler regions of the continent and is also offered for sale by garden centers.

represented by the American Plant Life Society, an organization specializing in amaryllids and other plants. It publishes *Plant Life*, devoted to various kinds of plants, and a special *Amaryllis Year Book* edition. The Society sponsors trial gardens in co-operation with municipal and state agencies. Other activities include the awards for achievement in its field, the introduction of new plants, and the sponsoring of exhibitions. Dues are $5 per year and should be sent to the Executive Secretary, The American Plant Life Society, Box 150, La Jolla, California, 92037.

Amaryllis hallii. See *Lycoris squamigera*.

Amaryllis vittata. See *Hippeastrum vittatum*.

amateur—Nonprofessional. In horticulture, home gardeners, not florists, nurserymen, professional gardeners or instructors in horticulture.

Amazon-lily. See *Eucharis grandiflora*.

Amberbloom rhododendron. See *Rhododendron flavidum*.

ambiguus (am-*big*-yew-us), **-a, -um.** Uncertain (of origin).

AMELANCHIER (am-el-*lank*-ee-uhr). SHADBUSH. SHADBLOW. SARVICEBERRY. SERVICEBERRY. Rose Family (*Rosaceae*). Deciduous shrubs or small trees, found chiefly in N. America. Alternate, toothed leaves and profuse, airy clusters of white flowers briefly in early spring before the foliage appears. Effective at the edge of woodland or back of large-scale shrub plantings during spring bloom and when the foliage colors in autumn. In no case do they ever acquire a domesticated appearance. Will grow in almost any soil. Gray's *Manual of Botany* recognizes 19 species (some with several varieties); those listed below are most valuable to gardeners. Propagate by seeds, grafts or softwood cuttings. Serviceberry, *Amelanchier alnifolia,* is on the preservation list of Calif. and is protected, that is, is not to be picked or dug up; *canadensis* is protected in Conn., Washington, D.C., Ind. and Ky. Zone 4.

A. alnifolia (al-nif-*foh*-lee-uh). Leaves are obtuse and hairy on the underside. Native from Mich. to Wash.

● **A. canadensis** (kan-ad-*den*-siss). One of the most decorative small shrublike trees of early spring, this species grows to 30 ft. or more. The oblong leaves, 2 in. long, are silvery when young. The nodding clusters of flowers, to 2 in. long, appear before the leaves, filling the early woodlands where they are most effective with airy drifts of white. The small, sweet, dark purple fruits make good jam despite the seeds.

A. florida (*flor*-id-uh). PACIFIC SARVICEBERRY. Grows as a columnar bush, bare below, to 25 ft. Flowers typical. Zone 2.

A. x grandiflora (grand-if-*floh*-ruh). A natural hybrid of *A. canadensis* and *A. laevis*. Shrub or small tree with purplish leaves and flowers larger than those of the parents. There is a rose-colored form, x *grandiflora rubescens*, but the white is generally most effective, especially in casual plantings or the edges of woodlands.

● **A. laevis** (*lee*-viss). Grows to 40 ft., with oval leaves to 3 in. long, purplish when young. Flowers in drooping clusters. Dark purple, juicy fruit. An ornamental tree of more compact form than *A. canadensis* but with no greater charm.

Flowers of *Amelanchier* appear before the leaves in early spring and give this small tree a silvery silhouette. The tree is particularly effective as a naturalized or woodland subject. Small purple fruits are sweet and make good jam. Amelanchier grows in almost any soil.

A. stolonifera (stoh-lon-*nif*-er-uh). June-berry. Thicket-forming shrub to about 6 ft. Makes sprawling patches as it spreads by underground stolons. Sweet, purplish fruits ripen in late summer and make edible jelly. Better in a naturalistic setting.

ament. Botanist's term for what a gardener knows as a catkin, such as is part of the inflorescence of birch.

American aloe. See *Agave americana.*

American alum-root. See *Heuchera americana.*

American arborvitae. See *Thuja occidentalis.*

American beachgrass. See AMMOPHILIA. For other plants suitable for beach culture see index, Plant Finder section, Volume 16.

American beech. See *Fagus grandifolia.*

American bittersweet. See *Celastrus scandens.*

American chestnut. See *Castanea dentata.*

American crab apple. See *Malus coronaria.*

American cranberry. See *Vaccinium macrocarpum.*

American cranberry bush. See *Viburnum trilobum.*

American cyrilla. See *Cyrilla racemiflora.*

American dog violet. See *Viola conspersa.*

American elm. See *Ulmus americana.*

American filbert. See *Corylus americana.*

American ginseng. See *Panax quinquefolium.*

American holly. See *Ilex opaca.*

American hop-hornbeam. See OSTRYA.

American hornbeam. See *Carpinus caroliniana.*

American larch. See *Larix laricina.*

American lotus. See *Nelumbo pentapetalum.*

American maidenhair fern. See *Adiantum pedatum.*

American mulberry. See *Morus rubra.*

American parsley-fern. See *Cryptogramma crispa.*

American pennyroyal. See *Hedeoma pulegioides.*

American plane tree. *Platanus occidentalis.*

American Plant Life Society. This organization popularizes information available about amaryllids and similar plants. It publishes *Plant Life* devoted to amaryllids and a special *Amaryllis Year Book* edition. The Society also sponsors trial gardens in cooperation with many municipal and state run agencies. Other activities with which it has associated members include awards given for achievement in its field, the introduction of new plants, and the sponsorship of plant exhibitions. Dues are $5 per year. Requests for information should be addressed to The American Plant Life Society, Box 150, La Jolla, Calif. 92037.

American red elder. See *Sambucus pubens.*

American senna. See *Cassia marilandica.*

American wood anemone. See *Anemone quinquefolia*.

American yellow-wood. See *Cladrastis lutea*.

amethystinus (am-eth-*ist*-in-us), **-a, -um.** Amethyst- or violet-colored. (Plants are grouped by color in lists in the Plant Finder section, Volume 16.)

AMIANTHIUM (am-ee-*an*-thee-um). FLY POISON. Lily Family (*Liliaceae*). This genus, native to eastern N. America, includes a single species.
A. muscaetoxicum (moos-kee-*tox*-ee-cum). A bulbous plant, leaves and flower spikes resembling *Camassia*, but white flowered. Foliage and scapes tend to be limp. Entire plant is poisonous. Plant bulbs 4 in. deep in sandy soil in the garden. Propagate by division or sow freshly gathered seed immediately. Zone 4.

Ammate. A nonselective weed killer. It is especially recommended for poison ivy and other woody plants but is no longer packaged for home use. See *weeds* for a complete discussion of weeds, their identification and how to control them safely.

AMMOBIUM (am-*moh*-bee-um). Composite Family (*Compositae*). A small genus of tender perennials from Australia, usually treated as annuals. One species is grown principally for the dried flowers used in winter bouquets. Alternate, velvety leaves. Full sun and a sandy soil are needed. Sow seeds outdoors in May or when the ground has warmed up where plants are to stand. Do not transplant. Thin plants to stand 1 ft. apart. For other flowers suitable for drying see Plant Finder index, Volume 16.
A. alatum (al-*lay*-tum). WINGED EVERLASTING. A bushy plant, 2 to 3 ft. high, with prominently winged branches. Needs a long season to come to bloom and should not be pinched back. For best results in dried bouquets, cut the whitish flowers before they are fully opened. Hang upside down in small bunches to dry. The variety *grandiflorum* (gran-di-*floh*-rum) has larger flower heads.

ammonia. A chemical combination of nitrogen and hydrogen. Ammonia gas (NH₃) dissolves in water to form ammonium hydroxide; this, greatly diluted, becomes household ammonia water. Another chemical reaction results in ammonium nitrate, a soluble crystalline material rich in nitrogen and valuable as a fast-acting nitrogenous fertilizer. A similar fertilizer, ammonium sulfate, supplies less nitrogen and gives a slightly acidic reaction.

In round figures, the percentage of nitrogen in some common ammonium fertilizer is:

ammonium nitrate, 33⅓ per cent

monobasic ammonium phosphate, 12 per cent (12-61-0)
dibasic ammonium phosphate, 21 per cent (21-53-0)
ammonium polyphosphate, 16 per cent (16-61-0)
ammonium sulfate, 21 per cent.

ammonium nitrate. A chemical compound, often and importantly used to furnish nitrogen to plants. A slightly acid-forming constituent of fertilizers containing nitrogen and one that is quickly assimilated by plants when in solution. See *fertilizer*.

ammonium sulfate. A chemical compound frequently used to furnish nitrogen to plants. More strongly acid-forming than ammonium nitrate and slower to become available to plants. See *fertilizer*.

AMMOPHILA (am-*moff*-il-uh). Grass Family (*Gramineae*). Perennial grasses, highly valued as ground covers for dry, sandy soil, especially along seacoasts. These sturdy plants will stand any amount of salt spray and spread quickly by means of creeping rootstocks. Conservationists use these to prevent wind erosion of dunes and beaches. Propagate by rootstock division. Zone 5. Other plants suitable for shore culture will be found in the Plant Finder lists located in Volume 16.
A. arenaria (are-en-*nay*-ree-uh). EUROPEAN BEACHGRASS. MARRAM. Tough, wiry grass, growing about 4 ft. high, with leathery leaves to 1 ft. long.
● **A. breviligulata** (brev-il-ig-yew-*lay*-tuh). AMERICAN BEACHGRASS. Found wild along the Atlantic Coast, this species is similar to *A. arenaria*, but slightly larger.

amoenus (am-*meen*-us), **-a, um.** Charming, pleasing.

AMOMUM (am-*moh*-mum). Ginger Family (*Zingiberaceae*). An East Indian genus with a single species.
A. cardamon (*car*-dah-mun). CARDAMON AMOMUM. With tough, fibrous rhizomes that give rise to clustered 8-ft.-high canes furnished along their length with lance-shaped leaves 8 to 12 in. long by 3 in. wide. Tubular, dirty-yellow flowers are followed by nutlike capsules. This plant is aromatic, reminiscent of true cardamon which is *Elettaria cardamomum*. Zone 10.

AMORPHA (am-*morf*-uh). FALSE INDIGO. Pea Family (*Leguminosae*). Deciduous shrubs of N. America that are of some ornamental value during their flowering season and in sunny, dry locations or where winters are harsh. Propagate by seeds, cuttings or layers. These are difficult in cultivation but suitable for the sunny, arid wild garden. They are excellent bee plants. Gray's *Manual of Botany* describes five species which show horticultural value. For other plants suitable for the wild garden, see Wildflowers index, Plant Finder section, Volume 16. Lead plant, *Amorpha canescens*, is on the preservation list of Iowa and is protected, that is, is not to be picked or dug up.

● **A. canescens** (kan-*ness*-senz). LEAD PLANT. Shrub, growing to 4 ft., with grayish or whitish stems, distinctive season-long foliage and pretty purplish flower spikes. The alternate leaves consist of up to 45 leaflets. Dark indigo-blue flowers dusted with orange pollen open in dense spikes up to 6 in. long, blooming in early summer. A more rewarding plant than its individual assets would indicate. Zone 4.

A. fruticosa (fruh-tic-*coh*-sah). BASTARD INDIGO. A leggy coarse shrub to 10 ft. or more. Pinnate foliage dull gray-green, flowers in spikes similar to the above species but duller. Gray's *Manual of Botany* recognizes four natural varieties.

A. nana (*nay*-na). Also, *A. microphylla*. Grows from Minn. to the Rocky Mts. and in spring produces flowers that are purplish in racemes to 6 in. long. Grows about 12 in. high.

AMORPHOPHALLUS (am-mor-foh-*fal*-lus). Arum Family (*Araceae*). A small genus of eerie-looking plants from the South Pacific. These seldom survive in cultivation. The huge (over 100 lb.) fleshy corm produces, first, an almost treelike, green and pink blotched, slick naked petiole bearing a crown of much-divided, umbrella-like leaflets. After this dies down, a monstrous, ill-smelling, callalike inflorescence appears, the spathe extending to 4 ft. or more. Greenhouse specimens are grown from collected corms and usually die after flowering.

A. rivieri: *Hydrosme rivieri*.

A. titanum (tie-*tay*-um). From Borneo, this is the largest of the species. Longwood Gardens, Kennett Square, Pa., has flowered (and lost) this species and Kew Gardens, London, displays a plaster model of the one that once flowered there.

AMPELOPSIS (am-pel-*lop*-siss). Grape Family (*Vitaceae*). Deciduous, tendril-climbing shrubs, native to

UPPER: *Amorphophallus* is a large tropical plant from Asia usually seen only in greenhouse collections. It belongs to a small genus of strange-looking plants with extraordinarily large corms, some over 100 pounds. The spathe of some varieties extends over 4 feet.

LOWER: *Amorpha canescens* is the lead plant, a shrub that is useful for its season-long foliage and pretty purple flower spikes. This species grows wild and is on the preservation list of Iowa.

N. America and Asia. Delicate, finely divided leaves, each leaf usually with three lobes. These vines are vigorous and fast-growing, excellent for covering walls, arbors, fences or trellises, but sometimes hard to restrain. Colorful berries appear in the fall. Any good garden soil in sun or partial shade. Poor foliage may be the result of leaf spot (spray with ferbam or zineb). Sometimes attacked by caterpillars (spray with diazinon or malathion). Propagate by seeds, cuttings or layers.

A. aconitifolia (ak-oh-nye-tif-*foh*-lee-uh). MONKSHOOD VINE. Slender climber with compound, five-parted leaves. Small bluish berries turn orange as they mature. One of the most ornamental species. Zone 4.

A. arborea (ar-*boh*-ree-uh). PEPPER VINE. ARKANSAS TRAVELLER VINE. A fast-growing vine (if left alone, will cover up to 15 ft. the first year). Finely cut large, pinnate leaves and dark purple fruit. The new growth is handsome, rich red. Zone 7 (hardy to 5° but root hardy making rapid spring growth, to Zone 5).

● **A. brevipedunculata** (brev-ip-ed-unk-yew-*lay*-tuh). PORCELAIN VINE. A strong, rampant climber with coarsely toothed leaves to 4 in. across. Especially handsome in the summer and fall with the berries that appear in a striking color range of greens, blues, pinks and purples. Zone 4.

A. humulifolia (hew-mew-lee-*foh*-lee-uh). HOP AMPELOPSIS. A sturdy Chinese species with lobed, grapelike leaves to 4 in. across, whitish underneath. The pale yellow to pale blue fruit is small and not produced as abundantly as on some of the other species. Zone 5.

A. megalophylla (meg-al-*loff*-ih-luh). SPIKENARD AMPELOPSIS. Another Chinese species, this with compound leaves 10 to 25 in. long that are of considerable ornamental value. Blue fruits are sparsely produced. Zone 6.

LEFT: *Ampelopsis* species are among the fastest of the climbing vines and are excellent for covering walls, arbors, fences or trellises. A drawback is that that they sometimes take over. Colorful berries appear in the fall, but the plant is used less than its speedy growth warrants. It is a deciduous vine and offers no winter cover.
RIGHT: *Ampelopsis brevipedunculata* is the porcelain vine, and takes its name from the porcelain-blue color of the fruits borne in the fall. Berries are pea-sized, and change from pale blue to yellow to porcelain-blue, providing an everchanging display that few other vines can offer.

UPPER: *Amsonia tabernaemontana* is a trouble-free perennial native to N. America and easy to grow. This species is the willow amsonia and produces light blue flowers in May. LOWER: A view of the willow amsonia plant. Hardy to Zone 5, it is a useful flower for the perennial border.

A. quinquefolia: *Parthenocissus quinquefolia.*
A. tricuspidata: *Parthenocissus tricuspidata.*

amphibius (am-*fib*-ee-us), **-a, -um.** Amphibious; able to live on land or in water. Plants suitable for water culture will be found in Aquatic Plants, Plant Finder section, Volume 16.

AMPHICARPA (am-fi-*car*-pa). HOG-PEANUT. Pea Family (*Leguminosae*). Low, slender eastern N. American and Asiatic perennials with twining stems clothed with brownish hairs. Leaves pinnately trifoliate, flowers mostly purplish. One species is known in America.

A. bracteata (brak-tee-*ay*-ta). This vine produces pea-like flowers on the aerial stems which mature into thin walled pods with three or four small seeds. At the same time, creeping stems produce flowers with no petals, and these develop, underground, into fleshy pods, each with one large, meaty seed. The Indians used these for food. Propagate by seed or division. Zone 3.

AMPHICOME (am-*fik*-om-ee). Bignonia Family (*Bignoniaceae*). These are tender perennials from the Himalaya Mts., related to and resembling *Incarvillea*, but far more difficult to grow well. These are best pot-grown the year round. The compost is two parts loam, one third part each fine sand, leafmold and decayed manure. Water freely in summer, sparingly autumn and winter. In winter put them in the cool greenhouse, in summer plunge the pots in a shaded bed. Propagate by seeds (sow in spring, 55°) or cuttings of half-ripe shoots in summer. Zone 9.

A. arguta (ar-*gew*-tuh). Rose-red flowers on stems 1 to 3 ft. high in Aug.

A. emodi (*em*-oh-dye). Rose flowers with orange throats on 18-in. stems, Aug. to Oct. This frequently is in the trade as Incarvillea emodi.

amplexi-. Prefix meaning clasping.

amplexicaulis. A botanical term meaning stem-clasping, as when the base of a sessile (no petiole) leaf wraps around the stem.

AMSONIA (am-*soh*-nee-uh). Dogbane Family (*Apocynaceae*). Easily grown perennials with small, funnel-shaped flowers. Native in N. America, the species below are useful in the flower border and as a filler in shrub borders as they thrive in full sun or half-shade. Ordinary garden soil, well turned to a spade's depth. Propagate by seeds, root division in spring, or by stem cuttings in spring or summer. Dogbane, *Amsonia ciliata*, and *tabernaemontana* are on the preservation list of N.C. and are protected, that is, are not to be picked or dug up. It is not protected in states where it grows wild in greater numbers.

A. ciliata (sil-ee-*ay*-tuh). Species 3 to 5 ft. tall with purple-blue flowers found from N.C. to Fla. and in Tex.

A. tabernaemontana (tab-bur-nee-mon-*tay*-nuh). WILLOW AMSONIA. Grows 2½ to 3 ft. high, in partial shade or in full sun. The light blue flowers, ½ to ¾ in. long, in dense terminal clusters, make a fine display in May and June. Zone 5.

Amur honeysuckle. See *Lonicera mackii*.

Amur maple. See *Acer ginnala*.

Amur privet. See *Ligustrum amurense*.

amurensis (am-moor-*ren*-siss), **-e.** From the Amur River region. The Amur forms the northern boundary of Manchuria.

Amygdalus communis. See *Prunus amygdalus*.

ANACAMPSEROS (an-ak-*kamp*-ser-oss). Purslane Family (*Portulaceae*). A genus of slow-growing, greenhouse succulents grown for both their attractive leaves and pretty flowers. Pot up in March in a mixture of two parts loam, and one-third part each old, crushed brick, old, crushed mortar and sand. Grow in a cool window or the cool greenhouse near the glass. A dry atmosphere is desirable. Water sparingly over winter but freely in summer. Propagate by seeds (sow in spring, equal parts crushed brick and sandy loam; warm) or summer cuttings (allow to dry for three days, then stick in fine, damp sand). Zone 10.

ANACAMPSEROS SPECIES IN CULTIVATION		
SPECIES	FLOWER	HEIGHT
A. albissima	White, in clusters, midsummer	9 in.
A. arachnoides	Pink, in early summer	12–18 in.
A. filamentosa	Pink, in late summer	9–12 in.
A. lanceolata	Reddish, poor, in midsummer	12 in.
A. papyracea	Yellow, in clusters, summer	10–12 in.
A. telephiastrum	Pink, in midsummer	12 in.
A. tomentosa	Bright red (good), midsummer	6–12 in.

Anacardiaceae. See Cashew Family.

ANACARDIUM (an-ak-*kard*-ee-um). Cashew Family (*Anacardiaceae*). One species, yielding the edible cashew; another, with no commercial application, sometimes is grown as an ornamental in hot, dry, tropical regions. These gnarled, semi-evergreen trees originate on the arid "*tabolerios*" of eastern Brazil. Leaves are large, to 10 in., subject to wind scald. Flowers are small, pinkish or white, in terminal clusters, neither showy nor persistent. The oil from the plants, particularly from the fruit, causes dermatitis resembling a poison-ivy rash. Propagate by seed or soft-wood cuttings. Zone 10.

A. occidentale (ok-sid-en-*tay*-lee). CASHEW. Mostly grown in India, which exports great quantities (the U.S. imports more than 25 thousand tons of cashews

Anacharis canadensis, or elodea, is an excellent aquarium oxygenator. Usually sold in bunches of cuttings without roots. Submerge in water with lower inch or two of stems in sand. Sometimes weedy in outdoor ponds.

annually). The curved seed or "cashew-nut" is borne at the end of a pearlike swollen receptacle. In Brazil natives eat the "pear" raw or ferment it to make caju wine, esteemed throughout Brazil. The raw cashew is astringent but becomes edible when roasted. The cashew tree tolerates no frost and is damaged by chill.

A. excelsum (ex-*sel*-sum). Growing to 30 ft. or more in tropical U.S., this species presents a gnarled, wind-swept appearance but actually suffers from continuous, drying wind. Useful for planting on dry, sandy soil where rainfall is scanty.

ANACHARIS (an-*nak*-ar-iss). Frogs-bit Family (*Hydrocharitaceae*). Aquatic perennials with soft, leafy stems and tiny flowers. Native to N. America, they are widely naturalized in Europe and often become pests if allowed to spread. Useful only in an aquarium or a pool where their graceful, feathery foliage is an attractive addition. Propagate by cuttings.

A. canadensis (kan-ad-*den*-siss). WATER-WEED. Sometimes listed in catalogs as Elodea canadensis. The tiny leaves, 1/4 to 1/2 in. long and barely 1/12 in. wide, are densely crowded on the stems, which may be as much as 3 ft. long if the water is deep enough. A common aquarium plant, usually sold in rootless bunches. Zone 4.

ANACYCLUS (an-ass-*sye*-klus). MOUNT ATLAS DAISY. Daisy Family (*Compositae*). Hardy rock-garden plants from the Atlas Mts. of N. Africa. These require a deep, gravelly, alkaline soil, ample drainage and full sun. Where winters are severe protect after first frost with loose evergreen boughs. Propagate by spring-sown seed. Zone 6.

A. atlanticus (at-*lan*-tik-us). Prostrate, daisylike white blossoms on a flat rosette of gray-green leaves. Flowers are 1 1/2 to 2 in. across, white petals are sometimes red below, appearing in early summer. From Morocco.

A. depressus (dee-*press*-us). Very similar to the above species; reverse of petals crimson. N. Africa.

ANAGALLIS (an-ag-*gal*-liss). PIMPERNEL. Primrose Family (*Primulaceae*). Small annuals and perennials from Europe and Asia. Opposite or whorled leaves and small colorful flowers in shades of red, blue and white. They tend to be weedy and must be controlled. Useful in rock gardens or as edgings for borders. Light, well-drained soil and full sun are needed. Propagate by seeds, division, or cuttings.

A. arvensis (arr-*ven*-siss). A small spreading annual with scarlet or occasionally white flowers usually borne singly and blooming in summer. Likely to become weedy, but good on walls in warm, sunny positions.

A. grandiflora: *A. linifolia.*

A. linifolia (lye-nif-*foh*-lee-uh). Often listed in catalogs as A. grandiflora. A perennial usually grown as an annual. Narrow, lance-shaped, linear leaves to 1 in. long and blue flowers tinged with red. Blooms in June. There are many varieties. Zone 5.

A. tenella (ten-*nell*-uh). BOG PIMPERNEL. Annual, native to western Europe and the Mediterranean. To 6 in. with 1/2 in. leaves and red flowers on longer stems than *A. arvensis.*

ANANAS (an-*nan*-ass). Bromelia Family (*Bromeliaceae*). The only recognized species is the common pineapple, which can be grown in the southernmost regions of continental U.S. (Zone 10), in any good, well-drained soil. Propagate by suckers, or by cutting off the rosette of leaves with a thin slice of fruit which, after drying 24 hrs., is placed on slightly damp sand. Grows indoors in sun.

A. comosus (kom-*moh*-sus). PINEAPPLE. A principal crop of Hawaii. The flowering stalk grows from 2 to 4 ft. high, with sword-shaped leaves in basal rosettes to 3 ft. long. *A. c. variegatus* (var-ee-eg-*gay*-tus), with striped leaves, is the only variety grown for ornament. Today Fla.-grown plants, standard, variegated and, especially, a dwarf form are marketed in the North with small fruits ready to mature. Keep

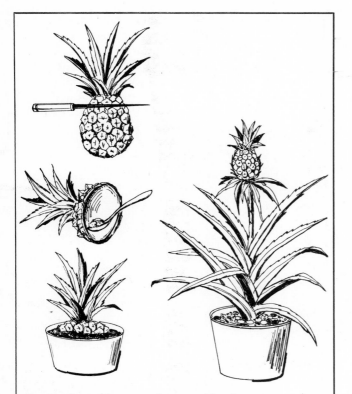

ABOVE: *Ananas comosus*, the pineapple of commerce, may be propagated by rooting the leaf rosette that forms on the mature fruit. Slice off the top; scrape away the fruit; air-dry 24 hours. Plant in a pot of soil. Keep barely moist until top growth indicates the new plant has rooted. Fruiting will occur in about 18 months to 2 years. BELOW: *A. c. variegatus*.

the plant indoors until quite warm; grow in a sunny window, water to maintain damp soil and apply dilute house plant fertilizer solution each month.

ANAPHALIS (an-*naff*-al-iss). Composite Family (*Compositae*). Gray-white, fuzzy-leaved perennials, valued for dried arrangements. They are also good in the hot, dry border of the sunny wild garden. Any soil and full sun. Propagate by seeds or root division.
A. margaritacea (mar-gar-it-*tay*-see-uh). PEARLY EVER-LASTING. CAD-WEED. RABBIT-TOBACCO. Found in all North Temperate regions, this species has tiny white flowers, ¼ in. across, closely packed in small heads and blooming from mid-spring to early summer. Grows 2 to 3 ft. high. Ky. and Ozark-region people smoke the dried leaves for asthma. Zone 3.
A. nubegina (noo-bay-*geen*-uh). This species comes from Tibet and usually grows no taller than 10 in. high. It is a perennial that blooms late in the summer and has lance-shaped leaves that are ½ in. wide and quite woolly. The flower heads are off-white and bunched together on their stalks. Zone 2.

ANASTATICA (ann-a-*stat*-ih-cuh). Mustard Family (*Cruciferae*). One species of this eastern Mediterranean genus is sometimes cultivated. It grows in ordinary garden soil as a half-hardy annual. Sow seed in place in early spring or start in flats.

Anaphalis nubegina is cultivated for heads of whitish flowers which may be cut just before or at the time they are fully open and air-dried for winter bouquets.

LEFT: *Anastatica hierochuntica*, is called resurrection plant because its dried leaves appear to live again when moistened. RIGHT: *Anchusa* in bright blue bloom. Plants are easy to grow and very effective in large masses.

A. hierochuntica (he-ro-*chun*-ti-ca). ROSE-OF-JERICHO. RESURRECTION PLANT (though this term is properly reserved for *Selaginella lepidophylla*). With a tap root, and a rosette of somewhat leathery, finely divided leaves, this resembles many other mustards. The small, greenish-white flowers on 12-in. stems in summer are not showy. When soil is moist, leaves lie out flat; during drought, they become brownish and roll inward, forming a ball; with renewed soil moisture, these resume a normal aspect and growth continues. When the rosettes are gathered, dry, they continue to respond to dampness and drought much like the living plants, though they actually are quite dead.

anceps (*an*-seps). Two-headed or two-edged.

Anchor plant. See *Colletia cruciata*.

ANCHUSA (an-*kew*-suh). ALKANET. BUGLOSS. Borage Family (*Boraginaceae*). Annuals, biennials and perennials mostly from Europe, some found escaped from cultivation and naturalized in eastern N. America. Plants are coarse, usually with hairy leaves and stems. Showy clusters of shallow funnel-shaped flowers, usually a fine, clear blue. These sturdy plants are most effective when planted in large groups. Easily grown in ordinary garden soil and full sun. Propagate by seeds or root division.

● **A. azurea** (az-*yew*-ree-uh). ITALIAN ALKANET. ITALIAN BUGLOSS. Sometimes listed in catalogs as A. italica. A tall perennial, 3 to 5 ft. high. The cultivar 'Dropmore' has brilliant blue flowers in large clusters. Other cultivars are 'Pride of Doves' and 'Opal.' The blooming season begins in June and may be extended into early autumn by cutting faded sprays. Zone 3.
A. barrelieri (bar-el-*yeer*-eye). Perennial to 2 ft., with lovely, small blue flowers, forget-me-not-like in appearance, with yellow or white eyes. Blooms in May and June. Fine with bulbs in the border. Zone 3.
A. caespitosa (seess-pit-*toh*-suh). TUFTED ALKANET. An almost flat little plant from Crete for the rock garden. Blooms May to July, with a few small blue flowers above the strap-shaped, fuzzy little leaves. Zone 5.
A. capensis (kap-*pen*-siss). A tender biennial from S. Africa that self-sows and therefore, once established, often proves permanent and hardy. The small blue flowers, with red edges and white centers, bloom from late May into midsummer. Makes an attractive pot plant indoors. There is an all-white variety. Sow the cultivar 'Blue Bird' when tulips bloom for late summer blossoms. Zone 7.
A. italica: *A. azurea*.
A. myosotidiflora: *Brunnera macrophylla*.
A. officinalis (off-iss-in-*nay*-liss). Biennial or perennial, depending on climate. Grows 2 ft. high, with sprays of tiny blue, purple or pink flowers. Zone 6.

ANCISTROCACTUS (ann-*sis*-tro-*cac*-tus). Cactus Family (*Cactaceae*). Small, slightly ribbed, very spiny globe-shaped or cylindrical cacti from Tex. and Mexico. Small flowers occur at the apex of the plant in summer. These were, until recently, classified as *Echinocactus* species (which see); cultivation is the same.
A. megarhizus (meg-ar-*rye*-zus). Flowers pale yellow.
A. scheeri (*shear*-ee). Flowers greenish yellow.

androgynus (an-*drog*-in-us), **-a, -um.** Having both staminate (male) and pistillate (female) flowers in one cluster. Hence, perfect-flowered.

ANCISTROCHILUS (ann-sis-*trock*-ih-lus). Orchid Family (*Orchidaceae*). Seldom encountered, small epiphytic orchids from the west African rain forests. Grow these in the warm, humid orchid house in pans near the glass. The potting mixture is equal parts chopped (fine) osmunda, tufts of sphagnum, crushed crocks and chipped charcoal. Propagate by division. Zone 10.
A. rothschildianus (roth-*shild*-ee-*ay*-nus). Spikes of two to four 3-in. flowers, white, flushed rose with greenish-brown lip mottled purple. Winter.
A. thomsonianum (tom-*sohn*-ee-*ay*-num). Arching spike with few 2-in. blossoms, white with green lip marked purple. Late fall.

Andorra juniper. See *Juniperus horizontalis plumosa.*

ANDROMEDA (an-*drom*-ed-uh). Heath Family (*Ericaceae*). A small genus of hardy, low-growing, evergreen shrubs of northern N. America. Useful in the bog garden or in specially prepared places in the rock garden. They need peaty, moist soil. Propagate by seeds, division or layering.
A. glaucophylla (glaw-koh-*fill*-uh). DOWNY ANDROMEDA. A bog plant to 1 ft., with evergreen leaves, narrow edges rolled under. Globe-shaped white flowers in drooping clusters of five or six at the tips of branches. Zone 2 (hardy to −50° but intolerant of hot summer weather).
● **A. polifolia** (pol-if-*foh*-lee-uh). BOG-ROSEMARY. The most familiar species, this pleasant little shrub grows only to 1 ft., with creeping rootstocks. Very narrow convex leaves, to 1½ in. long, downy and bluish beneath. Small, pink, urn-shaped flowers in nodding clusters bloom in May and June. Good only in moist, sharply acid ground. Zone 2 (hardy to −50° but intolerant of hot summer weather).
Several other ericacious species are commonly called andromeda. See *Cassiope, Leucothoe* and *Pieris.*

ANDROSACE (an-*dross*-ass-ee). ROCK-JASMINE. Primrose Family (*Primulaceae*). Attractive rock-garden

Androsace helvetica belongs to the Primrose Family and is called rock-jasmine. The plants are small and many species, as this one, form tiny cushionlike clumps that are suited to the rock garden. They grow best in gritty soil.

plants, widely distributed in North Temperate Zones, these annuals and perennials require plenty of moisture and very good drainage. Do not let them dry out. Many species are grown by experienced rock gardeners and fanciers of rock plants, but the ones below are generally preferred. These grow best in sandy or gritty soil with plenty of stone chips, in a location that is shaded part of the day where summers are hot. All are difficult where summer temperatures exceed 90°. Propagate by seeds, division or cuttings.

For rock-garden enthusiasts the cushion-forming androsaces offer a great challenge. Though all of these require a stone chip bed (or a crevice in larger stones) some want an acid gravel root run, others require neutral to limy gritty soil below the chip layer. Among the most attractive of tiny cushion-forming species are *A. alpina, A. helvetica, A. hirtella, A. imbricata, A. jacquemontii* and *A. pyrenaica.* These are not for the beginning gardener. The species listed in the table below, however, are suitable for amateur rock gardening. Other plants suitable for the rock garden will be found in the Plant Finder section, Volume 16. In the table of *Androsace* species recommended for the amateur, which follows on page 132, are seven species which have proven reasonably amenable to culture outside their native aeries. They may be grown in a rock-garden scree, or in clay flowerpots in the alpine house or sun-heated pit.

ANDROSACE SPECIES RECOMMENDED FOR THE AMATEUR

NAME	PLANT FORM	FLOWERS	SOURCE	SOIL	RANGE
A. carnea	Small rosette.	Loose umbel of white to pink flowers on naked 4 in. scape.	Europe	Rock garden gritty, moist pocket, neutral to slightly acid.	Zone 5.
A. chamaejasme	Small, fuzzy rosette.	Loose, airy umbel of tiny white to pink flowers on 3 in. naked scape.	Europe, Asia, N. America (Alpine)	Cool, gritty pocket, always damp below.	Zone 5, intolerant of summer heat.
A. foliosa	Loose cluster of 1½ in. long leaves at base of stem.	Pink flowers with rose centers in an open spray on 5 in. stem.	Himalaya Mts.	Coarse stony layer overlying gritty, neutral soil.	Zone 6.
A. lanuginosa	Mat-forming creeper with small silver-haired leaves.	Small, bright rose-red flowers on 2 in. naked scapes in late spring.	Himalaya Mts.	Gritty rock-garden soil overlaid with stone chips.	Zone 6.
A. sarmentosa	Small, hairy rosettes.	Showy rose-pink flowers in open umbels on 6 to 8 in.-high naked scapes.	Himalaya Mts.	Gritty rock-garden pocket, neutral, damp.	Zone 3.
A. sempervivoides	Very small, tight rosettes of shiny leaves.	Pink blossoms, very small, in clusters in 2–4 in. naked scapes.	Himalaya Mts.	Deep, gravelly soil with some peat.	Zone 5. This species tolerates some shade.
A. villosa	Rosettes of hairy, silvery leaves.	Showy little flowers in open umbels, white on a sturdy 3 in. scape.	Europe, Asia (Alpine)	Deep gravelly soil, damp beneath and overlaid with stone chips.	Zone 4. Intolerant of hot summer weather.

-andrus. Suffix meaning stamen.

ANEIMIA (ann-a-*ee*-mee-ah). A genus in a family of tropical ferns (*Schizaeaceae*). From Central and S. America and the Caribbean Islands, these ferns are seldom encountered outside botanic garden collections or on tropical estates. Some do best with a winter night temperature of 70°, others thrive at 55° to 60°. All require high humidity and frequent syringing of foliage. Pot up in late winter, equal parts loam, peat, leafmold, sand and charcoal. Water freely spring and summer, moderately other times. Propagate by spores or division. Zone 10.

High-temperature species include: *A. adiantifolia*, 1 to 1½ ft., tropical America; *A. collina*, 8 to 12 in., Brazil; *A. dregeana*, 9 to 12 in., Natal; *A. rotundifolia*, 6 to 9 in., Brazil.

Warm-temperature species include: *A. phyllitidis*, 1 ft., Cuba, Peru; *A. tomentosa*, 1 to 2 ft., Central America. The latter also is known as A. chelianthoides, A. deltoides and A. flexuosa.

ANEMONE (an-*nem*-on-ee). WINDFLOWER. Buttercup Family (*Ranunculaceae*). A large genus of perennials, many of them rhizomatous or tuberous rooted. Some are among our loveliest and most delicate native spring woods flowers. Others, native in Europe or Asia, bloom in summer and autumn. Enormously varied in size, form and flowering characteristics, they are valuable in borders, rock gardens, the wild garden and the cutting garden. All like rich, well-drained soil, plenty of moisture and partial shade. *All portions of these plants usually are quite poisonous.* Propagate by seeds sown when ripe in the fall or by offsets.

Pasque-flower, *Anemone patens* var. *wolfgangiana*, was declared the official flower of S. Dak. in 1903; is on the preservation lists of Washington, D.C., and Iowa and is protected, that is, is not to be picked or dug up; *Pulsatilla hirsutissima* is protected in N. Mex.

A. alpina (al-*pye*-nuh). ALPINE ANEMONE. From high in European mountains, this windflower grows to 18 in. under ideal conditions. The slightly cupped, 1- to 1½-in. white flowers stand above ferny leaves.

A. apennina (ap-pen-*nye*-nuh). ITALIAN WINDFLOWER. A tiny plant from Italy, 4 to 9 in. high. Dark green leaves and sky-blue flowers, with various pink and white cultivars, 1½ in. across, blooming in early spring. For shady places. Zone 6.

A. baldensis (ball-*den*-sis). MORAINE WINDFLOWER. A 6-in.-high species from Alpine altitudes in Europe, this grows from tuberous roots. With dark green, ferny foliage and pink-tinged white blossoms, this belongs in an always moist pocket of the rock garden where soil is gravelly, rich in organic matter and slightly acid. Zone 6.

● **A. blanda** (*bland*-uh). GREEK ANEMONE. A delicate little plant from Greece and Asia Minor. Grows about 4 to 8 in. high, with deeply divided leaves and star-shaped, bright blue flowers with many narrow petals. It blooms in early spring, after which the leaves disappear. An excellent rock-garden plant. Should have full sun, but since its growing season is so early, it may be grown under deciduous trees. White and pink varieties are marketed, as are several named cultivars. Zone 6.

A. canadensis (kan-ad-*den*-siss). MEADOW ANEMONE. A showy native American wild flower of the moist, open woodlands. Deeply cut, basal leaves and white flowers, 1 to 2 in. across, in May and June, on plants that grow 1 to 2 ft. high. Useful in the border, the wild garden and under overhanging shrubbery but may be extremely invasive. Zone 3.

A. caroliniana (ka-rol-in-ee-*ay*-nuh). CAROLINA WINDFLOWER. A delicate-appearing little plant of moist woodland areas, with graceful white and purplish flowers, 1 in. across, blooming in April and May. Not particularly showy except in large plantings. Best in the wild garden or as specimens in a glady cranny of the rock garden. Zone 5.

● **A. coronaria** (kor-oh-*nay*-ree-uh). POPPY-FLOWERED ANEMONE. This lovely European plant, about 1½ ft. high, can be grown outdoors in the warmer sections of Calif. and Fla. Elsewhere it is satisfactory greenhouse pot plant. The ruffled blooms range in color from white to red, blue and purple. 'St. Brigid' and 'De Caen' are the varieties usually grown. Sometimes recommended as house plants, these do not tolerate the heat and dry air of modern homes. There are both single and double forms. Zone 8.

Poppy anemones are grown in countless numbers both here and in Europe for the cut-flower trade, yet

UPPER: Anemones aren't all like the intensely colored flowers bought at the florist shop. There are many species having different forms and colors. This one, *Anemone alpina sulphurea*, is the mountain anemone and prefers rocky soils and heights.
LOWER: This is the Greek anemone, *Anemone blanda*. It blooms in early spring and looks very much like a small daisy.

we seldom think of cultivating them at home. The green-ruffed flowers in vivid hues of blue, pink, purple and red, also in creamy white, come from hybrid strains known as 'De Caen' and 'St. Brigid.'

Outdoors these anemones need a partially shaded to sunny situation where the soil has been enriched with sand and leafmold. In the Deep South, plant the tubers in autumn or early winter; in colder regions where severe freezing occurs, plant out in early spring. Position the corms 4 to 6 in. apart, and cover with 2 to 3 in. of soil. Avoid extremely wet soil until growth is active.

To grow anemones indoors, you will need a sunny place where nighttime temperatures can be kept on the cool side, preferably around 55°. Pot the corms in Sept. or Oct., 1 in. deep and about 2 in. apart, using a mixture of equal parts garden loam, peat moss and sand. Set the pots in a dark, cool place and keep moist, but not wet, until growth starts. Then transfer to a sunny place, and water freely as the plants grow. At this time begin feeding every two weeks with a liquid house-plant fertilizer. Watch the leaves for signs of green aphids; if detected, spray carefully.

Anemones are ideal subjects for a home green-

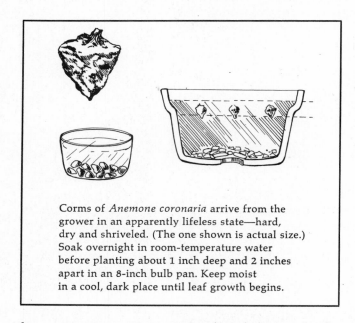

Corms of *Anemone coronaria* arrive from the grower in an apparently lifeless state—hard, dry and shriveled. (The one shown is actual size.) Soak overnight in room-temperature water before planting about 1 inch deep and 2 inches apart in an 8-inch bulb pan. Keep moist in a cool, dark place until leaf growth begins.

house or sunny, airy sunroom, but they can also be grown successfully in a bright but cool window garden. Tecolote hybrid *Ranunculus* (buttercups) require the same culture.

A. deltoidea (del-*toy*-dee-uh). Species grown from Wash. to Calif. To 1 ft. tall with a single white flower.

A. demissa (dee-*miss*-uh). From eastern Asia, a rock-garden species, difficult to keep. With ferny foliage to 6 in., the slightly cupped white flowers are borne on 9-in. stems in early to midsummer. Zone 6.

A. fulgens (*full*-jenz). Scarlet windflower. From France, this tuberous-rooted species grows about 1 ft. high, with divided leaves rather like those of a buttercup. Brilliant scarlet flowers, up to 2½ in. across, with a black center, bloom in early summer and forces easily in the greenhouse as tulips. This species needs full sun. Zone 5.

A. glaucifolia (glaw-sif-*foh*-lee-uh). From China and Tibet, a variable, summer-blooming species. Forms a buttercup-like clump and bears slightly cupped lavender-blue flowers sparingly 1 to 3 ft. high. Zone 6.

A. halleri (*hall*-er-ee). Haller's anemone. An alpine European species with a tap root. Presents a 6 in.-high mound of finely divided, soft foliage with silky hairs. The cupped, 1½ in. lavender flowers stand above the foliage in early spring. This species requires a rock-garden site, full sun and alkaline soil. Zone 5.

A. hortensis (hor-*ten*-siss). Garden anemone. A native species of southern Europe despite the species name that indicates garden origin. Flowers white, and in all shades of red, pink and purple, all with brownish stamens. Cup-shaped blossoms to 3 in. across open in mid-spring. Much used by florists; often forced in the cool greenhouse for cut flowers. Zone 5.

A. hupehensis (hoo-pay-*en*-siss). Dwarf japanese anemone. This species, 1½ to 2 ft. high, has pale pink flowers in late summer. *A. h. japonica*, Japanese anemone, often listed as A. japonica, blooms up to a month later, is somewhat taller and has more varied coloring. Most of the varieties known as Japanese anemones fall into this sizable group. The handsome plants grow 2 to 4 ft. tall and have large flowers from pure white through many pink and rose shades to dark red. They begin blooming in Aug. and make a fine display in the fall border along with chrysanthemums and asters. Plants may take two years to establish, but are well worth the effort and occasional loss. Protection from north winds and a winter covering of salt marsh hay, pine needles, or excelsior are needed. The blossoms are attractive for cutting. The variety *alba* (*al*-buh) is white-flowered. Good cultivars include: 'Alice,' rosy-carmine; 'September Charm,' pale semidouble pink, 'Queen Charlotte,' darker semidouble pink and 'Whirlwind,' semidouble white.

A. japonica: *A. hupehensis japonica.*

A. narcissiflora (nar-sis-ih-*floh*-ruh). Narcissus windflower. Among the most beautiful and most difficult to grow anemones, this is worth considerable effort. Fresh seed offers the best chance of getting good plants. This is late spring-blooming, white, pale pink, rarely pale yellow, to 1 ft., with coarsely ferny foliage. From the European mountains. Zone 6.

● **A. nemorosa** (nem-or-*roh*-suh). European wood

ABOVE: *Anemone coronaria*,
poppy-flowered anemone,
succeeds in warm sections of the
South or in a greenhouse.
UPPER RIGHT: *Anemone pulsatilla*
grows to 12 inches.
UPPER CENTER: Dwarf Japanese
anemone. LOWER
RIGHT: Narcissus windflower
is pretty and difficult to grow.
LOWER LEFT: European wood
anemone is similar to species
that grow wild in America.

Anemone hupehensis variety *japonica*, the Japanese anemone, grows 2 to 4 feet tall and begins to bloom in August. It makes a handsome display in the fall border. Hardier than others of this species.

ANEMONE. Grows to 6 in., with single, white or purplish-tinged flowers, blooming in April and May. This species is similar to our native wood anemone (*A. quinquefolia*), and is a good plant for an acid-soil pocket in the rock garden or the wild garden. Natural varieties and several cultivars include single- and double-flowering plants in various colors. Zone 3.

A. patens (*pay*-tenz). SPREADING PASQUE-FLOWER. Grows 3 to 6 ft. tall, with hairy leaves and stems. Flowers are blue to violet. The variety *wolfgangiana* was declared the official flower of S. Dak. in 1903.

● **A. pulsatilla** (pul-sat-*till*-uh). EUROPEAN PASQUE-FLOWER. This European species grows to 1 ft. high; hairy, pinnately divided foliage and with blue, purple or reddish blooms, 1½ to 2½ in. across. Effective in the early spring garden. Many varieties, including white and bicolors, are available. A hairy variety, *hirsutissima*, is protected in N. Mex. Given a protected location, Zone 6.

A. quinquefolia (kwin-kwef-*foh*-lee-uh). AMERICAN WOOD ANEMONE. One of our ornamental native woodland plants, carpeting moist, deciduous woods from

April to June with delicate, white or slightly pink-tinged flowers, ½ in. across. As it grows only to 8 to 10 in., it must be planted in large patches to make an effective show in the wild garden. Zone 4.

A. ranunculoides (ran-un-kew-*loh*-eed-eez). YELLOW WOOD ANEMONE. The tuberous root throws up a cluster of deeply cut leaves with an 8- to 10-in. stem bearing, in early spring, a single, golden-yellow flower about 1 in. across. From Europe and Siberia, this species grows best in woods soil with deciduous tree shade. An excellent carpeting plant for shady areas. Zone 4.

A. sylvestris (sil-*vess*-triss). SNOWDROP WINDFLOWER. From Europe and southwestern Asia. Fragrant, white flowers, 2 in. across, bloom in April and May or June on plants that grow to 1½ ft. Useful in the wild garden, shady border or rock garden. Zone 4.

A. tomentosa (toh-men-*toh*-suh). Sometimes in the trade as A. hupehensis tomentosa or A. japonica tomentosa, this late summer-blooming sort from western China resembles the *A. hupehensis* varieties, with rose-colored flowers on 3 to 5 ft.-high stems. Zone 6.

A. tuberosa (too-ber-*roh*-suh). From Ariz., Nev. and Utah, this tuberous-rooted species, not showy, remains a collector's item for western U.S. wildflower specialists. The small white or purplish flowers rise to 1 ft., blooming in early summer. Zone 6.

A. virginiana (vir-jin-ee-*ay*-nuh). VIRGINIA ANEMONE. Native to much of eastern N. America, this grows in open or lightly shaded, dry, rocky sites. Small nondescript white flowers rise 2 to 4 ft. above the rather harsh compound leaves in midsummer. The plant resembles a white-flowered field buttercup. Zone 4.

A. vitifolia (vye-tif-*foh*-lee-uh). GRAPE-LEAVED WINDFLOWER. A rather tender sort (Zone 7) from northern India and northwestern China, this late summer-blooming species produces 2 in. white flowers on stems 3 to 4 ft. high. The cultivar 'Robustissima,' with silvery-pink flowers on 2 to 3 ft. stems is much hardier, growing to Zone 5.

ANEMONELLA (an-em-on-*nell*-uh). RUE-ANEMONE. Buttercup Family (*Ranunculaceae*). There is only one species, native to eastern N. America, a delicate-appearing perennial with tuberous roots. Good for shady nooks in the rock garden; best in the wild garden. Grows well in a moist, woodsy soil, lightened with sand. Flowers are composed of five to ten petal-like sepals. Propagate by fresh seed or by root division in spring. Rue-anemone, *Anemonella thalictroides*, is on the preservation list of Washington, D.C., Iowa, Md., and R.I. and is protected, that is, is not to be picked or dug up. Zone 4.

A. thalictroides (tha-lik-*troh*-eed-eez). A small perennial, 4 to 10 in. high, found in shady woodlands and useful as a ground cover. White to pink blossoms, to

1 in. across, in a loose terminal cluster early to late spring, growing above low, fernlike leaves. There is a variety with double flowers and one with reddish flowers.

ANEMONOPSIS (uh-nem-moh-*nop*-sis). Buttercup Family (*Ranunculaceae*). A genus of but one species, from Japan. Zone 6.
A. macrophylla (mac-row-*fill*-uh). A hardy, herbaceous perennial for the shaded wild-garden margin. Requires deep, rich loam, ample water during dry spells. Anemonelike blossoms, 2 in. across, purple or lilac, on 2- to 3-ft.-high stems in midsummer. Propagate by seed (spring) or division (fall). Most successful when conditions of its native habitat are reproduced in the garden in which it is planted.

ANEMOPAEGMA (a-*nee*-mo-*peeg*-ma). Bignonia Family (*Bignoniaceae*). *A. chamberlaynii* (*cham*-ber-*lain*-ee-eye) is a tender clambering or vining woody plant for the tropical garden (full sun, deep humus, moist soil) or in the warm greenhouse, large tub, with Basic Potting Mixture with doubled peat. This Brazilian species has petunialike yellow flowers, often striped purple and white in the throat.

anerobic. Living without oxygen; referring to bacteria, for example, that are active under airless conditions, such as the bacteria of putrefaction.

ANETHUM (an-*neeth*-um). Carrot Family (*Umbelliferae*). Annual and biennial herbs, native to Europe but rarely naturalized in N. America. Some are slender plants with delicate, feathery foliage and small, lacy, yellow flowers that develop into seeds, widely used in flavoring. The best-known species is easily grown in the herb garden. Any good garden soil and full sun or partial shade. Sow seeds where plants are wanted and thin to stand 6 in. apart. They do not transplant well.
A. graveolens (grav-*vee*-ol-enz). DILL. Annual, 2 to 3 ft. high, with aromatic, fernlike leaves and small yellow flowers in umbels. The leaves, flowering tops and seeds are used as condiments. Seeds shallowly sown in Basic Potting Mixture, in a 6-in. pot, produce usable foliage and sometimes seeds. Grown in a sunny window, dill often is spindly, but it flourishes in the open sun in a well-tilled garden. Snip ferns as needed for summer salads. Use maturing seed heads to flavor pickles. Or harvest seeds, dry on screens and store in tightly capped bottles. For other herbs see Plant Finder section, Volume 16.

ANGELICA (an-*jell*-ik-uh). Carrot Family (*Umbelliferae*). Tall, handsome, perennial or biennial herbs,

with large, decorative, light green leaves and large clusters (umbels) of small white or greenish flowers on hollow stems. Both seeds and stems are used for flavoring, the stems often candied for decorating pastry. Propagate by seeds sown when fresh, sometimes by division.
● **A. archangelica** (ark-an-*jell*-ik-uh). HOLY GHOST. A native of Europe and Asia, this species is a sturdy biennial, 4 to 6 ft. high, with large, divided leaves at the base of the plant. Celerylike, this aromatic plant with ribbed stems creates a bold effect in the back of borders or in the herb garden, where it is most often grown. Moist, well-drained soil, light shade. The large heads of small flowers bloom in July. Perennial if flowers are removed before they go to seed. Zone 5.
A. atropurpurea (at-roh-per-*pew*-ree-uh). PURPLE-STEM ANGELICA. A native species of east and central N. America. This biennial species closely resembles *A. archangelica* but has dark purple stems and the thrice-compound leaves are dark green with purplish veins and petioles. Flowers in early summer. Zone 4.
A. sylvestris (sill-*vess*-tris). Native to Europe and naturalized in the eastern U.S. in abandoned fields and shady roadsides. This species has relatively slender, round stems and the thin leaflets are sharp-toothed. Produces heads of small white flowers in late summer. May be poisonous. Zone 4.
A. venenosa (ven-en-*oh*-sah). A perennial species very similar to *A. sylvestris* but the slender, round

Harvesting dill: Just before seed heads are completely ripe, cut and air-dry. Shake seeds on plastic sheet; sift to remove foreign matter; seal in glass jars. For fresh dill weed, snip leaves onto cookie sheet; put in freezer; when frozen, store in containers and keep in freezer until needed for seasoning.

stems are minutely fuzzy toward the top. *This plant is extremely poisonous.* Small, greenish white flowers in flat heads to 8 in. across in late summer. Zone 4.

Other, rarely encountered, N. American species are *A. triquinata,* and *A. laurentiana.*

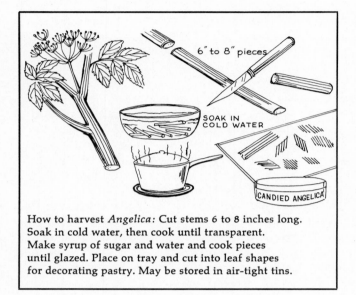

How to harvest *Angelica:* Cut stems 6 to 8 inches long. Soak in cold water, then cook until transparent. Make syrup of sugar and water and cook pieces until glazed. Place on tray and cut into leaf shapes for decorating pastry. May be stored in air-tight tins.

Angelica-tree. See *Aralia chinensis; Aralia elata.*

ANGELONIA (an-jel-*loh*-nee-uh). Figwort Family (*Scrophulariaceae*). Seldom encountered, tender herbaceous perennials from S. America. Grow in a warm greenhouse over winter, in pots outdoors in summer. Pot up in March, Basic Potting Mixture with doubled peat; water freely March to Oct., moderately Oct. to March. Propagate by seed (spring), cuttings of tender shoots (April) or division (March). Zone 10.
A. grandiflora (grand-if-*floh*-ruh). Moderate-sized, mimulus-like lilac flowers on a sparsely branched plant 1½ to 2 ft. high. Blooms in late summer.
A. salicarifolia (sal-ih-car-ih-*fohl*-ee-uh). Similar to the above species, but leaves narrower, flowers blue, in Aug.

Angel's tears. See *Narcissus triandrus.*

Angel's trumpet. See *Datura arborea.*

ANGIOPTERIS (ann-gee-*op*-ter-iss). Tree-fern Family (*Marattiaceae*). From the South Pacific islands, Ceylon and Java, these treelike fern relatives are sometimes encountered in the hot, humid jungle rooms of botanic gardens. They are not manageable in the home or the home greenhouse. Pot up in equal parts loam, peat, leafmold, sand and chipped charcoal in late winter. Deep containers should always stand in shallow (3 in.) water, in shade, no wind or

drafts. Water freely spring and summer, moderately other times. Propagate by offsets. Only Zone 10, but need humid atmosphere. Ferns suitable for indoor culture will be found in Plant Finder section, Volume 16.
A. evecta (ee-*vek*-tah). Coarse trunk 10 to 15 ft. high crowned with palmlike spray of tough, yellowish green fern fronds.
A. teysmanniana (*tays*-man-ee-*ay*-nah). Usually taller than *A. evecta,* the fibrous, dark green fronds reach to more than 6 ft.

angiosperm. A plant that produces seeds inside a closed ovary, which may take the form, for example, of a pod, berry or fleshy fruit. Contrast *gymnosperm.*

anglicus (*an*-glik-us), **-a, -um.** From England.

ANGRAECUM (an-*greek*-um). Orchid Family (*Orchidaceae*). A genus of evergreen, epiphytic (tree-perching) orchids with very beautiful flowers. Mostly from tropical Africa, these plants are characterized by a central stem bearing thick leaves and long sprays of waxy, star-shaped, usually white flowers that have the unusual feature of a very long spur. They need a warm, humid greenhouse and show to best effect in orchid baskets or cribs. Keep them evenly moist and in partial shade. Use fir bark or osmunda fiber mixed with tufts of sphagnum moss and charcoal chips for the potting mixture. Propagate by air layering or by the side shoots that appear at the base of old plants. Recently this genus was revised and much divided; horticulturists still follow the older classification. Zone 10.
A. eburneum (ee-*burn*-ee-um). The leafy stem or stems rise 3 to 4 ft. high with gracefully arching, leathery green leaves to 2 ft. long and 2 in. wide. The fragrant, ivory-white flowers, to 4 in. across, are inverted and bloom neatly in two ranks along the flower stalks. The flowers are long-lived and usually bloom from Dec. to March.
A. sesquipedale (ses-kwip-ed-*day*-lee). This species usually has a single stem about 1½ ft. high. The dark green, wavy-margined leaves are closely arranged in two ranks (distichous) and are up to 1 ft. long and 2 in. wide. Large, star-shaped, white flowers with a long greenish spur to 1 ft. long. In bloom from Nov. to March.

angularis (an-gew-*lay*-riss), **-e.** Angular.

ANGULOA (an-gew-*loh*-uh). CRADLE ORCHID. Orchid Family (*Orchidaceae*). Terrestrial orchids from tropical S. America, with fanlike leaves and grotesque, deep-cupped fragrant flowers that are produced singly on scaly scapes that arise from new growths. When growth begins pot in clay pot with three parts composted sod, one part coarse brown peat chunks or chopped osmunda and ¼ part each sphagnum moss tufts and chipped charcoal. Water freely May to Sept., seldom afterwards, as plant rests. Minimum winter night temperature 60°. Leaves must remain dry at all times, unlike most orchids. Propagate by division.

ANGULOA SPECIES IN CULTIVATION		
SPECIES	FLOWER	SOURCE
A. brevilabris	Twisted, small demitasse shape and size, greenish, blotched dull red; in summer.	Peru
A. cliftonii	Deep, twisted cup-shaped, yellow and gold, splotched crimson-purple; in spring.	Colombia
A. x rolfei	A natural hybrid of two species above, flowers intermediate, variable.	Peru
A. ruckeri	Twisted, tulip-shape, yellow with crimson blotches and speckles; in May; and variety *sanguinea*, crimson blotches larger, darker.	Colombia
A. uniflora	Like a twisted tulip, cream or white, often with pink speckles; in May.	Colombia

angusti-. Prefix meaning narrow.

ANIGOZANTHOS (an-ig-oh-*zanth*-os). Amaryllis Family (*Amaryllidaceae*). Rarely encountered herbaceous perennials from Australia. In March pot up in Basic Potting Mixture with doubled peat. Grow in full sunlight; water freely spring and summer, moderately fall and winter. Hold at barely above 40° in winter, no extra heat spring or fall. Propagate by division of roots in spring. Zone 10.
A. flavidus (*flay*-vid-us). Scarlet flowers in June.
A. manglesii (man-*gless*-ee-eye). Greenish flowers marked red, in July; plant to 3 ft.
A. pulcherrimus (pull-*kehr*-im-us). Flowers yellow and white, in May; plant to 2 ft.
A. rufus (*roof*-us). Flowers purple, in June; plant to 2 ft.

animal injury. See entry for the animal causing damage and the article on Pests and Diseases.

Animated oat. See *Avena sterilis*.

Anise. See *Pimpinella anisum*.

Anise, Chinese. See *Illicium verum*.

Anise, star. See *Illicium verum*.

Aniseed. Fruit of *Pimpinella anisum*, which see.

Anise-tree. Name for many of the *Illicium* species.

Annatto. See *Bixa orellano*.

ANNONA (an-*non*-nuh). Custard-apple Family (*Annonaceae*). Broadleaf evergreen trees and shrubs with fragrant, laurel-like foliage cultivated in the tropics for their edible fruits. Outdoors (Zone 10 only) grow in fertile, sandy soil. Water during dry periods. For the warm conservatory, tub in Basic Potting Mixture with double, fibrous loam. Grow in full sun in winter, part shade in summer, water freely March to Oct., moderately afterwards. Syringe the foliage daily April to Sept. Night temperature in winter is 60°. Propagate by seed (spring) or firm shoots in moist sand under glass (summer). Zone 10.
A. cherimola (care-*im*-oh-luh). CHERIMOYER. Tall shrub or small tree to 18 ft., with brown flowers in Aug. A tropical American species.
A. montana (mon-*tay*-nuh). MOUNTAIN SOURSOP. Yellow flowers in midsummer followed by prickly, kidney-shaped, heavy fruits, 6 to 8 in. long. The juice from the yellowish pulp is used in beverages.
A. muricata (mew-rik-*kay*-tuh). SOURSOP. Small tree or shrub to 30 ft., flowers yellow in midsummer, heavy, pebbled fruit with edible pulp.

Anigozanthos manglesii grows wild in western Australia where it is enjoying great popularity. It may one day be a favorite all over the world. Although usually propagated by division, seeds planted in the spring will bloom in 18 months to 2½ years.

A. palustris (pal-*lust*-riss). ALLIGATOR-APPLE. From tropical America, a tree or shrub to 20 ft., with yellow flowers in summer followed by massive, heavy fruits with rindlike green alligator hide.

A. reticulata (ret-ik-yew-*lay*-tuh). CUSTARD-APPLE. BULLOCK'S-HEART. A spreading tree to 25 ft.; yellowish-green flowers marked brown or purple. Fruits are edible, heart-shaped, 6 in. long, yellow-brown or yellow with russet cheek. The pulp is creamy white, sweet, custardlike, enclosing several beanlike seeds. A garden ornamental in southern Fla.

A. squamosa (skwam-*muh*-suh). SWEETSOP. SUGAR-APPLE. A deciduous, S. American species to 25 ft. with eucalyptus-like leaves and yellowish flowers followed by pine-cone-shaped fruits that are a delicacy. The flavor is unlike that of any other fruit and delicious. The fruit is highly perishable.

Annona Family (*Annonaceae*). A mostly tropical family of shrubs, vines and trees, often with edible fruit, alternate leaves and inconspicuous flowers. The genus *Asimina* contains hardy shrubs or small trees native to N. America.

Annonaceae. See Annona Family.

Annual poppy. See *Papaver caucasium.*

annual ring. The layer of wood formed each year just beneath the bark of a woody plant and retaining distinctive coloration. By counting the number of rings in a stump, you can tell how old the tree was. Thin rings are formed in poor growing seasons, wide rings in good seasons. Some seasons, with alternating wet and dry periods, stimulate the production of two or more rings. Scientists correlate annual ring patterns in several species to establish past rainfall amounts. By matching series of rings in old wood, continuous rainfall records have been established for given areas for more than 3,000 years.

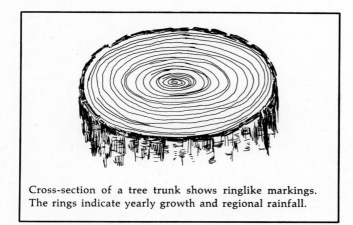

Cross-section of a tree trunk shows ringlike markings. The rings indicate yearly growth and regional rainfall.

Annuals: Flowers for a Season

By GEORGE TALOUMIS

An annual plant completes its life cycle from germination to seed formation within a single year. Following seed formation, the plant, exhausted of energy reserves, dies. Some annual plants complete their life cycles in a remarkably short time; desert species, stimulated by a brief rainy season, germinate, flower and make seed in a few weeks. Horticulturists have, by selection and breeding, extended the blooming period of flowering annuals and, likewise, extended the useful period of annual vegetable crops.

Not every plant that we set in the annual bed is truly an annual. Tender perennial plants are used as annuals for display bedding, for window boxes and in many other ways. Geraniums, lantanas, marguerites, fuchsias, periwinkles, wax begonias—these and more all live for several years in their frost-free native habitats. But, as they bloom quickly from seed or from cutting, we use them as single-season plants, and group them with the annuals.

Some plants that grow from bulbs, corms and tubers also have come to be used as annuals. By its very nature, no "bulbous" plant is a single-season grower. But many of the inexpensive, frost-sensitive sorts sometimes are handled as annuals. Dahlias from seed and from tubers, inexpensive gladioli, tuberoses, montbretias, acidantheras, tigridias and the like make a grand summer show. If you are dollar-conscious dig and store these over winter; however, it is a great saving in time and trouble to let the winter take them, and buy more next spring.

Annuals thrive during the summer months, or complete their life cycles from fall to early spring. Lobe-

This display of annual flowers gives an indication of the wide range of colors and forms available. In size they vary from ground-carpeters like sweet alyssum, and dainty fernleaf edgers like the Dahlberg daisy (*Thymophylla*), to 6-foot hybrid sunflowers with refined apricot-colored flowers, and castor bean plants which rush to grow 15 feet high in one season. Among the annuals shown are marigold, cosmos, gaillardia, aster, zinnia, larkspur and dahlia.

lias, petunias, marigolds, cosmos and most other ornamental garden annuals grow through the summer months. But many species, notably native "weeds" such as chickweed, shepherd's purse, *Poa annua* (the small, clumpy grass that plagues greenskeepers) and others germinate during cool, fall weather, grow intermittently over winter, and make seed sometime after January. Hardy annuals stand frost; you may enjoy an early burst of color from bachelor's buttons, larkspur, Shirley poppies and other winter (hardy) annuals if you sow seed of these in the fall.

Uses of Annual Flowers

The greatest use of annual flowers is for summer bedding. Apparently it all started during the eighteenth century when palace owners wanted something brighter than colored stones in their scrollwork-hedged gardens. By Victorian days public parks were filled with extremely complicated geometric flower beds. Highly trained gardeners made endless lists—lists of flowers by height, hue and month of bloom; lists of plants with colored foliages; plants with flowers that opened or closed at specific hours—to use in a sort of floral sundial—and plants compatible with various growing conditions. Annual vines, tender perennials used as annuals, bulbs, corms and tubers to be used as annuals, all of these went into the lists. These old and hard-to-find notebooks make wonderful reading, recalling an age of abundant, low-cost labor in the gardening world.

Annual flowers quickly became the backbone of the cottage garden because packets of seeds were cheap. "Penny packets" sell for twenty-five cents or more today, but still they are a bargain. A hundred and fifty seeds for a quarter, yielding at least one hundred blooming plants—that's a real buy in any age. Cottagers and mansion dwellers alike use annuals.

We use lots of annuals and it is not just a matter of price. Annual flowers tolerate a wide range of soil conditions; properly handled, they bloom for week after week, and they do not require the degree of year-round care and attention essential for longer-lived species. You draw open a furrow and sow seed, or you buy plants in the spring, you cultivate and water only a few weeks before the first blossoms come, you enjoy bright flowers throughout summer,

OPPOSITE: By carefully providing moisture drainage, essential to most annuals, this garden thrives beside a stream, with a pink ivyleaf geranium (*Pelargonium*) cascading to reflect in the water. With it are other geraniums, petunias, daisies and marigolds; also lavender *Verbena rigida*, pink *Astilbe chinensis* (both hardy perennials) and *Calceolaria integrifolia* (tender perennial that needs a cool summer climate).

and you clean off the bed after the first frost in the fall.

Annuals fit into modern gardens in several ways. We plant bright drifts of them at the doorway and around the terrace. We fill our window boxes and hanging baskets with them. They look fine and grow well in various sorts of planters and containers. Apartment dwellers, gardening on a balcony or on the roof, depend almost entirely on annuals for color. Even the twentieth-century nomad brightens the front step of his mobile home with annuals when he settles down for a few weeks, and that burgeoning breed, the summer cottager, stops increasingly at the roadside stand for a few trays of annuals as he heads for his hideaway.

There are annuals for full sun, for part sun and for growing in the shade. While most annual flowers grow best on well-drained soil, a few will thrive in damp places. With fairly modest root systems in most cases, annuals may be closely planted for a solid display of color. For the same reason, they are quite suitable for window and porch boxes and for growing in pots. The greenhouse enthusiast relies heavily on annuals for winter color in many cases. Cineraria, some greenhouse primulas, and schizanthus are examples of annuals for the backyard greenhouse.

Early Sowing, Indoors

Most annuals can be sown directly in the garden where they are to bloom. Many of us, however, like to start seedlings early, indoors. Seeds of annuals usually germinate quickly, and the seedlings tolerate a wide range of conditions. Use the sophisticated John Innes germinating compost, the Cornell mix, sieved dry sphagnum moss or a germinating medium of your own concocting. Shallow clay pots (bulb pans), compressed paper plant trays, three-inch-deep wooden flats or almost any other shallow container with drain holes holds the germinating medium. Fill to within half an inch of the rim; the medium should be only slightly compacted. Sprinkle seeds sparsely over the surface of the germinating medium. Fine seeds (petunia, forget-me-not, lobelia, snapdragon, for example) are pressed gently into the medium; cover larger seeds with an eighth-inch of the germinating medium or with crumbly, damp, sieved sphagnum or peat, or with clean sand. Set the container in a tray of tepid water for two or three hours (water droplets should glisten on the surface of the germinating mix), then stretch a piece of clear plastic over the face of the container and secure it with a rubber band. Place in dim light, at moderate room temperature. My choice is to lay slats on the tops of the reflectors of my fluorescent plant light units and

FLOWER SEEDLINGS IDENTIFIED

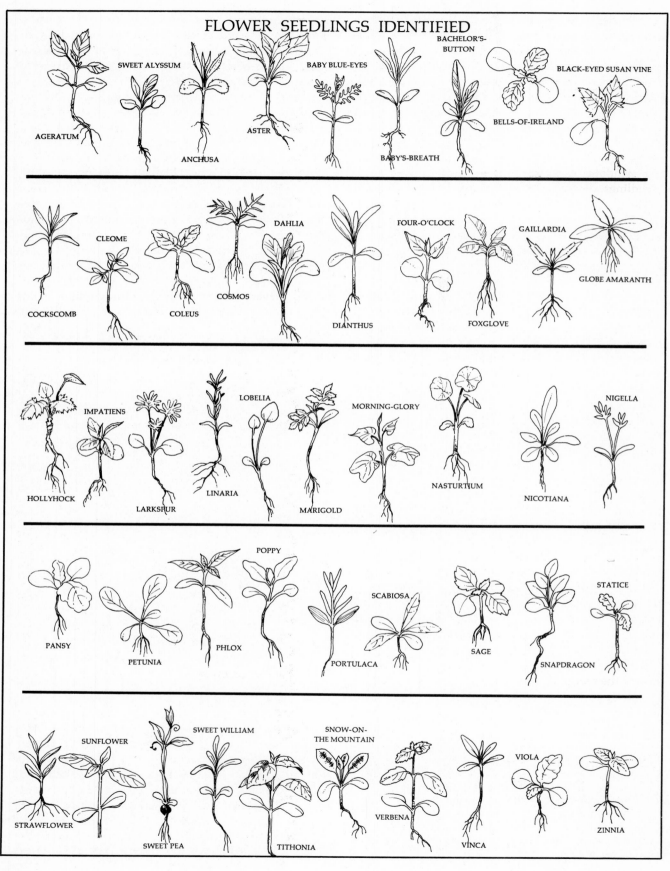

AGERATUM

SWEET ALYSSUM

ANCHUSA

ASTER

BABY BLUE-EYES

BABY'S-BREATH

BACHELOR'S-BUTTON

BELLS-OF-IRELAND

BLACK-EYED SUSAN VINE

CLEOME

COCKSCOMB

COLEUS

COSMOS

DAHLIA

DIANTHUS

FOUR-O'CLOCK

FOXGLOVE

GAILLARDIA

GLOBE AMARANTH

IMPATIENS

HOLLYHOCK

LARKSPUR

LINARIA

LOBELIA

MARIGOLD

MORNING-GLORY

NASTURTIUM

NICOTIANA

NIGELLA

PANSY

PETUNIA

PHLOX

POPPY

PORTULACA

SCABIOSA

SAGE

SNAPDRAGON

STATICE

STRAWFLOWER

SUNFLOWER

SWEET PEA

SWEET WILLIAM

TITHONIA

SNOW-ON-THE MOUNTAIN

VERBENA

VINCA

VIOLA

ZINNIA

set the seeded flats on these. The mild bottom heat brings the seedlings right out.

New germinating gadgets, such as Jiffy-Sevens, come in handy for certain seeds. I soak up a batch of them, poke two seeds each of morning glory, cardinal creeper, cypress vine or other ornamentals into every container. The seedlings grow in these and container and all goes into the garden.

As quickly as germination begins, give the seedlings dim light for a day, then bright light—a south-facing window, fluorescent or greenhouse daylight. As seedlings develop the second set of true leaves, prick them off into flats, spacing them two inches apart. As growth resumes, apply half-strength liquid fertilizer.

Seeding in the Garden

In the garden work up the soil in a well-drained bed; dress prior to turning with one-fourth cup of 5-10-5 fertilizer and two cups of dehydrated manure per square yard (this is a general rule of thumb, and may be modified to meet local conditions), then spade deeply. Rake down the soil, working it to crumble the clods and to develop a reasonably well settled, even surface.

Plan your annual bed with low-growing sorts in front, intermediate heights in the center and higher varieties at the rear if the bed backs up to shrubbery or a building. A freestanding bed is high in the center and low at the edges or low all the way across. With a hoe handle, scratch out roughly rectangular, trapizoidal or triangular "patches" for each sort of seed. Then, with a fine-pointed cultivating tool or with a small Warren hoe, mark out shallow drills. At the front of the bed the drills ought to run at acute angles to the face of the bed. Drills in a given patch are parallel, but those in adjacent patches are not parallel.

For a modest-sized bed, say one 10 feet by 25 feet for the home garden, plan on three or four low-growing annuals for the front, four or five annuals of intermediate height, and, perhaps, three tall-growing kinds for the rear of the bed.

OPPOSITE: It is important to know a flower-seedling from a weed-seedling. Note that the first leaves to appear—cotyledons—are usually quite different from the true leaves which follow. Seedlings sown directly where they are to grow in the garden or in a seed frame outdoors need light cultivation and weeding shortly after germination. Seedlings grow so thickly that they compete with one another for light, moisture and nutrients and need to be thinned. If you've planted an annual flower not shown here and can't decide what to pull and what to encourage, ask a friend who gardens.

In all cases, make the drills roughly 6 inches apart (closer for very fine sorts such as Dahlberg daisy or 'Twinkle' phlox, wider for large kinds such as tithonia, castor-bean or annual hollyhock). Sow seed generously in the drills and plan to thin later; the excess plants may be discarded or transplanted. Cover all seed two to three times its diameter with finely crumbled soil.

As seedlings appear, keep the bed in clean cultivation, and, when of a size to be well established but before they begin to crowd badly, thin them.

Plants you have grown yourself or purchased from the garden shop may be planted in the same carefully organized, informal manner. Push young annuals with biweekly feeding of balanced, low-nitrogen liquid fertilizer, keep the soil loose and free of weeds. Most annuals require one or two pinchings to make them branch well. Water often enough so the soil never dries completely throughout the top inch. When buds begin to show color, discontinue fertilizing.

Maintaining the Annual Flower Bed

Cultivate annuals frequently; use a scuffle hoe or just rake the soil; avoid deep cultivation as it may injure roots. Stake larger kinds when half-grown. An easy way is to use brushy, leafless, dry branches. Stick these among the growing plants, butts downward, shoving them firmly into the soil. As buds show color, with a pruning tool clip off twigs that show. Stems and branches supported throughout by a mesh of twigs are much more secure than those tied to single stakes.

Remove spent blossoms when it is practical. For example, when most snapdragons are fairly bloomed out, step into the bed and clip back the flower stalks just above a leaf. Probably new secondary shoots will develop shortly, particularly if the plants get a light feeding. On the other hand, you should nip off zinnia heads, spent petunia blossoms and spent cosmos once or twice each week, so the plants bloom continuously. Shear back sweet alyssum after each flush of flowering, and it will renew itself.

Insect and Disease Control

Watch for signs of aphids and other piercing-sucking insects. You will see them clustered on leaves, tender shoot tips or buds, or these parts of the plants will be crippled-looking and, perhaps, discolored. Spray immediately with a recommended garden insecticide. Malathion, Spectracide and nicotine sulfate are favorite insecticides for the control of piercing-sucking insects. Other insect pests chew the leaves; the insecticides listed above, among others, will give con-

Begonia semperflorens, one of the most popular low growing edgers, blooms almost continuously.

trol of chewing insects, though two or more sprayings at five-day intervals may be required. Methoxychlor is a low-residue insecticide of great value for combating chewing beetles and beetle larvae, as well as lepidopteran (mothlike) insect pests, and it has low toxicity to warm-blooded creatures. If you are seriously plagued with insect pests consider applying a foliar-absorbed or a granular (root-absorbed) systemic insecticide.

Few diseases, either bacterial or fungal, attack most annuals. Damping-off, a fungus disease, sometimes kills seedlings and may be controlled by quick use of Pano-Drench or a Dexon solution. Crown rot of annual plants may be a serious fungus problem where summers are hot and the soil is heavy with clay. Pretreat the bed in early spring with a Terrachlor drench, or water in the newly set (or thinned) annuals with a solution of Dexon. See Pests and Diseases.

Selection of Annuals

The list of annuals is legion. The beginning gardener is likely to wander into the seed shop or pick up a seed catalog, and, completely confused, select a number of varieties quite unsuited for growing in his locality. If you are not sure which kinds to order, visit the park department and see what they use; go on home-garden tours and make notes of which annuals recur garden after garden; get a list of recommended sorts from your County Extension Agent's office. But then, take a flier at two or three kinds you never heard of or that nobody mentioned. With luck, you may enjoy a patch of unusual and lovely flowers.

Just a word to help you with names. We recognize common names, horticultural names and scientific names. For example, the correct common name for any of the familiar annual asters is China aster. The scientific name for China aster is *Callistephus chinensis,* and, correctly used, this cognomen always is italicized with the first letter of the genus (*Callistephus*) capitalized and the species (*chinensis*) in all lowercase letters. But there are lots of kinds of China asters. There are the Giant Crego strain, the Powderpuff strain, the American Branching strain, the Perfection strain, and so on. These strains of asters are identified by capital first letters; we write Giant Crego aster. Sometimes a specific pure-line color and form of a plant is selected and given a special name; for example, one of the American Beauty asters, a cerise-scarlet sort, is offered as the 'Scarlet Beauty' aster. Notice the single quotes and capitalized first letters. This tells us that 'Scarlet Beauty' aster is a cultivar, that is, a hybrid sort of aster that was developed in cultivation. Another example, 'Cherry Belle' nasturtium is a cerise-rose cultivar of the Dwarf Double strain of garden nasturtiums, *Tropaeolum majus.*

(Plant Finder section, Volume 16, lists annuals by size, color, growth habits, blooming periods and in many other categories designed to help the home gardener plan flowering borders.)

Mr. Taloumis, the author of this article, is a successful home gardener who has distinguished himself in all areas of horticultural communications; as a newspaper columnist, lecturer, photographer, author of the book The Movable Garden, *magazine contributor and former editor of* Horticulture.

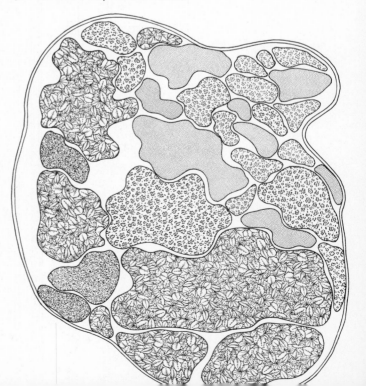

The sketch opposite indicates the irregular planting areas used to achieve masses of different kinds of flowers in a mixed border like that shown above. To prepare for planting, mark off entire plot. Work soil to a spade's depth; rake smooth. Outline spaces for each kind of flower with shallow drill made with hoe. Broadcast seeds or set out started plants. The border shown features annuals for garden display and cutting. Plants include 'Golden Ball' feverfew, French and African hybrid marigolds, purple sweet alyssum, blue bachelor's-buttons and echium, pink petunias and annual asters, gray-leaved cineraria or dusty miller, nasturtiums and orange calendulas. The dahlias are grown from tubers planted each spring. Tables at the end of this article group the most popular annuals by height.

ANNUAL FLOWERS BY HEIGHT, BLOOMING SEASON, HARDINESS AND COLOR

AVERAGE HEIGHT	NAME	DURATION OF SPRING BLOOM	DURATION OF SUMMER BLOOM	DURATION OF AUTUMN BLOOM	HARDINESS	COLOR OF TYPE AND VARIETIES
To 6 in.	Arctotis breviscapa		■		Tender	Orange or yellow, blue-centered.
	Calandrinia umbellata	■	■		Tender	Crimson-magenta.
	Dorotheanthus bellidiformis	■	■		Tender	Pink, red, white, rose, apricot, orange or crimson.
	Dorotheanthus gramineus	■	■		Tender	Red, pink, white or rose.
	Eschscholtzia caespitosa	■	■	■	Hardy	Bright yellow.
	Gilia dianthoides		■		Hardy	Lilac, pink or white.
	Gypsophila muralis	■	■	■	Hardy	Rose or white.
	Layia gaillardioides	■	■	■	Hardy	Orange-yellow.
	Linaria amethystina	■	■		Hardy	Lilac and yellow.
	Lobelia erinus		■		Tender	Blue, white, rose or crimson.
	Lobularia maritima	■	■	■	Hardy	White, lilac or yellow.
	Mimulus bigelovii	■	■		Hardy	Red, white or yellow.
	Mimulus tricolor	■	■		Hardy	Yellow, purple-spotted.
	Myosotis welwitschii	■			Hardy	Bright blue, cream-centered.
	Nemophila maculata	■	■		Hardy	White, spotted purple, or deep purple.
	Sanvitalia procumbens	■	■		Hardy	Bright yellow, purple-centered.
	Sedum caeruleum	■	■		Tender	Pale blue, white-centered.
	Ursinia pygmaea	■	■		Tender	Bright orange.
	Viola hybrida	■			Hardy	Violet, yellow, white, purple, etc.
	Viola tricolor	■			Hardy	Violet, yellow, white, purple, etc.

ANNUAL FLOWERS BY HEIGHT, BLOOMING SEASON, HARDINESS AND COLOR

AVERAGE HEIGHT	NAME	DURATION OF SPRING BLOOM	DURATION OF SUMMER BLOOM	DURATION OF AUTUMN BLOOM	HARDINESS	COLOR OF TYPE AND VARIETIES
6 in. to 1 ft.	Abronia umbellata	▬	▬		Tender	Pink or rose.
	Ageratum houstonianum	▬	▬		Tender	Bright blue.
	Anagallis linifolia		▬	▬	Hardy	Dark blue, rose or scarlet.
	Antirrhinum majus	▬	▬	▬	Hardy	All colors except blue.
	Arctotis acaulis		▬		Tender	Yellow, orange or red.
	Coreopsis bigelovii	▬	▬		Hardy	Golden-yellow.
	Dianthus chinensis var. heddewigii		▬		Hardy	Lilac, red or white.
	Diascia barberae	▬	▬	▬	Tender	Rose, pink or orange.
	Dimorphotheca cuneata	▬	▬		Tender	Scarlet-orange.
	Godetia grandiflora		▬	▬	Hardy	Red, pink, crimson, scarlet, lilac or white.
	Iberis umbellata	▬	▬		Hardy	White, red, lilac, purple or rose.
	Lychnis haageana	▬	▬		Tender	Scarlet, orange-red, salmon, white or crimson.
	Nemesia strumosa		▬		Tender	Cream, yellow, carmine, scarlet, pink, crimson or orange.
	Nemophila menziesii	▬	▬		Hardy	Blue and white.
	Petunia hybrida		▬		Tender	All colors.
	Phacelia linearis	▬	▬		Hardy	Violet or white.
	Portulaca grandiflora		▬		Tender	White, orange, rose, pink, scarlet, yellow or red.
	Tagetes patula		▬	▬	Tender	Red, yellow or orange.

ANNUAL FLOWERS BY HEIGHT, BLOOMING SEASON, HARDINESS AND COLOR

AVERAGE HEIGHT	NAME	DURATION OF SPRING BLOOM	DURATION OF SUMMER BLOOM	DURATION OF AUTUMN BLOOM	HARDINESS	COLOR OF TYPE AND VARIETIES
6 in. to 1 ft.	*Thymophylla tenuiloba*		▬▬▬▬	▬▬▬	Tender	Golden-yellow.
	Tropaeolum majus		▬▬▬▬	▬▬▬	Tender	Yellow, orange, red, crimson, scarlet, purple or white.
	Ursinia cakilefolia	▬	▬▬▬		Tender	Yellow or orange.
	Venidium decurrens		▬▬▬▬	▬▬▬		Golden-yellow, purple-centered.
	Venidium hirsutum		▬▬▬▬	▬▬▬	Tender	Orange, dark-centered.
	Verbena hortensis		▬▬▬▬	▬▬▬	Tender	Pink, red, yellow, blue, lilac, salmon, crimson, purple, rose, scarlet or white.
	Vinca rosea		▬▬▬		Tender	Rose or white.
	Zinnia linearis		▬▬▬		Tender	Golden-yellow, orange-tipped.
1 to 1½ ft.	*Adonis aestivalis*	▬▬			Hardy	Crimson or yellow.
	Alonsoa linifolia		▬▬▬▬	▬▬▬	Tender	Bright scarlet, spotted with black.
	Anagallis linifolia		▬▬▬▬	▬▬▬	Hardy	Deep blue or scarlet.
	Anchusa capensis	▬	▬▬▬		Hardy	Blue, white-throated, edged red.
	Antirrhinum majus	▬▬▬	▬▬▬▬	▬▬▬	Hardy	All colors except blue.
	Arctotis hybrida		▬▬▬		Tender	Cream, yellow, orange, red, crimson or purple.
	Brachycome iberidifolia	▬	▬▬▬		Tender	Rose, white, lilac or pink.
	Calendula stellata	▬▬▬	▬▬▬▬	▬▬▬	Hardy	Yellow.
	Chrysanthemum parthenium		▬▬▬		Hardy	White or yellow.
	Clarkia pulchella		▬▬▬▬	▬▬▬	Hardy	Lilac, white, red, etc.

Among the annuals are many flowers of the type called everlastings or strawflowers–kinds that mature and air-dry like those in the bouquet above without any special effort on the part of the gardener. The general rule is to cut them just before the blooms are fully open. Strip away excess foliage and hang to dry in loose bunches in an airy, dry, dark place. When completely dry they may be kept dust-free until needed for an arrangement by storing in large cardboard cartons or plastic bags. Favorite annual everlastings include strawflower (*Helichrysum*), statice, globe amaranth (*Gomphrena*), acroclinium (*Helipterum*), pearl ever-lasting (*Anaphalis*), immortelle (*Xeranthemum*), ammobium and rhodanthe. Ornamental grasses such as *Avena sterilis*, *Coix lachryma* and *Lagurus ovatus* are showy dried.

ANNUAL FLOWERS BY HEIGHT, BLOOMING SEASON, HARDINESS AND COLOR

AVERAGE HEIGHT	NAME	DURATION OF SPRING BLOOM	DURATION OF SUMMER BLOOM	DURATION OF AUTUMN BLOOM	HARDINESS	COLOR OF TYPE AND VARIETIES
1 to 1½ ft.	Collinsia grandiflora	▄	▄▄▄	▄	Hardy	Blue and white or red-violet.
	Dianthus armeria		▄▄▄		Hardy	Rose or pink.
	Dimorphotheca aurantiaca	▄	▄▄▄		Tender	Orange-yellow.
	Dimorphotheca calendulacea	▄	▄▄▄		Tender	Lemon-yellow, blue-centered.
	Dimorphotheca chrysanthemifolia	▄	▄▄▄		Tender	Pale yellow.
	Dimorphotheca sinuata	▄	▄▄▄		Tender	Orange-red.
	Eschscholtzia californica	▄	▄▄▄	▄	Hardy	Yellow, orange, crimson, rose, apricot, yellow or white.
	Gaillardia pulchella		▄▄▄		Hardy (or) Tender	Yellow, red or purple.
	Gomphrena globosa		▄▄▄	▄	Tender	White, yellow, rose, red, purple, violet.
	Heliotropium arborescens		▄▄▄		Tender	Violet, purple, blue, pink, rose or white.
	Layia calliglossa	▄	▄▄▄	▄	Hardy	Yellow, white-tipped.
	Linaria gharbensis	▄▄	▄▄▄		Hardy	Cream and violet.
	Linaria maroccana	▄▄	▄▄▄		Hardy	Violet, purple, white, rose, pink or yellow.
	Lychnis coeli-rosa		▄▄▄		Hardy	Rose, red, white or blue.
	Lychnis coronata		▄▄▄		Hardy	Red, pink, white or scarlet.
	Matricaria inodora		▄▄▄		Hardy	White.
	Mentzelia lindleyi	▄	▄▄▄	▄	Hardy	Golden-yellow.
	Nemesia strumosa		▄▄▄		Tender	Cream, yellow, carmine, scarlet, pink, crimson or orange.

ANNUAL FLOWERS BY HEIGHT, BLOOMING SEASON, HARDINESS AND COLOR

AVERAGE HEIGHT	NAME	DURATION OF SPRING BLOOM	DURATION OF SUMMER BLOOM	DURATION OF AUTUMN BLOOM	HARDINESS	COLOR OF TYPE AND VARIETIES
1 to 1½ ft.	Omphalodes linifolia	■	■		Hardy	White or blue.
	Papaver glaucum	■	■		Hardy	Brilliant scarlet.
	Petunia hybrida		■		Tender	All colors.
	Phacelia ciliata	■	■		Hardy	Lavender-blue.
	Phacelia minor	■	■		Hardy	Blue or purple.
	Phlox drummondii	■	■		Tender	Purple, rose, red, scarlet, pink or violet.
	Reseda odorata	■	■	■	Hardy	Orange, yellow, gold, crimson or white.
	Salvia horminum		■	■	Hardy	Purple, violet, lilac, white, blue or red.
	Silene armeria	■	■		Hardy	Pink, rose or white.
	Tagetes lucida		■	■	Tender	Yellow or orange.
	Torenia fournieri		■		Tender	Blue, purple and gold or white.
	Ursinia anthemoides	■	■		Tender	Yellow.
	Ursinia pulchra	■	■		Tender	Orange or yellow.
1½ to 2 ft.	Alonsoa warscewiczii		■	■	Tender	Brilliant scarlet.
	Antirrhinum majus	■	■	■	Hardy	All colors.
	Arctotis hybrida		■		Tender	Cream, yellow, orange, red, crimson or purple.
	Browallia americana	■	■		Tender	Blue, violet or white.
	Calendula officinalis	■	■		Tender	Cream, yellow or orange.
	Callistephus chinensis	■	■		Tender	All colors.
	Centaurea moschata	■	■		Hardy	White, yellow, rose, red or purple.
	Chrysanthemum segetum		■		Hardy	Golden-yellow.

ANNUAL FLOWERS BY HEIGHT, BLOOMING SEASON, HARDINESS AND COLOR

AVERAGE HEIGHT	NAME	DURATION OF SPRING BLOOM	DURATION OF SUMMER BLOOM	DURATION OF AUTUMN BLOOM	HARDINESS	COLOR OF TYPE AND VARIETIES
1½ to 2 ft.	Collinsia bicolor	▓▓▓	▓▓▓	▓▓▓	Hardy	White or violet.
	Dahlia hybrida		▓▓▓	▓▓▓	Tender	Yellow, rose, pink, scarlet or lilac.
	Delphinium ajacis		▓▓▓		Hardy	Blue, violet, lavender, rose, lilac, pink or white.
	Emilia sagittata	▓▓▓	▓▓▓		Tender	Scarlet or yellow.
	Gilia tricolor		▓▓▓		Hardy	Violet, rose-pink or white.
	Gypsophila elegans	▓▓▓	▓▓▓	▓▓▓	Hardy	White, pink, rose, carmine or red.
	Heliophila linearifolia	▓▓▓	▓▓▓		Tender	Blue, yellow-centered.
	Limonium sinuatum	▓▓▓	▓▓▓		Tender	Blue, white, rose or carmine.
	Limonium suworowii	▓▓▓	▓▓▓		Tender	Rose or white.
	Lonas inodora		▓▓▓		Tender	Golden-yellow.
	Nemesia strumosa		▓▓▓		Tender	Cream, yellow, carmine, scarlet, pink, crimson or orange.
	Nigella damascena		▓▓▓		Hardy	Blue or white.
	Rudbeckia hirta		▓▓▓	▓▓▓	Hardy	Yellow, purple-centered.
	Salpiglossis sinuata		▓▓▓		Tender	All colors.
	Salvia patens		▓▓▓	▓▓▓	Tender	Blue, white or lilac.
	Senecio elegans	▓▓▓	▓▓▓		Tender	Purple, white, rose or blue.
	Silene compacta	▓▓▓	▓▓▓		Tender	Bright pink.
	Tagetes tenuifolia		▓▓▓	▓▓▓	Tender	Yellow.
	Zinnia elegans		▓▓▓		Tender	Rose, pink, lilac, red, crimson, scarlet, orange, yellow or white.
2 to 3 ft.	Agrostemma githago	▓▓▓	▓▓▓		Hardy	Magenta-purple.

ANNUAL FLOWERS BY HEIGHT, BLOOMING SEASON, HARDINESS AND COLOR

AVERAGE HEIGHT	NAME	DURATION OF SPRING BLOOM	DURATION OF SUMMER BLOOM	DURATION OF AUTUMN BLOOM	HARDINESS	COLOR OF TYPE AND VARIETIES
2 to 3 ft.	Alonsoa acutifolia		▬▬▬	▬▬	Tender	Dark red or white.
	Amaranthus caudatus		▬▬▬		Tender	Bright red, white or yellow.
	Ammobium alatum	▬	▬▬▬		Hardy	Silvery-white.
	Antirrhinum majus	▬▬	▬▬▬	▬	Hardy	All colors.
	Arctotis hybrida		▬▬		Tender	Cream, yellow, orange, red, crimson or purple.
	Bidens coronata		▬▬▬		Hardy	Golden yellow.
	Bidens ferulaefolia		▬▬▬		Tender	Bright yellow.
	Calandrinia grandiflora	▬	▬▬▬		Tender	Pale purple.
	Callistephus chinensis		▬▬▬		Tender	All colors.
	Campanula medium	▬▬	▬▬▬	▬	Tender	Blue, white, pink or rose.
	Celosia argentea		▬▬▬		Tender	Yellow, orange, red, crimson, purple or white.
	Centaurea cyanus	▬	▬▬▬		Hardy	Blue, pink, rose, purple or white.
	Chrysanthemum carinatum		▬▬▬		Hardy	White, red, purple and yellow mixed.
	Clarkia elegans		▬▬▬	▬	Hardy	Rose, purple, white, pink or lilac.
	Convolvulus tricolor		▬▬▬		Hardy	Blue, white and yellow mixed.
	Coreopsis grandiflora	▬	▬▬▬		Hardy	Golden-yellow.
	Crepis rubra	▬	▬		Hardy	Rose-purple, pink or white.
	Delphinium ajacis	▬	▬▬▬		Hardy	Blue, violet, lavender, lilac, rose, pink or white.
	Delphinium orientale	▬	▬▬▬		Hardy	Violet-purple.
	Gilia capitata		▬▬▬		Hardy	Blue or white.

ANNUAL FLOWERS BY HEIGHT, BLOOMING SEASON, HARDINESS AND COLOR

AVERAGE HEIGHT	NAME	DURATION OF SPRING BLOOM	DURATION OF SUMMER BLOOM	DURATION OF AUTUMN BLOOM	HARDINESS	COLOR OF TYPE AND VARIETIES
2 to 3 ft.	Godetia amoena		███████	███████	Hardy	Lilac-crimson to reddish pink.
	Impatiens balsamina	█████	████████		Tender	White, pink, crimson, red or yellow.
	Impatiens holstii	█████	████████		Tender	Scarlet.
	Linum grandiflorum	████████	████████		Hardy	Red, crimson, scarlet, rose or violet.
	Linum usitatissimum	████████	████████		Hardy	Sky-blue.
	Lupinus hartwegii	█████	████		Hardy	Blue, white, rose or red.
	Malope trifida	█████	████████		Hardy	Rose-purple, red or white.
	Mirabilis jalapa		████████		Tender	Yellow, red, crimson, white or rose.
	Nicotiana alata		████████		Tender	Rose, mauve, violet, pink, crimson or scarlet.
	Papaver rhoeas	████████	█████		Hardy	Pink, scarlet, carmine, crimson, salmon or white.
	Papaver somniferum	████████	█████		Hardy	White, pink, red or purple.
	Rudbeckia bicolor		██████	██████	Hardy	Yellow, black-centered.
	Salvia splendens		██████	██████	Tender	Scarlet or white.
	Scabiosa atropurpurea		████████		Hardy	Crimson, blue, lavender, pink, purple, salmon, rose, scarlet or white.
	Schizanthus hybridus	█████	████		Tender	All colors.
	Tagetes erecta		██████	██████	Tender	Yellow or orange.
	Venidium fastuosum	█████	████████		Tender	Orange, yellow or white, black-centered.

ANNUAL FLOWERS BY HEIGHT, BLOOMING SEASON, HARDINESS AND COLOR

AVERAGE HEIGHT	NAME	DURATION OF SPRING BLOOM	DURATION OF SUMMER BLOOM	DURATION OF AUTUMN BLOOM	HARDINESS	COLOR OF TYPE AND VARIETIES
2 to 3 ft.	Zinnia elegans		▬▬▬▬▬		Tender	Rose, pink, lilac, red, crimson, scarlet, orange, yellow or white.
3 to 4 ft.	Arctotis hybrida		▬▬▬		Tender	Cream, yellow, orange, red, crimson or purple.
	Argemone grandiflora		▬▬▬▬		Tender	White or yellow.
	Chrysanthemum coronarium		▬▬▬▬		Hardy	White, cream or yellow.
	Cleome spinosa	▬▬	▬▬		Tender	Rose-purple, white or rose.
	Coreopsis tinctoria	▬▬	▬▬▬▬		Hardy	Yellow, crimson and purple mixed.
	Cosmos bipinnatus		▬▬▬▬	▬▬	Tender	White, crimson, pink or rose.
	Cosmos sulphureus		▬▬▬▬	▬▬	Tender	Yellow or orange.
	Datura metel		▬▬▬▬		Tender	White, blue, yellow, or red.
	Helichrysum bracteatum		▬▬▬▬		Hardy	Yellow, orange, red, pink, white, scarlet or purple.
	Lavatera trimestris		▬▬▬▬		Hardy	Red, rose or white.
	Solanum warscewiczii	▬▬	▬▬		Tender	White.
4 to 5 ft.	Centaurea americana	▬▬	▬▬▬		Hardy	Rose, pink or purple.
	Helianthus debilis		▬▬▬	▬▬	Hardy	Yellow, red, pink, rose or purple.
	Tithonia rotundifolia		▬▬▬▬	▬▬	Tender	Orange-yellow or scarlet.
	Tithonia tagetifolia		▬▬▬▬	▬▬	Tender	Dark orange or orange-yellow.
5 to 6 ft.	Althaea rosea		▬▬▬▬		Hardy	Red, pink, rose, yellow or white.
Over 6 ft.	Helianthus annuus		▬▬▬	▬▬	Hardy	Yellow, magenta or red, purple-centered.

BORDER DESIGNS FEATURING ANNUALS

ABOVE: This plan for a corner area, measuring approximately 28 feet across the top, suggests a raised retaining wall about 18 inches high along the front, with comfortable seating. Using the accompanying tables, select low- to medium-growing annuals for the front of the border and around the flowering tree, which might be an ornamental crab apple, dogwood or redbud. Use taller flowers at the back of the border. To develop this plan as an all white and yellow summer border, select varieties of sweet alyssum, wax begonia, baby's-breath, candytuft, celosia, cleome, marigold, nicotiana, snapdragon, thymophylla and zinnia. In autumn interplant bulbs of tulip, daffodil and hyacinth.

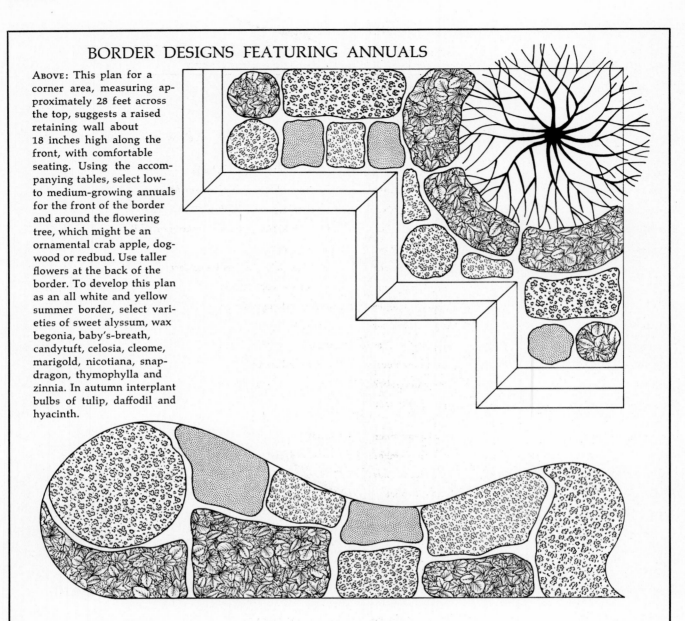

ABOVE: A border plan like this one can be laid out easily with a length of garden hose to help establish the curves. Depending on space and personal preference this could be developed with fragrant annuals, kinds for cutting or in a color scheme. RIGHT: For a partly shaded nook that receives only early morning or late afternoon sun, try begonia, browallia, clarkia, impatiens, nicotiana and salvia. Scented flowers for shady positions include lunaria, mimulus, the viola species, myosotis and *Monopsis campanulata*.

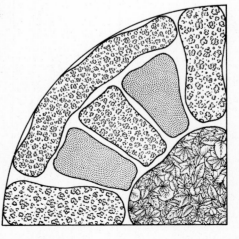

ANNUAL CLIMBERS

NAME	HARDINESS	TIME OF FLOWERING	COLOR OF TYPE AND VARIETIES	HEIGHT
Calonyction aculeatum	Tender	July–September	White	10–20 ft.
Convolvulus aureus superbus	Tender	July–September	Golden-yellow	5–6 ft.
Eccremocarpus scaber	Tender	June–August	Orange-red, yellow-tipped; yellow, red, scarlet or carmine	6–15 ft.
Humulus japonicus	Hardy	(Foliage vine)	For quick screening and shade	12–20 ft.
Ipomoea hederacea	Tender	May–September	Pale blue or blue with white border	6–12 ft.
Ipomoea nil	Tender	May–September	Blue, purple, rose or white	8–12 ft.
Ipomoea purpurea	Hardy	May–September	Purple, pink, blue, crimson, scarlet or white	10–15 ft.
Ipomoea setosa	Tender	May–September	Rose-purple	10–15 ft.
Ipomoea tricolor	Tender	May–September	Dark blue, pale blue, white or rose	8–12 ft.
Lathyrus odoratus	Hardy	June–September	All shades except yellow	4–10 ft.
Maurandia barclaiana	Tender	August–October	Purple, white or rose	To 6 ft.
Maurandia erubescens	Tender	August–October	Rose-pink	To 6 ft.
Maurandia scandens	Tender	August–October	Purple	To 6 ft.
Pholistoma auritum	Hardy	July–September	Blue, lavender or violet	To 6 ft.
Quamoclit coccinea	Tender	June–September	Scarlet, yellow or orange	To 10 ft.
Quamoclit coccinea var. *hederifolia*	Tender	June–September	Scarlet	To 10 ft.
Quamoclit grandiflora	Tender	June–September	Scarlet	To 10 ft.
Quamoclit lobata	Tender	June–September	Crimson to yellow	6–12 ft.
Quamoclit sloteri	Tender	June–September	Crimson and white	8–12 ft.
Thunbergia alata	Tender	June–October	White, purple-throated, orange or yellow	6–7 ft.
Thunbergia fragrans	Tender	June–October	White	To 5 ft.
Thunbergia gibsonii	Tender	June–October	Orange	To 5 ft.
Tropaeolum majus	Tender	July–October	Various colors	To 8 ft.
Tropaeolum peltophorum	Tender	July–October	Various colors	To 6 ft.
Tropaeolum peregrinum	Tender	July–October	Golden-yellow, spotted crimson	To 8 ft.

LOW-GROWING BORDER ANNUALS

(Including tender perennials and biennials used as annuals)

AGERATUM	CINERARIA	GAILLARDIA	NASTURTIUM (Tom Thumb)
ALONSOA	CLARKIA	GILIA	NEMESIA
ALYSSUM	COLLINSIA	GODETIA (dwarf)	NEMOPHILA
AMARANTHUS	COREOPSIS	GOMPHRENA	NIEREMBERGIA
ANAGALLIS	CUPHEA	HELIOPHILA	OMPHALODES
ANTIRRHINUM (dwarf vars.)	DAHLIA (Coltness vars.)	HELIPTERUM	PETUNIA
ASPERULA	DELPHINIUM	IBERIS	PHACELIA
BEGONIA	DIANTHUS	IMPATIENS	PHLOX (Drummondii)
BELLIS	DIASCIA	LAYIA	PLATYSTEMON
BRACHYCOME	DIMORPHOTHECA	LINARIA	RESEDA
CALANDRINIA	ECHIUM	LOBELIA	TAGETES
CALCEOLARIA (bedding vars.)	EMILIA	LYCHNIS	URSINIA
CALENDULA	EMMENANTHE	MATRICARIA	VERBENA (dwarf)
CELOSIA	ERYSIMUM	MESEMBRYANTHEMUM	VIOLA
CHEIRANTHUS	ESCHSCHOLTZIA	MYOSOTIS	ZINNIA (dwarf)

ANNUALS FOR WINDOW-BOXES

ABRONIA	GRAMMANTHES	PETUNIA
AGERATUM	IPOMOEA	PHLOX (dwarf)
ANTIRRHINUM (dwarf)	LINARIA	RESEDA
ASTER (dwarf)	LOBELIA	SALVIA
BEGONIA	MATTHIOLA	STATICE (dwarf)
CELOSIA	MESEMBRYANTHE- MUM	TROPAEOLUM (dwarf)
COLEUS	NEMESIA	URSINIA
ESCHSCHOLTZIA	NIEREMBERGIA	VERBENA

SOW WHERE THEY ARE TO FLOWER

ADONIS	DOWNINGIA	LINARIA
ALYSSUM	ECHIUM	LINUM
ANCHUSA	EMILIA	LUPINUS
BORAGO	ERYSIMUM	MALCOMIA
CALENDULA	ESCHSCHOLTZIA	MALOPE
CALLIOPSIS	EUPHORBIA	MATTHIOLA
CAMPANULA	GILIA	NEMOPHILA
CENTAUREA	GLAUCIUM	NICOTIANA
CHRYSANTHEMUM	GODETIA	NIGELLA
CLARKIA	GYPSOPHILA	PAPAVER
CLEOME	HELIANTHUS	PHACELIA
COLLINSIA	IBERIS	RESEDA
COLLOMIA	IPOMOEA	RUDBECKIA
CONVOLVULUS	LATHYRUS	TAGETES
CYNOGLOSSUM	LAVATERA	TROPAEOLUM
DELPHINIUM	LEPTOSYNE	VISCARIA
DIMORPHOTHECA	LIMNANTHES	ZINNIA

BEDDING ANNUALS FOR PARTLY SHADED PLACES

ANCHUSA	ESCHSCHOLTZIA	NICOTIANA
ANTIRRHINUM	GODETIA	OENOTHERA
BEGONIA	IMPATIENS	OXALIS
BELLIS	LINARIA	PAPAVER
CALLISTEPHUS	LOBULARIA	PETUNIA
CAMPANULA	MATRICARIA	SALVIA
CLARKIA	MIMULUS	VIOLA
CYNOGLOSSUM	MYOSOTIS	
DELPHINIUM	NEMOPHILA	

ANNUALS WITH SCENTED FLOWERS

ABRONIA UMBELLATA	LOBULARIA MARITIMA
ASPERULA ORIENTALIS	LUNARIA ANNUA
BRACHYCOME IBERIDIFOLIA	LUPINUS MUTABILIS
CENTAUREA MOSCHATA	MATTHIOLA INCANA
CLEOME SPINOSA	MENTZELIA LINDLEYI
DIANTHUS BARBATUS	MYOSOTIS SYLVATICA
ERYSIMUM ASPERUM	NICOTIANA ALATA
HEDYSARUM CORONARIUM	RESEDA ODORATA
HELIOTROPIUM ARBORESCENS	TAGETES LUCIDA
HESPERIS FRAGRANS	VIOLA CORNUTA
HESPERIS MATRONALIS	VIOLA HYBRIDA
IBERIS AMARA	VIOLA TRICOLOR
LIMNANTHES DOUGLASII	

Shady Positions

ANDROSACE ARMENIACA	MONOPSIS CAMPANULATA
COLLINSIA GRANDIFLORA	MYOSOTIS SPP.
IONOPSIDIUM ACAULE	NEMOPHILA SPP.
LUNARIA ANNUA	TORENIA FOURNIERI
MIMULUS SPP.	VIOLA SPP.

ANNUALS FOR CUT FLOWERS

ACROCLINIUM	DIANTHUS	MATTHIOLA
ANTIRRHINUM	ESCHSCHOLTZIA	NIEREMBERGIA
CALENDULA	GAILLARDIA	NIGELLA
CALLIOPSIS	GODETIA	PENSTEMON
CALLISTEPHUS	GYPSOPHILA	RESEDA
CENTAUREA	HELICHRYSUM	RHODANTHE
CHEIRANTHUS	HELIPTERUM	RUDBECKIA
CHRYSANTHEMUM	LATHYRUS	SALPIGLOSSIS
CLARKIA	LEPTOSYNE	SCABIOSA
COSMOS	LINARIA	STATICE
CYANUS	LUPINUS	TROPAEOLUM
DAHLIA	LYCHNIS	VERBENA
DELPHINIUM	MATRICARIA	ZINNIA

annularis (an-yew-*lay*-riss), **-e.** Annular; ringed.

Annual larkspur. See *Delphinium ajacis.*

annuus (*an*-yew-us), **-a, -um.** Annual; living only one year.

Photographers, Volume 1

COVER: GEORGE DE GENNARO   MOST COLOR ILLUSTRATIONS FROM I. G. A.

MOLLY ADAMS
RALPH BAILEY
BODGER SEEDS, LTD.
PAT BRINDLEY
RALPH D. CORNELL
J. E. DOWNWARD
CHARLES MARDEN FITCH
PAUL E. GENEREUX

HAL HARRISON
HAMPFLER
GRANT HEILMAN
HORT-PIX
EMIL JAVORSKY
ANDRÉ KERTESZ
WARD LINTON
ELVIN MCDONALD
PAN-AMERICAN SEED CO.

PAUL J. PEART
ROCHE
O. PHILIP ROEDEL
JOHN ROGERS
H. SMITH
GEORGE TALOUMIS
U.S. FOREST SERVICE
TOM WIER

GARDENER'S READY REFERENCE CHART

BASIC POTTING MIXTURE

4 parts coarse builder's sand
2 parts sedge peat pr peatmoss
1 part dried cattle manure
1 part vermiculite

add to each bushel:
8 level tb. superphosphate
8 level tb. cottonseed meal
4 level tb. sulfate of potash
4 level tb. ground limestone

To increase drainage:
double the sand

To increase moisture retention:
double the peat

PLANTING DEPTH FOR SEEDS

Small seeds
broadcast over soil surface and tamp

Large seeds
plant at 3 times depth of seed diameter

Bloom in Spri

Bloom in Early Spring

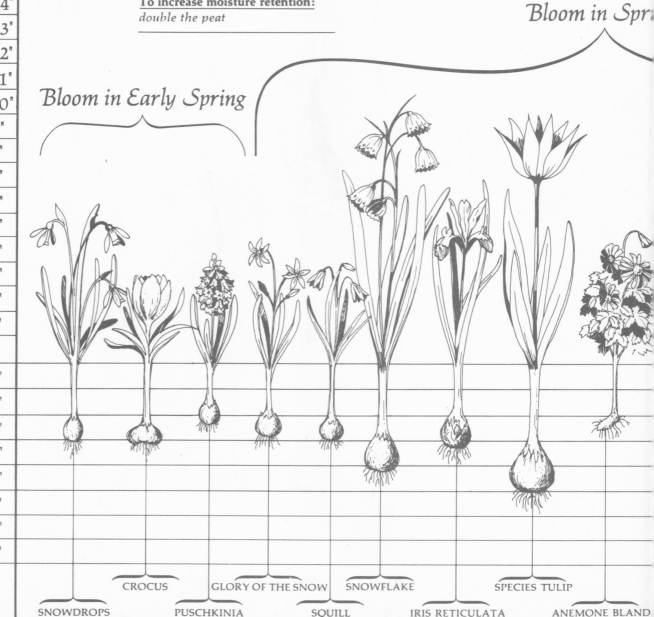

SNOWDROPS CROCUS PUSCHKINIA GLORY OF THE SNOW SQUILL SNOWFLAKE IRIS RETICULATA SPECIES TULIP ANEMONE BLAND